THE EVERYTHING GUIDE TO DIVORCE

Dear Reader,

If you're reading this book, you are probably going through or about to go through a very painful period in your life. I hope the information in this book will help you go forward armed with knowledge about the road ahead. Having experienced divorce for myself and having held the hands of many clients as they ended their marriages, I have had a unique perspective of the scorched earth left behind after a contested divorce.

If you take only one thing from reading this book, learn to compromise and be tolerant. If you can master these traits, your divorce and postdivorce life will be far more pleasant and your children will grow up happier, kinder people.

Milinda J. Reed, Esq.

Welcome to the EVERYTHING® Series!

These handy, accessible books give you all you need to tackle a difficult project, gain a new hobby, comprehend a fascinating topic, prepare for an exam, or even brush up on something you learned back in school but have since forgotten.

You can choose to read an *Everything®* book from cover to cover or just pick out the information you want from our four useful boxes: e-questions, e-facts, e-alerts, and e-ssentials.

We give you everything you need to know on the subject, but throw in a lot of fun stuff along the way, too.

We now have more than 400 *Everything®* books in print, spanning such wide-ranging categories as weddings, pregnancy, cooking, music instruction, foreign language, crafts, pets, New Age, and so much more. When you're done reading them all, you can finally say you know *Everything®*!

QUESTIONS?
Answers to
common questions

FACTS
Important snippets
of information

ALERTS!
Urgent
warnings

ESSENTIALS
Quick
handy tips

PUBLISHER Karen Cooper

DIRECTOR OF ACQUISITIONS AND INNOVATION Paula Munier

MANAGING EDITOR, EVERYTHING SERIES Lisa Laing

COPY CHIEF Casey Ebert

ACQUISITIONS EDITOR Katie McDonough

ASSOCIATE DEVELOPMENT EDITOR Elizabeth Kassab

EDITORIAL ASSISTANT Hillary Thompson

Visit the entire Everything® series at *www.everything.com*

THE
EVERYTHING®
GUIDE TO DIVORCE

2ND EDITION

All you need to navigate this
difficult transition and get on with your life

Milinda J. Reed, Esq.

Avon, Massachusetts

For Bob—
thanks for all the words that mattered. I think of them often.

For my family near and far—
thanks for believing in me and helping me find my way.

An Everything® Series Book.
Everything® and everything.com® are registered trademarks of F+W Media, Inc.

Published by Adams Media, a division of F+W Media, inc.
57 Littlefield Street, Avon, MA 02322 U.S.A.
www.adamsmedia.com

ISBN 10: 1-59869-866-4
ISBN 13: 978-1-59869-866-4

Printed in the United States of America.

J   I   H   G   F   E   D   C   B   A

Library of Congress Cataloging-in-Publication Data
is available from the publisher.

This publication is designed to provide accurate and authoritative information with regard to the subject matter covered. It is sold with the understanding that the publisher is not engaged in rendering legal, accounting, or other professional advice. If legal advice or other expert assistance is required, the services of a competent professional person should be sought.

—From a *Declaration of Principles* jointly adopted by a Committee of the American Bar Association and a Committee of Publishers and Associations

Many of the designations used by manufacturers and sellers to distinguish their products are claimed as trademarks. Where those designations appear in this book and Adams Media was aware of a trademark claim, the designations have been printed with initial capital letters.

The material in this book is provided for informational purposes only. Readers should consult with their personal financial or legal advisors before utilizing the information contained in this book. The author and the publisher assume no responsibility for any damages or losses incurred during or as a result of following this information.

This book is available at quantity discounts for bulk purchases.
For information, please call 1-800-289-0963.

Contents

Acknowledgments

Most people think that lawyers learn to be lawyers in law school, but I disagree. Lawyers learn to be lawyers from their interactions with people. Thanks to all the people who taught me about the law, from professors to judges to chief court clerks, who kindly and sometimes sternly helped me understand how to practice law. Thanks to all my clients, who taught me about people and the complicated and messy intricacies that shape intimate relationships.

Special thanks to Katie McDonough, my editor from Adams who shaped the book's format and kept me focused, and to Patricia, for introducing us and always being a great friend.

Top 10 Things You'll Learn after Reading This Book

1. What to consider before deciding to divorce.

2. Who needs a lawyer and how to choose the right lawyer to represent you.

3. How to avoid a lengthy legal battle and ensure a fair settlement.

4. How to handle the emotions that accompany the breakup of a marriage.

5. How to manage your finances and protect your assets before and during a divorce.

6. The ways to tell children about a divorce and how to get what's best for them.

7. How courts decide custody issues.

8. What legal paperwork you will need and how to prepare it.

9. How to develop a parenting plan after you've split up.

10. What issues are involved with child support or alimony expenses that you may be faced with.

Introduction

▶ EVERYONE HAS HEARD the statistics: Half of all first marriages in the United States end in divorce. The success rate for second marriages is even lower. When people marry for the first time, they rarely think about the possibility of divorce. They make a commitment "til death do us part," and they intend to honor that commitment. Why, then, do so many marriages end in divorce? There's no simple answer.

Some marriages end because the parties married when they were very young. As the parties matured, their hopes, dreams, and goals changed and moved in different directions. Some of these young people may have been expecting a baby and weren't ready for the hard work and commitment marriage demands. Other marriages end because one of the parties becomes emotionally involved with someone new. Long-term marriages may end when children grow up and move away, and the parents realize they've grown too far apart to have a marriage.

Some people think the U.S. divorce rate is so high because the laws of divorce make it too easy to get divorced. These folks must never have gone through a divorce; even under the best of circumstances, divorce is an emotionally upsetting process that brings with it many changes.

Other people think the high divorce rate results from changes in how people view making a commitment to marriage. Instead of gritting their teeth and hanging in there, people put themselves first and think more in terms of what they should be getting from marriage. If their expectations aren't met, they choose divorce.

Some marriages end when a victim of domestic violence finds the resources to safely escape an abusive partner. Domestic violence is a serious issue and states have enacted laws to help protect victims of domestic violence from further abuse. Public education over the last twenty years has emphasized that neither party to a relationship has the right to control the other with force or threats. Today, most people believe domestic violence is wrong and must not to be tolerated. More victims have access to supportive services, to safe shelter, to jobs, and, ultimately, to independence.

Whatever the reasons for the breakup, people do choose to divorce. Often, they make this choice with little or no knowledge of what lies ahead. However, it's hard to get information to couples contemplating divorce. Courts don't know about these divorcing couples until they file their papers with the court. Community divorce education programs provide helpful information, but divorcing couples don't always know about these programs.

You, too, may have precious little information about divorce. This book will take you through the entire process, from contemplation to implementation, with a lot of side trips into the little issues that may rear their heads along the way.

This book will be helpful if you're trying to decide whether to get a divorce, if you've made the decision and are about to begin, if you're in the middle of a divorce, or if the legal part of the divorce is over. It will help you handle being the person on the receiving end of divorce papers. It will also be useful if you're looking at a second (or third, or . . .) divorce.

Many judges and lawyers have a bias when it comes to the divorce process. They feel very strongly that litigation is rarely the right way to get divorced. It is usually contrary to your best interests to take your divorce to court and let a judge decide your disputes. It's extraordinarily expensive and seldom produces the results you were seeking. These judges and lawyers believe a negotiated settlement is the way to go. So, although this book will explain everything you need to know about the litigation process, it will emphasize staying in charge and making the decisions you'll have to live with once the divorce is done. It is much better to make those decisions yourselves than to have them imposed on you by a stranger, the judge.

Divorce is a painful and scary process. You can make it less scary by reading this book. If you can learn what's ahead and how to take care of yourself, you will reduce the pain. Knowledge is a powerful tool.

Read this book. Gain knowledge. Then move on to your new life.

CHAPTER 1

Do You Really Want a Divorce?

Making a marriage work is hard. Many factors contribute to marital stress and dissatisfaction, but before you shout "divorce," you need to decide whether the marriage needs serious help or whether it's truly over. This chapter will help you find ways to reach and cope with this important decision. It will outline your options for trying to save your marriage, and it includes resources for ending your marriage if that is your ultimate decision.

Identify the Problem(s)

A successful marriage often requires work and effort. Sometimes the problems of the marriage make divorce look like a good choice, but surviving a divorce is difficult as well. Be sure that you've given your marriage every possible chance before deciding to end it. You should first pinpoint the reasons why you're unhappy or dissatisfied with the marriage. Sometimes these problems can be fixed, and sometimes they can't. You'll never know unless you first identify them.

The Thrill Is Gone

People have expectations about marriage. They believe marriage will be like courtship except that no one has to go home at the end of the evening. There's no way to appreciate the effort that goes into making a marriage work until you actually get married and live with the day-to-day reality of sharing your life with another person.

When partners in a relationship do nice things for each other and say nice things to each other, they can more easily ignore the little things about the other person that they don't like very much. When the nice things and the nice words become few and far between, the little annoyances get much bigger. When you surprise each other with little presents, go out dancing on Saturday nights, and often say, "I love you," the work of taking care of your home and each other is more fun than drudgery.

FACT

Even couples who live together before they marry are often unprepared for the long-term commitment the formal union requires. Couples who live together but aren't married may keep more of the elements of courtship in their relationship than couples who marry. This may be because their partners aren't yet a sure thing, and the couple needs to put some energy into keeping romance alive.

Home and family responsibilities can feel quite different when you're awakened by a sick child at 3 A.M. for the third night in a row and your spouse rolls over and tells you to deal with it. It can be disappointing when you've gone out of your way to do something special for your spouse and your efforts go unnoticed. Over time, the day-to-day responsibilities of home, spouse, and children become heavier and heavier. The happy moments become rarer and rarer. It becomes easier and easier to keep a score sheet of the times your spouse has disappointed you, and to create a mental list of your spouse's shortcomings. You feel overwhelmed by what's wrong with your marriage and find it harder and harder to find anything that's right.

Money Troubles Can Sabotage Marriages

Maybe you and your spouse have different ideas about finances. Maybe you both like more of the good life than you can afford or one of you is controlling and penny-pinching while the other has a casual attitude toward spending. Is chronic unemployment an issue? Is there tension because she makes more than he does?

Financial issues can add a lot of stress to a marriage. If your money issues are attitudinal—that is, how you feel about spending and saving—you may be able to resolve them in counseling. If your money issues have led you into significant debt, you will need to do more than talk. You will probably need to meet with a financial counselor and develop a plan to pay off the debts.

Children Can Be the Breaking Point

Do you have children? It's not unusual for the imminent arrival of a baby to be the basis for a wedding. Many people really want to have children, so they expand their families early in the marriage. Kids are wonderful, but they can also increase the stress on a marriage. Do you and your spouse agree on how to raise children? Do you have similar goals and objectives for your kids? Do you agree on safety needs and appropriate supervision? Do you share the responsibility of caring for the children? Parenting disagreements can be incredible land mines in a marriage. If things are shaky for starters, fights over children can bring a marriage down.

Trapped in an Abusive Marriage

If your partner is verbally, emotionally, physically, or sexually abusive, you need to seriously consider ending the marriage. Statistics show that domestic violence typically increases in frequency and severity over time. It can be dangerous for you and your children to remain in a marriage where your spouse engages in abusive behaviors. In some cases, it can be lethal. The news is full of stories about murder/suicides, missing spouses, and violence perpetrated by one spouse against another. If you are trapped in an abusive marriage, there are resources that can help. Find them. You can start by calling the National Domestic Violence hotline at 1-800-799-SAFE (7233). Domestic violence will be discussed in greater detail in Chapter 17.

Can the Marriage Be Saved?

Does anything you've read so far strike a chord for you? Probably, or you wouldn't be reading this book. When you're feeling low, it's easy to make a list of what's wrong in your marriage. So what should you do?

First, make a list of what's right in your marriage. What about the good times? What about the qualities that attracted you to your spouse in the first place? On a good day, are they still there? If good moments still happen in your marriage and there is no abuse, especially if you have children, you might consider giving the marriage one more try. If the list doesn't help, don't lose heart; there are other options out there.

Marriage Counseling

Your spouse is probably aware the marriage is in trouble, but that's not always the case. If you tell your spouse you're unhappy, he may or may not be surprised. You need to have a talk at a time when neither of you is angry or upset. Send the children off to Grandma or to the neighbors, have a relaxing dinner, and afterward raise some of your concerns. When it feels like the appropriate time, tell your spouse what's troubling you.

With any luck, your spouse will agree to go to marriage counseling. If you choose counseling, you should both make a commitment to give it a real try. Don't use marriage counseling as a way to tell your spouse the marriage is over. You'll need to put your energies into learning new ways to deal with each other and unlearning old ways that have been destructive. This is hard work. It's too easy to give up when you aren't really committed to saving the marriage.

You can pursue marriage counseling even after you begin a divorce, as long as both of you want to do so. Most courts are willing to grant an adjournment while the parties seek counseling. In some cases, time limits may prevent lengthy adjournments, so consult with your lawyer to discuss your options. The most important thing is saving your marriage if that is what you and your spouse want.

The purpose of counseling is to help spouses work together to solve problems and improve their relationship. It assumes that each partner is an equal in the relationship. If your spouse is abusive, do not consider marriage counseling. In an abusive marriage the abuser holds the power and control in the relationship. Counseling in this situation could result in increased abuse. If you decide to try counseling anyway, at least tell the counselor about the abuse so she is in a better position to help.

Finding a Marriage Counselor

Many communities have marriage counselors. How can you find the right one? Ask your friends, your pastor, priest, rabbi, or a friend who is also a divorce lawyer. If you can, it is always best to get a reference from someone you know who has used the counselor. If you are unable to get any referrals, try the Internet or directory assistance. Always be sure to check the counselor's qualifications. If cost is a concern, you may need to talk to your health insurance provider to see whether your insurance covers such counseling. If it does, you'll probably have to select a counselor from the provider's list.

Meet two or three times with the counselor you select. Do you feel comfortable with this person? Are you getting helpful feedback? Are you and your spouse able to discuss issues with the counselor's help? Does the counselor give you homework? Are you seeing any changes in how things are going at home? If you can answer "yes" to these questions, you're on the right track. If not, you may need to look for a different counselor.

Getting into Therapy

If your spouse refuses to go to marriage counseling, what can you do? You can go to counseling by yourself. You may find it very helpful to get a sense of what's going on with yourself before you tackle what's going on in your marriage. If your spouse won't go to marriage counseling, at least you can take care of yourself. Find a therapist.

ALERT!

Don't use your own therapist as a marriage counselor. Your spouse may be reluctant to do marriage counseling in the first place and is likely to see your therapist as someone who is biased in your favor. Besides, you don't want to compromise your relationship with your therapist by asking him to wear two hats. Get the names of some neutral, new therapists for marriage counseling.

The same rules apply here as for finding a marriage counselor. Get referrals. Meet with the therapist a few times. Make sure you're comfortable, and see whether you're making progress.

Your therapist may suggest participating in a group. It's often comforting to know you aren't the only one experiencing marriage problems. Sometimes hearing how others see you and your marriage provides useful information—and it can be a bit of a shock. You may hear that some of the problems are yours. This kind of feedback from people outside the marriage is often better received than when it comes from your spouse.

What a Therapist Can Do

A therapist can help you see the big picture. A divorce may sound like a way out, but maybe it's too drastic a remedy right now—like having major surgery when a little physical therapy would do the trick.

Sometimes a therapist will suggest making a list of your spouse's good points. When was the last time you thought about what you like about your spouse? What have you been doing to encourage these positive attributes? A therapist can also teach you how to talk to your spouse in a nonblaming way. Instead of saying, "You make me so mad when you come home late," you can try to use what the therapists call "I" statements. You can say "I feel really sad (disappointed, worried) when I don't get to spend the evening with you."

If you and the therapist work well together, chances are good you'll start to feel better about yourself. This may lead to feeling better about your marriage. However, it can also go the other way. Therapy may make it clearer that something in the marriage needs to change or you'll have to end the relationship. For example, addiction to alcohol, drugs, or gambling may be a major problem in the marriage. Use and abuse of money may also be a major problem. You can try to address these issues before taking the divorce plunge.

Treating Addictions

Your counselor may be able to help you or your spouse get into treatment for whatever addiction is affecting your family. Sometimes it works better to have this recommendation come from an outsider—a nonfamily member—than from a spouse. However, sometimes it takes an intervention of family and friends to get the dependent spouse into treatment.

What is an intervention? Typically it's three sessions with someone trained in this type of work. The first two meetings prepare concerned family and friends for the third meeting with the addicted person. At the third meeting, family and friends tell the addict their concerns about his behavior, hoping to persuade him to get help. Hopefully the addict does agree to treatment.

Managing Finances

Are finances your big problem? How about consulting a financial adviser? Here again, outside advice often produces better results than arguing with your spouse about money. A financial adviser can help you set a budget, reorganize or consolidate debt, and stick to the plan. It's kind of like going to Weight Watchers; you need to check in regularly to review your spending habits until you're sure you can live within your incomes on your own.

Rarely is too much money the problem, although it has been known to happen. Usually the money available to your household doesn't meet your needs and desires, and debts keep growing. Sometimes bankruptcy is the only option, but be careful.

FACT

Debt management and financial planning are two different things. Debt managers help you consolidate your debt and pay it off in affordable monthly payments. If you choose this route, make sure you are using a legitimate debt consolidation provider. Financial planners help you develop an investment program. They charge a commission on the investments you make through them.

Helpful Resources Abound

If there's hope for the marriage, by all means first put your energies into trying to save it. All kinds of help are out there in your community. Check out local United Way agencies, Catholic Charities, Lutheran Brotherhood, Jewish Family and Children's Services, and your local county's social services. Ask the court for a referral to a mediator who can help you and your spouse resolve some of your differences.

If you can't save your marriage, then you may want to utilize the resources available to you to help you through the hard times. Psychologists who work with families going through divorce say most people need three years to complete the emotional divorce. To go through the process and emerge ready to begin anew means experiencing some enormous mental ups and downs. This is a bit easier when you ask for and accept outside help. A divorce isn't so different from a death in terms of adjustment stages people go through. Divorce is not to be entered into casually.

Moving Toward Divorce

Maybe you've been in counseling for several months, and your spouse has refused to work with you in any way—no individual or marriage counseling, no financial planning. Indeed, your spouse may refuse to see anything amiss in the marriage. The only thing that has changed is that you're feeling better about yourself and feeling clearer about what happens next.

If you have children, consider their developmental levels before making the final decision to divorce. Infants need to see their parents every day. They have no sense of time and become very anxious when separated from a caregiver. Make sure you have planned for your children's needs, including counseling if that is necessary.

Maybe at this point you decide you need to live separately from your spouse. Before discussing a separation, you would be wise to consult a financial adviser or debt manager to develop a budget. You need to know what it will cost to live on your own, either in the place you now share with your spouse or somewhere new. If you have children and want them to live with you, you will need to figure their expenses into your budget.

When you work out a budget, you may find you don't have enough income to support yourself and your children. If your spouse has no income or doesn't make much, you can't expect much help there. You may have to support your spouse, too. If you have no income and will have to look to your spouse, can she support two households? What if there isn't enough money?

Because you haven't dropped the separation bomb yet, you have the option of staying in the marriage—and the marital home—until there is more money. You or your spouse can get jobs. You both could do a better job of managing the income of the family—whatever it takes to get into a financial position to live apart.

What about a Separation?

If you're not sure that a divorce is in your future, you can also consider a separation. If you have talked to your spouse and you both have doubts about a divorce, you might suggest a trial separation. A trial separation period can allow you both time to decide whether to make it permanent. Separation from your spouse can provide some time to think about the marriage, the children, and the finances. Think of it as a trial period, a test run to see if your problems are really so bad that there is no hope for your marriage. Since a separation of this type does not have any legal status, you need to make sure that you have agreed about the details.

1. Where will the children live? How much time will they spend with each parent?
2. If one spouse earns more than the other, what amount should they contribute to the other's expenses?
3. If there are joint debts, how will they be paid and by whom?
4. If you have joint financial accounts, will they be separated or maintained, and by whom?

There will be a thousand details to resolve along the way, so it's important to try and keep the lines of communication open. You must have a clear and comprehensive understanding of your assets and debts for this to be a good option. There are no legal protections when you separate voluntarily, so if your spouse spends all the money, there may be nothing you can do about it.

ALERT!

Even if you think everything you want is in the separation agreement, you should consult a lawyer. The last thing you want at the time of a divorce is for the support provisions in your agreement to be invalid. If this happens you could end up paying double the amount to which you had agreed.

Most states provide a formal mechanism for couples to enter into a separation by agreement, usually referred to as a separation agreement. What this means is that the parties would put in writing all the things they have agreed to regarding sharing of children and division of assets. The agreement is absolutely binding on the parties, so you should not sign a document of this kind without having it reviewed by a lawyer.

The separation agreement option offers couples a more formal way to separate, which can be revoked should they choose to reconcile. In some states, an agreement of this kind, when made pursuant to the laws of the state, can substitute for fault after a given time period and can be easily used and incorporated into a divorce.

The Role of Family Court If You Do Not Divorce

If you're not ready to divorce but need to resolve issues related to custody, child, or spousal support, family court can be a good option. Family court is usually designed to be more user friendly than a supreme or superior court; a lot of people go there without a lawyer. You may be able to work out your issues with the help of a family court judge. While there may be some limited filing fees, there are often no costs associated with family court.

If you call or go down to your local family court, the clerks will probably be able to give you forms, answer procedural questions, and tell you how long things will take to get your case in front of a judge. As in other courts, they will not give legal advice.

Even if you and your spouse have agreed about custody and visitation and feel you don't need a lawyer, you may need some help deciding issues of child support. Most states have statutes that govern child support, so determining the right amount is straightforward. The court will ask you and your spouse to bring some financial information, including tax returns and pay stubs. Once the judge has this information, it is easy for him to tell you what the state requires each spouse to contribute. Having a judge tell you what the law requires may make the bite of child support a little more palatable if you are the one having to pay.

Although family court can also make an order of spousal support, determining the right amount is usually more complicated than with child support. Even so, a judge can probably help you sort out what is fair given your respective incomes and debts of the marriage.

Everyone Needs Legal Advice

Before making any decisions, get some legal advice. The best place to get legal advice is from a family or divorce lawyer. This seems pretty obvious, but many people get their information from friends, family, clergy, and even their local librarian!

Do not seek legal advice from your friends and family. Do not ask your hairdresser for help. In fact, do not ask your friends and family for advice about your divorce, period. Some of your friends may have gone through a divorce. Their information will be based on their experiences, and their situations were different from yours.

Use Friends and Family for Support

Friends and family mean well, but they just can't give you the advice you need. They are biased in your favor. They are most likely not divorce lawyers, and they don't—or shouldn't—have all the facts of your marriage. If you haven't discussed separation or divorce with your spouse, you sure don't want someone else to break the news.

You should use friends and family as your support system. They can be there for you when you're feeling low, help with the kids, and maybe provide financial assistance. Keep your focus on maintaining their friendship and support; try not to force your friends to take sides. You may want to work with your therapist on managing your need to vent appropriately.

Arm Yourself with Knowledge

You need to know whether it's safe to move out with the kids or whether the law will see this act as abandoning your spouse. You need to know what kind of support you are entitled to. You need to know how you will meet your financial needs during the separation. You need to know how to protect the assets of the marriage.

You and your lawyer need to talk about these matters as they apply to you. You need to hear about the laws of divorce and separation in your state. This knowledge will give you a better sense of the many issues you need to address.

Hiring a lawyer isn't going to be cheap. To protect your interests and your wallet, read the chapters on finding and using a lawyer before looking for one to talk to about separating. Go over them thoroughly before you hire a lawyer to handle your divorce.

Protective Steps

Make sure you make copies of important household financial documents before you leave. Remove the originals to make your copies and then replace them. Put your copies in a safe place, such as a safety deposit box in your name alone or at a friend or family member's house. If you and your spouse each have a set of these documents, you won't have to spend time and money fighting over getting this information.

If you have financial accounts together, do what you can to protect your share. If you have joint checking and savings accounts, you can take part of each account and open new accounts in your name alone. If your spouse uses the checking account, you will need to notify your spouse that you removed the funds and why so that the account doesn't get overdrawn. Also be sure to make copies of investment account and credit card statements, showing the balances at about the time you're planning to separate.

Any money or assets you use that come from joint accounts typically belong to both parties. A divorce will divide all of the assets you share with your spouse. Depending on your particular financial situation, you may have to pay back money or assets that you use or remove from joint accounts.

If you've had little to do with the finances of your household, now is the time to learn about them as fast as you can so you can protect your interests. If your spouse has managed the finances from a joint account you rarely use, you'll need to borrow the records and make copies of the entries so you can figure out what it costs to run your household.

CHAPTER 2

You've Decided to Divorce

At this point you're convinced you've taken all possible steps to save the marriage, and they didn't work. You've made the difficult decision that your marriage is probably over and you want to separate and probably divorce. Now you need to tell your spouse. There is not a right time to do this, and the longer you drag it out, the harder it will likely be on your spouse. Be sensitive because your spouse may be taken by surprise, especially if there's been denial about marital problems.

Breaking the News to Your Spouse

If you have children, it's very important to tell your spouse you want a separation when the children are somewhere else. You don't know how your spouse will react, so you want to give her time to calm down and digest the information. A big scene can be frightening and harmful to your children. If you pick a fight with your spouse and one of you leaves the house (and the marriage), you will leave each other frozen in rage. It's very hard to negotiate when you're both so angry.

Involving a Counselor

Your spouse may now suggest counseling. You'll have to decide whether this is too little too late, or whether you're willing to try it. You may be convinced the marriage is over, but the opportunity to actually communicate with your spouse by working with a counselor can help both of you deal better with whatever lies ahead.

FACT

If your issues are major—say chemical addiction or adultery—they may still be resolvable without a divorce, but they will take a lot of hard work. The work it takes to solve problems within a marriage may be far less than the work needed to make a new life after divorce. Make sure you've exhausted all possible alternatives before choosing divorce.

If you do agree to counseling, be clear to your spouse that either you're participating in marriage counseling to save the marriage, or you're going to divorce (or exit) counseling to help your spouse accept that the marriage is over. Some marriage counselors do both marriage counseling and exit counseling. Exit counseling assists a couple in dealing with the death of their marriage and helps them develop tools to cope in the least harmful way.

When people use divorce counseling to get a handle on the emotional issues, they're better able to focus on the legal and practical issues of their divorce and make good decisions. Emotional baggage creates most of the problems in a divorce for everyone involved—you, your spouse, and your kids. Get rid of it if you can.

Don't announce your decision to divorce when you're angry. Don't pack a bag and leave in anger, because you're inviting retaliation. If you leave, your spouse is in control of the house, the children, and the marital assets. Besides, you're likely to say things you'll regret. Things said in anger may come back to haunt you during the divorce.

Allowing Time for Acceptance

If the spouse who wants the divorce pushes too hard, the spouse being left may use desperate tactics to try to prevent it from happening. The left spouse may become irrational or threatening. This spouse may try to hide important papers, bring unnecessary motions in court, or try to convince the children that the other parent is immoral or otherwise unfit. It is wise to give the left spouse time to accept the fact of the divorce. While this may take some time and patience, it will pay off if he stops trying to keep the divorce from happening and cooperates in resolving the issues.

Some states retain vestiges of fault in their divorce laws, but those states apply fault in specific ways. For instance, in some states, a spouse who has been unfaithful can't get alimony. In some states, claims of mental cruelty or desertion may have an impact on the final property division. The American Bar Association website, *www.abanet.org*, offers a number of helpful resources, including a state-by-state summary of the residency and grounds requirements to get a divorce.

Taking Steps to Protect Yourself

If your spouse has been abusive to you or the children during the marriage, and you have reason to expect a violent reaction to your announcement, you must take precautionary steps for your protection. Discuss the nature of the violence and abuse that you've experienced with the lawyer you've selected, and find out what rights and protections you have under the law.

Most states have civil, as opposed to criminal, laws that make it possible for you to get a restraining order, also called an order of protection, to get the abuser out of the house. A judge can order your spouse to stay away from you, your home, and even the children. Telling an abusive spouse that you want a separation may be very dangerous. You may need to get that restraining order to get the separation you want. Violation of a restraining order is a criminal offense.

The most dangerous time for victims of domestic violence is when they leave the abuser. Be careful. Protect yourself and your children.

QUESTION?

Do you have to prove your spouse did something wrong to get a divorce?
Most states now have no-fault divorce. Each state that does has its own requirements but will grant a divorce based on "irretrievable breakdown" or "irreconcilable differences." Under no-fault law, if your spouse says it's over, it's over. When one spouse says the marriage can't be saved, the marriage is irretrievably broken.

If Your Spouse Wants the Divorce

So far, we've assumed that you're in the driver's seat in this divorce. What if, instead, your spouse surprises you with the announcement that he wants a divorce? You'll probably feel as if you've been punched in the stomach. You may react by denying what you've just heard. You may get very angry. You may well spend the night of the announcement sleepless, going over and over your marriage and wondering where it went wrong. In the days and weeks that follow, you'll be on an emotional roller coaster. Your world is in chaos. Even so, you need to pull yourself together enough to take action to protect yourself. How quickly you need to move depends on your relationship with your spouse. If you don't trust your spouse, you need to act sooner rather than later.

Considering Your Options

What can you do if you don't want a divorce? You can ask your spouse to go to counseling. If your spouse is willing to go to counseling, you may be able to save the marriage. If counseling can't save the marriage, it can give you some insight into your spouse's issues. It can also give you some time to adjust to the likelihood that there will be a divorce.

FACT

If you don't want to get a divorce, don't simply ignore the matter and assume your lack of cooperation will stop the proceedings. Your spouse may be able to get a divorce without your consent and may be able to get whatever she wants unless you take steps to protect yourself and your interests.

It is not uncommon for one spouse to decide the marriage is over long before the other has any idea that the marriage is in trouble. Lack of communication is a major factor in many divorces. When the spouse who wants the divorce pushes to move forward, the other spouse may use all kinds of tactics to delay the process. The spouse who is being left may plead and bargain with the other spouse to reconsider. Counseling can be very useful in helping the reluctant spouse accept the fact that a divorce will occur.

Steps to Protect Your Assets

Consider the worst-case scenario. Suppose you've hidden things from each other. You have some credit cards your spouse doesn't know about. Your spouse hides extra spending in the grocery budget. The bottom line is that you trust each other very little. Now your spouse is very angry and threatening to leave or to make you leave the house. You need to act quickly. At a minimum, you need to do the following things if you and your spouse have accumulated assets during the marriage:

- Go through your home and collect every possible financial paper that you can lay your hands on. Don't overlook anything. Something as simple as an ATM receipt may tell you that your spouse has an account you don't know about. Copy them as soon as possible.

- Write down the name of every financial institution, address, and account number for every document you find and keep this list separate from the financial papers. The list will help you in case your spouse takes the papers back before you have a chance to copy them.

- Get the balances on every account you know about—savings, checking, retirement, credit cards—right away and keep track of what goes on in the accounts in case you need to show that your spouse wrongfully withdrew funds or improperly ran up charges on the credit cards.

- Open an account in your own name and start putting some money in it. As long as there is not a restraining order or divorce in progress, you can take money out of your joint accounts and put it in a personal account for yourself. You do not need your spouse's permission. Do not take any more than half of the available funds in a joint account. Available funds are the money that has not yet been used. Make sure you have enough to pay for outstanding checks, monthly debits, or other charges. If you cause any checks to bounce or accrue other fees because of your withdrawal, you will probably have to repay these charges at some point.

- See a lawyer. Take every financial document you can find with you to show the lawyer. If you haven't already done so, ask the lawyer to make copies before these papers disappear. If you only have a list of accounts, ask the lawyer to make a copy and keep it on file in case your list disappears.

Your spouse may already have transferred assets into new bank accounts and may have tried to put various pieces of marital property out of your reach before telling you the divorce is imminent. While your spouse probably can't get away with this, you may have a long, costly legal battle to get what is rightfully yours. Knowing where the assets are located will help your lawyer get back what is rightfully yours.

Emotional Anatomy of a Divorce

Most divorcing couples experience something close to emotional break-down at the outset of a divorce. Psychologists say that next to a spouse's or child's death, divorce is the most stressful event for married people. It takes most people more than two years to regain their equilibrium and move on with their lives after they decide to divorce.

Some experts compare the emotions of divorce to those experienced when a loved one dies. The death of a marriage often generates feelings of sadness and loss, and a similar mourning period occurs. However, there are some important differences. Divorce has no ritual form of mourning, no memorial service that brings you the support of friends and family. In divorce, your friends tend to back away, hoping to avoid taking sides or getting caught in the middle. Divorce is often accompanied by a sense of failure that is rarely part of mourning a death. Also, the formerly loved one is alive and kicking and may be making your life miserable.

FACT

Emotions run very high during a divorce. You may find it helpful to speak with a counselor or therapist or even join a support group. There are many resources available through community-based programs that cost little or no money. There's help out there—you only need to ask for it.

The bad news is that this period of adjustment is very hard on the parties and their children. The good news is that most people do work through all the emotions of divorce and get on with their lives, and most of their children come through this turmoil without too many permanent scars.

Emotional Honeymoon Period

Despite having to adjust to the new structure of the family, it's common to feel pretty good the first month or two following a separation. You don't have the daily stress of dealing with your spouse, and that absence of tension is energizing. You and your spouse may consider reconciling and may go to marriage counseling with the hope of putting the marriage back together. You may become Super Parent, putting all your newfound energy into child-focused activities. Or you may become incredibly self-indulgent, focusing on yourself. Unfortunately, this sense of well-being will disappear all too soon.

Reality Returns

Marriage counseling isn't working. The relief of the first months transforms into loneliness. This loneliness is not so much missing your spouse as having a sense of panic that you'll be alone forever, that you'll never share happy moments with a special someone again. You may also experience depression that may affect your job performance. It can diminish your ability to concentrate. You may find yourself daydreaming on the job or simply unable to handle the daily routine at the office. Your health may suffer.

ALERT!

Statistics from a study in Washington state show that people going through a divorce had 82 percent more automobile crashes than the average driver. This may be related in part to their reduced ability to concentrate. Friends and family who can provide good emotional support will help reduce your stress during this process.

You may feel a tremendous sense of disappointment because your dreams for the future have been destroyed. Total responsibility for the children feels like drudgery, or not seeing the children leads to a profound sense of loss. You want to talk about your situation with your friends, but they lose interest just as you're warming up to your topic. Your initial high becomes an unpleasant low. A fair result seems nowhere in sight.

You feel a sense of failure. You see your kids missing their other parent and showing signs of anxiety or anger. You wonder, "What could I have done to save the marriage? Is there something wrong with me? Who changed?" Such thoughts plague sleepless, soul-searching nights, which are followed by cheerless days. You may feel abandoned and frightened of an unknown future. Sometimes you want to go back to the way it was while sometimes all you can think about is how to make your spouse hurt the way you hurt.

Acknowledge Your Anger

Some people mask their depression with anger. While depression can be paralyzing, anger tends to be energizing. However, using anger to avoid mourning the end of a marriage can be dangerous. It's normal to be angry; it's not normal to obsess about getting even with your spouse for causing you this pain. Some people get stuck in the hostility and anger phase and spend years blaming their ex-spouses for everything that goes wrong in their lives. Acknowledge your anger. Express it safely—in counseling or in conversation with a good friend. Never express anger without restraint. If you can recognize anger and accept it, you can control it, rather than letting it control you.

Six to Twelve Months after Separation

Your life still feels chaotic. Family routines are nonexistent or minimal. The financial reality of maintaining two households creates more stress. Custodial parents can become rigid, restrictive, and overprotective. They sometimes try to limit children's contact with the other parent, who they believe is too cavalier about the safety and well-being of the kids. Visiting parents want to have happy children during their limited time together, so they become overindulgent. Overindulgence can translate into having no rules. If the custodial parent learns that the other parent has no rules, visitation may be denied.

Depending on how difficult it is for your children to cope with the divorce, you may want to consider taking your children to a counselor. You're undoubtedly going through a tough time and may not be able to give your all to your children. A counselor can help.

If you are a custodial mother, you've probably gone to work, even if you stayed at home with the children during the marriage. Even with child support from your soon-to-be ex, your financial situation could be tenuous. You might find more often than not that you have to tell the children there's no extra money for a field trip at school or a new baseball glove. You might no longer be able to pay for child care, so your children come home to an empty house after school and are on their own until you get home from work. You might be exhausted when you get home and have little time and energy left for the kids. That lack of energy can translate into an inability to maintain any kind of consistency in the home. Meals can become erratic. Discipline can become inconsistent. Conflicts with the children might increase.

Into the Second Year

It is common to experience regret and ambivalence about the wisdom of getting divorced. An especially lovely sunset may remind you of the times your family spent at the lake. It's likely that you'll see less and less of the friends you shared during the marriage. If you're a woman, you're likely to put your energies into projects. Typically, women take classes, garden, or join groups. Men are more likely to socialize frenetically. Sociologists who have studied the behavior of men and women after separation say that this is the time when lust runs high and commitment low. It's a year when both men and women search for ways to avoid being at home alone. You're seeking confirmation that you're attractive and competent, and social relationships can help bolster your recovering self-esteem.

Many relationships that led to the breakup of the marriage may now break up as well. Maybe the person who was there for you and gave you the courage to announce that you wanted a divorce no longer looks like the person with whom you want to spend the rest of your life.

The Third Year Approaches

Household routines, often much different from those of the marriage, have evolved and stabilized. You've figured out how to manage with less money. You have a closer relationship with your children than you had during the marriage. If you're the visiting parent, you have blocks of uninterrupted time to talk more and do things together. If you're the custodial parent, you find yourself talking more to your children, in part because they are the only other people at home with you.

As you settle down, so do they, and a new equilibrium is established. If you've been able to work through your anger and recognize your role in the death of your marriage, you're probably ready to work with the other parent to develop a workable, affordable arrangement for you and your children's future. It's about time.

By the end of the third year after separation, most divorced people are ready to consider a new relationship. Before that time, they're working their way through the stages of adjustment needed to move on with their lives. Entering into a relationship with someone who is still struggling with the fallout from a divorce is probably not in your best interest.

Initiating the Divorce or Responding to It?

If you're the one who initiated the divorce, you probably gave this decision a lot of thought before telling your spouse. How you break the news may have a huge impact on how you go through the divorce itself, especially if your spouse is totally shocked and surprised. If you can tell your spouse your decision calmly and without placing blame, and if you then give your spouse time to catch up emotionally, you may be able to reach a point where the decision to end the marriage is mutual. When this happens, you have a much better chance of negotiating the terms of your divorce.

The person who begins the divorce discussion needs to realize it's too early to discuss long-term plans with the spouse who is just in the beginning stages of the emotional response to the idea of divorce. It will take your spouse some time to come to terms with your decision.

If you are on the other side of the equation and your spouse has told you he wants a divorce, you may feel you have less time to get ready for the divorce. You should still take the time you need to adjust to the idea. You have time to take care of your psyche, get personal counseling, and maybe even get marriage or divorce counseling.

Getting divorced is never easy. It is harder when you're the one being left, although both parties need time to adjust to the idea of divorce. The spouse who is pushed too hard too fast may react badly and cause the divorce to take longer and be more painful. While it may take some time for the spouse who is getting left to catch up, it's probably worth it in the long run to give that spouse the time she needs.

Don't try to play the hero and resist the urge to ask for help. This is a very trying time. If you need professional help to make it through, then by all means seek it out. However, keep in mind that everything you do during a divorce is fair game. It will be open to examination and inquiry by your spouse's lawyer and the court.

In some cases, the left spouse will not catch up. Instead, she will continue to be emotionally devastated throughout the process and even after the divorce. If you fall into this category, get some counseling and try and move forward. Holding onto the marriage when it is clearly over is only going to result in more emotional upset for you and your children.

Trying to Reconcile

If you're emotionally ready to divorce, you should say so. Hedging your position by saying you want to separate for a little while because you need some space is deceitful. If you hold out false hope to your spouse, your spouse will have a hard time trusting you once that hope is destroyed. Separation rarely leads to reconciliation.

It makes sense that couples would choose one last try to save a difficult relationship rather than face the unknown. Most couples make a significant investment in their relationship, and a sense of attachment continues even when the love and excitement are gone. That's why many divorcing couples try to reconcile even after one has filed for divorce.

Successful reconciliation requires the help of a talented therapist, and even then, the prospects for success are dim. Too many past hurts, too much damaged trust, too much focus on the shortcomings of the other spouse interferes. The most positive results of reconciliation counseling are often a better understanding of why the marriage failed and acceptance that it is over.

ALERT!

Successful reconciliation works only if both parties want the marriage to work. If your spouse truly wants the divorce and you try to force her into therapy to save the marriage, you're only going to end up hurting yourself. You can't force your spouse to stay with you if the decision has been made. You can't force your spouse to withdraw a divorce action.

Going to Court Is Stressful

You won't realize the stress of litigating a divorce until you do it. Going to court requires careful, time-consuming preparation. The time you have to spend preparing papers and documents for court is time away from your children and your job. Every time you have to see your spouse in court you will ride a roller coaster of emotions that will drain you physically and emotionally. Being in court is stressful because you're on unfamiliar ground dealing with your spouse, the person who you loved and trusted for years who is now acting like a stranger—and an angry stranger at that. You don't know the rules, and you don't know what a judge will do. When you're in court you can't do anything else but sit, wait, and avoid the stare of your angry spouse.

Waiting for a court order is stressful, because once again you're not in control. Getting that court order at long last can be stressful, too, because you may be very unhappy with it. Often it feels as if the judge didn't read your papers, didn't listen to your lawyer, or simply didn't believe you. Once again, your spouse is the winner and you are the loser. The court's order can turn your whole world upside down.

Let Reason Prevail

As you navigate the emotional waters of your divorce, let reason be your guide. Don't let your lawyer's goals become your goals. If you know what you want, stick with it even when your spouse makes you so angry your blood boils. Be reasonable and realistic. Your spouse is not going to magically become a different person because you are now getting divorced. If she couldn't keep a clean house before, she probably won't be able to now. If your children have survived so far with clutter around them and dirty dishes in the sink, chances are they will be fine even when you're not around.

Divorce is a very traumatic experience, especially if you spend a lot of time in the courts. You will undoubtedly suffer several ups and downs throughout the process, so you may want to join a support group to help you cope. Others in your situation can offer advice, relay their own experiences, or just be there to listen.

If your lawyer says you can get custody of the children by showing your spouse is emotionally unstable, think about whether this is what you really want. Would it be good for your children for you to drag their other parent through a battle about mental health? Whether you are successful or not, your children's opinion of you could be permanently altered. For example, what if you are the husband and you claim your wife is emotionally unstable or unfit in some way? If you are successful in proving this, the children may blame you for their mother's problems. It may cause your children to be more supportive and protective of their mother and more critical of you. If you are not successful, your children may hate you for lying about their mother. If your spouse truly has problems, you must act to protect your children, but make sure your actions are based on facts and not the desire for revenge.

Suppose you actually got custody of the children. Are you prepared to take time off in the middle of the day to go to the doctor or the dentist or get your child to soccer practice? Are you prepared to stay home from work on days that school is cancelled or when your children are too sick to go to a babysitter? Be careful what you ask for and make sure you are asking for the right reasons.

When Anger Turns to Abuse

Anger is a normal emotion that most people experience at some point during the divorce process. You should expect angry outbursts, negative comments, belittling, arguments, and even an exaggerated story about your shortcomings. What you should not tolerate is abuse. Domestic violence is a pattern of coercive behavior, not a couple of isolated incidents of anger in the context of a divorce. If you believe you are a victim of domestic violence you should tell your lawyer and seek help from a local domestic violence program.

If abuse is an issue for you, tell your lawyer. You may need to get a restraining order before you take the potentially dangerous step of beginning your divorce. If your spouse is emotionally abusive, take whatever steps you can to prepare her for your announcement that you want a divorce. Try to treat her with respect and civility, and don't let her behavior goad you into an angry response.

FACT

If your spouse's anger seems uncontrollable and he engages in behavior such as name calling, humiliation, and threatening you, you may be a victim of domestic violence. You do not have to sustain physical injury to be a victim of domestic violence. Verbal and emotional abuse can also be very damaging and could precede physical violence.

Even if you have never experienced domestic violence in your marriage, a spouse could become abusive during the course of a divorce. If you are a victim, you should find out what services are available to protect you and take steps to ensure the safety of yourself and your children. All states have laws that protect victims of domestic violence. Find out what they are and see if they apply to your situation.

Headed for Litigation

When one spouse refuses to let go and accept the reality of a divorce, it's unlikely that the parties will be able to negotiate a settlement. At some point, the initiator of the divorce will lose the ability to stay calm in the face of the spouse's behavior and fight back. When that happens, the divorce is headed for litigation, and lots of it. The angrier you or your spouse becomes, the longer the litigation will last. The more litigation there is, the angrier the parties become. It is a vicious circle that will cost you heartache and pain, not to mention a ton of money. Your best course of action is to try to avoid litigation if at all possible.

Emotional Component of a Divorce

Thankfully, for many people, the emotional component of a divorce doesn't rise to the level of abuse. But emotions are always a part of the divorce process. Whether you're motivated by anger or sadness, you'll find yourself wanting to make the other guy hurt, too. It's appropriate to recognize your anger—it's not appropriate to act on it.

ALERT!

Be aware that you can control only your own behavior. You may be surprised at how your spouse behaves, but you cannot control her behavior. All you can do is control how you respond, which may in time cause your spouse to behave differently.

Is Therapy Right for You?

Because of the emotional roller coaster you will experience throughout your divorce, you may want to consider therapy. There are many options available, including individual counseling with a social worker or psychologist, group therapy with other people who are going through a divorce, and peer support groups. Other types of counseling and supportive services are often available through local community organizations and churches.

If you are having trouble dealing with your divorce, therapy may be a good choice for you. A trained counselor can work with you to explore your feelings and develop positive ways to express your sadness and anger. There are many different approaches available, from talking about your problems to hypnosis. Finding a group session can also be very useful because you will be able to talk to other folks who are experiencing the same emotional roller coaster as you. Developing a positive support network can help you get through the hard times that you will experience during the divorce process.

If you are experiencing severe depression, anxiety, or sleeplessness as a result of your divorce, you may want to see a doctor who can prescribe medication that will help these symptoms. Don't be embarrassed or afraid to admit that you are having trouble. Many people experience depression and anxiety while going through a divorce. It doesn't mean that you have a long-term problem that will last past this difficult time in your life.

Although most therapy is confidential, your spouse may be able to access your records if your divorce is litigated. If you have children, your spouse can make your mental health an issue in the litigation. As a result, the court will want to make sure you are fit to parent and will probably order the counselor to turn over your records.

Finding a form of therapy that works for you may take some effort on your part, and you may have to try a couple of different options to find out what feels right. If you are in individual therapy, your sessions with your counselor are probably confidential. When you start therapy, you should ask your counselor about confidentiality and under what circumstances he will have to disclose what happens in your sessions.

If you have already been diagnosed with a mental illness, the divorce process will probably exacerbate your symptoms. You should consult with your regular doctor to see if she suggests any changes in your medication or has other options that might help you feel better.

CHAPTER 3

What about the Children?

Children will both enrich and complicate your divorce. They'll be there to hug you when the going gets tough, make you laugh when you most need it, and give continued meaning to your life. However, they will need your care, support, and reassurance at a time when you have little energy left after taking care of yourself. Parenting during this time is likely to present new challenges. Stay calm and make an effort to work with your spouse to make it as easy as possible on your children.

Telling Your Children

As your world is turning upside down, you're probably spending most of the time thinking about yourself. What will happen to you? How will you cope with your new status as a divorced person? Your emotions will run the gamut from relief to despair. Just think: If you are having a hard time dealing with the changes, what must be going on in the minds of your children? Fortunately, you have some control over what happens to you. Your children have no control; they depend on you and your spouse.

Both Parents Should Participate

It's important to tell the children what's going on. Think how devastating it is for a child to wake up one morning and find one of his parents gone. When this happens, children immediately start to worry that another morning they'll wake up to find the remaining parent gone. Ideally you and your spouse should tell children about the impending divorce together. If possible, you need to plan together how this will happen. Decide in advance what you will say. Pick a time when the family is normally together, say, Sunday dinner. If you don't have such a time, call a family conference when no one has to run off to an activity.

Both of you should participate. Tell the children you've decided to separate. Tell them the fact you're getting divorced doesn't change the fact you love them very much.

If you've made specific plans for your separation, tell the children what they are. If you're the parent who is moving out, be sure to tell the children they will always be welcome at your new place. Let them know you will spend as much time with them as you possibly can. Reassure them that you will always be there for them if they need you.

Reassure the children that you will always be their parents. Some children may feel it is their fault. Reassure your children that what is happening has nothing to do with them or anything they have done.

Use Simple Language

When you tell your children about the divorce, you need to use language they understand. All children old enough to understand language should be included in this process. While two-year-olds may not know the word divorce, they'll be able to understand when you say, "Mommy and Daddy aren't going to live together any more." Little kids don't have a good grasp of time, so it's better to say "I'll see you a lot," rather than "I'll see you in two weeks."

All children involved in a divorce wonder if they were so bad they drove their parents to it, so you need to be clear that the divorce is an adult decision for reasons having nothing to do with them. If children are old enough to understand, it's helpful to give them a concrete plan for the future. Kids don't do well with ambiguity. Most adults don't either, but kids especially need specifics. They need to know where you're going, when you're going, and when they'll see you. They need to know whether they'll move and with whom they'll live.

Even though your children may not drastically change their behavior or even act as though the news of divorce affects them, this doesn't mean that they're not suffering. Some children live in a state of shock or denial after hearing the news. If your child's behavior changes drastically, you may want to consult a mental health professional.

If you tell the children you're sad, you give them permission to be sad, too. While it's good to talk to your children about feelings, make sure you don't badmouth the other parent in the process. Children need to be able to express their emotions about the divorce and they need to know you'll continue to be their parents.

Give an Explanation

Tell your children why you are getting divorced. You might say, "You kids have probably noticed Mom and I have been arguing a lot recently. We haven't had many fun times, like we used to. We just can't seem to get along." It's probably not a good idea to tell children you're getting divorced because one of you has found someone else. Children will have enough on their plates without dealing with the idea that one beloved parent has dumped the other for someone else. This is not the time to place blame. The idea is to give the children a reasonable explanation to help them understand and to make it clear the divorce is not their fault.

Develop Your Parenting Plan Quickly

Once you've told the children about the divorce and reassured them you have a plan for taking care of them, you'd better develop that plan. If you're one of the lucky ones, you've been able to sit down with your spouse and work out how you'll take care of the children after you separate. Unfortunately, many divorcing parents are too caught up in their own issues to give much thought to a plan for their children until the separation is imminent or has already happened.

A parenting plan needs to cover a lot of material, and it may take you more than one meeting to hammer it out. Discuss where the children will live. When will the parent who is moving out get to see the children, and for how long? Also work out how you will communicate with each other in the future—by phone, through e-mail, or face to face?

It's common for a dad who has taken his role as a father for granted to suddenly realize how important his children are. He may want to spend every evening with them, either at the marital home or at his new place. He may want them to live with him, even though historically he has been mostly a Sunday afternoon parent.

Mom may be feeling overwhelmed and resentful of the responsibilities about to fall in her lap. She's probably facing taking care of the house, the kids, and her job—by herself. She's probably worrying about money, too. She may be feeling more protective toward the children and may not want the children to be out of her control. As a result she may not want Dad to have so much time with the children.

These are normal responses to a divorce, but they make it harder to negotiate a parenting plan, especially if you've never done it before. You need to know your options, and you need to evaluate your children's needs based on their ages and developmental levels.

The Legal Perspective

Before you separated, perhaps you made many decisions together. You chose an obstetrician for yourself or your spouse when a pregnancy was confirmed. After your children were born, you selected a pediatrician. You decided whether to raise your children in a religion. If you were both working, you selected child care. As the children grew older, you decided whether to send them to nursery school. When it came time for kindergarten, you decided when to start your children and picked their schools. You decided to put braces on your children's teeth. You probably planned to decide on high schools together and help your children make college choices. Divorce will complicate this, and you may find it challenging to figure out the laws that apply in your case. The American Bar Association website, *www.abanet.org*, offers a number of helpful resources, including a state-by-state summary of custody criteria.

FACT

There are several divorce education programs available in the United States today. If you're having difficulty helping your children understand certain aspects of divorce, such as custody issues, you may want to consider attending one of these programs to help both you and your children through these trying times. Check with your child's school to see if they have a support group for children or consult your church or local community agency for suggestions.

Legal Custody

The law calls making decisions about your children's health care, education, religious upbringing, and so on legal custody. As part of your divorce, you'll choose—or the court will decide—whether you'll have joint legal custody or whether one of you will have sole legal custody. Joint legal custody means you make these decisions together. Sole legal custody means one of you will have total authority over these decisions.

Physical Custody

Before you separated, maybe you divided responsibility for taking care of the children. One or both of you got the children up, fed them breakfast, and got them to school or to the school bus. One of you took them to soccer practice. One of you volunteered in your children's classrooms. Each of you spent time with your children. The law calls the actual time you spend with your children physical custody.

If both of you continue to share the actual hands-on care of the children, this is called joint or shared physical custody. If the children spend most of their time with one parent, that parent is said to have sole physical custody or primary physical custody. Sometimes parents divide responsibility by actually dividing the children. One parent takes the older children and one the younger. This arrangement is called split custody. Courts and psychologists agree this usually isn't good for children. Most take the position that children should stay together whenever possible.

A Responsibility to Your Children

You chose to take on the responsibility of children, and parenting is a big job in the best of circumstances. Divorce is not the best of circumstances. All the same, you want your children to make it through the divorce with as little damage as possible. Psychologists tell us over and over that parental conflict causes the most harm to children of divorce.

ALERT!

If you and your spouse are able to communicate well (at least in matters of the children) and live relatively close to each other, try to be flexible with visitation schedules. If children aren't able to see a parent when they feel they need to, they may become resentful toward both parents.

If you want to minimize parental conflict, you will need to develop a workable parenting plan. To develop such a plan you need to know something about the developmental needs of your children. Children at different ages and levels of psychological development have different needs. The kids who do the best when their parents divorce are the kids whose parents take those needs into account.

Boys and Girls React Differently

Psychologists who have studied the children of divorce report that boys at all ages are more likely to react with increased aggression and stubborn opposition to household rules. Experts report that boys seem to have a harder time dealing with their parents' divorce. Boys generally—in intact families as well—are resistant to authority, more demanding of their parents than girls, and more likely to get into trouble. These behaviors are intensified by divorce.

While there are certainly levels of psychological development that you need to be aware of, you must also remember that your children are individuals and will handle the divorce in their own ways. Emotional outbursts, sadness, and acting out are all to be expected of children living through a divorce.

Girls tend to turn their hurt inward. They try to be very, very good to make sure their remaining parent doesn't leave, too. They create a fantasy world where their parents are still together. They may be bossy and crabby at school and whiny and petulant at home, but they tend to get over this behavior quickly.

Society responds differently to boys and girls of divorce. When a little girl expresses her sadness, she is likely to be comforted. A little boy, on the other hand, is more likely to be told to act more like a man. Peers are more likely to forgive the bossy behavior of girls than the aggressive, angry behavior of boys.

Therapy for the Children

Many children whose parents are divorcing end up in therapy. The children may have difficulty with the divorce or with the behavior of one or both of their parents in the divorce context. Many parents send their children to a therapist, often because the children's behavior becomes worrisome or difficult during a divorce. Courts will usually leave this decision to the parents. However, in extreme cases, the court can order that children have a psychological exam or attend therapy even if the parents object.

Many therapists ask parents to sign a confidentiality agreement stating that conversations between a therapist and child are private. If you do go to court, the judge may order the therapist to turn over her notes and records. Exposing your child's confidences, shared in the belief that they were private, can have a devastating effect on his mental health.

If you think your child has said something that may benefit your case, it can be very tempting to allow your child's confidences to be violated. Try to remember that this could have devastating long-term effects on your child, particularly if one parent becomes alienated after the disclosure.

The process of divorce is an extremely emotionally unsettling time that can cause a lot of stress and anxiety. Try to find a way to reduce your stress and keep your emotions in check. You will find that you have a much better outcome overall if you can navigate your divorce with a level head. It is especially important in those cases where children are involved because you are going to have to deal with your spouse long after the dust has settled.

The Psychological Perspective

You'll want your parenting plan to fit the psychological needs of your children as well as meet the legal definitions. Experts say children have very specific needs, depending on their ages and levels of development. Even in the womb your child responds to what is going on. When a woman is pregnant, she shares her circulatory system with the fetus. If she is upset, her system sends out extra hormones and chemicals. These may circulate into the fetus, making it more agitated and active. Stress during pregnancy can result in premature birth. Add these stresses to the other stresses of divorce, and a baby's arrival can be more a nightmare than a dream come true.

Infancy to Age Two

Infants may not be able to understand words or recognize all the people in their world, but they're very aware of emotions. They respond to familiar faces. One of the first things they learn is trust. When they are wet or hungry, they cry and someone comes to care for them. Divorcing parents may be less responsive, and the infant may suffer. The interaction between infant and caregiver is critical to the baby's development. Infants and children up to about two years of age need a consistent caregiver. Their sense of security comes from the quality and consistency of care they get during this time.

At about a year old, children develop a fear of strangers. They also develop a deep fear of losing the parent who is their primary caretaker. This may make putting them in day care traumatic for child and parent.

Two-year-olds are just beginning to develop a little independence. If parents separate, children this age are likely to redevelop fears they had seemed to outgrow. They may resist going to bed, both because they're afraid of losing their primary caretaker and because their nightmares may have intensified. Having a parent move out may make these fears worse.

Little kids need to see their parents frequently. The absent parent should spend time with these little ones at least every third day. The visits should be frequent but short. Ideally, they should take place at the child's home, because small children aren't ready for overnights with the visiting parent. Children under two need consistent caregivers. This is the time when children bond, or develop human attachments.

One piece of good news: Very young children often are less affected by a divorce because they have a much shorter history of living with both parents and less exposure to fighting and stress in the home.

Ages Three to Five

Children from three to five may react to a divorce with regression, going back to a happier time when Mom and Dad lived together. They may deny their parents are divorced because it's too scary to admit they've lost one parent. They're afraid they may well lose the other. Children this age may believe they caused the breakup, and if they're just good enough their parents will get back together.

FACT

Regardless of their ages, never assume your children don't have at least some understanding of what's going on. Though you may believe they're too young to understand what you're saying, they'll often get the gist of the conversation, or at the very least pick up on the tension.

You need to give children this age a specific, concrete plan in language and concepts they can understand. They need frequent contact with both parents. They need predictability and consistency. It's extremely important that parents handle exchanges with a minimum of stress. By this age children can handle overnights and weekends with the visiting parent.

Ages Six to Eight

Children from six to eight experience enormous sadness when their parents divorce. They feel torn between their parents. When they're with Mom, they miss Dad. When they're with Dad, they miss Mom. They often cry when moving from one parent to the other. Despite these strong emotions at exchanges, they need to spend time with each parent. They often worry the other parent will forget about them. Frequent time with both parents helps them get past their feelings of loss and abandonment.

Divorced or separated parents often misread this behavior. The fact that your child misses her other parent when she's with you doesn't mean she loves you less. The fact that she cries when she leaves you doesn't mean she loves you more.

Children this age have strong and elaborate fantasies about their parents getting back together. At the same time, some children may welcome their parents' new partners, as long as the children themselves are included in the "new family." Other children may be adamantly opposed to a new partner and refuse to see a parent when the new partner is around. A danger here is that children can attach to the new partner. If this new relationship ends, the children will be devastated all over again.

Encourage your children to voice their feelings. Your children could be suffering silently, allowing the unspoken feelings to fester until they become too much for the children to handle. The buried emotions could then be released in unhealthy ways, particularly in older children.

While children this age will benefit from spending frequent time with each parent, they may not be ready for a shared arrangement that has them spending part of each week with each parent. They have a lot of sorting out to do, so managing such a schedule may be more than they can comfortably handle. The ideal arrangement is for parents to live near one another, so the children can easily spend time with each parent without actually moving from one house to the other for prolonged stays.

Children of this age are particularly troubled when their parents remain hostile. Fear of losing both parents may force a child to avoid mentioning one parent in the other's presence for fear of triggering an angry reaction. This can even result in a child refusing to see one parent to appease the other parent. It can also result in children making up negative stories about one parent in order to align with the other parent.

Ages Nine to Twelve

Kids from ages nine to twelve have rigid moral rules, and when they believe one parent has violated these rules, they get very angry. They may refuse to see or talk to that parent or may act hostile and revengeful when they're together. Sometimes they may take the side of the parent with whom they live, out of a sense of self-preservation, and never mention the other parent and act badly toward that parent.

The custodial parent needs to stress the absent parent's good points and try to defuse the child's anger, even if that parent secretly agrees the other parent has behaved badly. The parent who feeds into a child's anger may become the object of the child's anger in later years. The older child may blame that parent for depriving him of a relationship with the other parent.

While children this age have a better understanding of what led to the divorce and are less likely to blame themselves, they still want their parents to be figures worthy of veneration. When parents try to put children in the middle, the youngsters are resentful, and rightfully so. Boys at this age may become defiant toward their mothers and girls toward their fathers.

FACT

A divorce can sometimes cause a child to give up or lose interest in extracurricular activities. It is often recommended that the parents encourage their children to keep up with normal activities to help them move on with their lives. The more normal you can keep their schedules, the easier time they will have adjusting to their new living situation.

Kids this age may be well aware of the financial differences between their household and that of their other parent. This may make them even more protective of the parent with whom they live. In addition, adult responsibilities are too often imposed on children this age. If the custodial parent works, an older child may have to look after a younger one until the parent gets home. A son living with his mother may be told he's now "the man of the house" and may worry unnaturally about keeping his household safe.

It's important to remember children perceive themselves as "part-Mom" and "part-Dad." When Mom criticizes Dad, or vice versa, children hear it as criticism of themselves. It's important for children this age to make peace with both parents so they can get on with their development.

The Teen Years

As children get older, their activities at school and with friends become very important to them. Parents need to accommodate these activities, but they shouldn't be used to limit their time with the visiting parent.

Teenagers want to be adults, so they are constantly testing family limits and values. At the same time, they want a secure home base from which to operate. The teenage years are turbulent in any family. One moment teens want to be treated as adults, and the next they want to have their parents' advice and guidance.

While these older children may understand the reasons for a divorce—and may be better able to distance themselves from guilt—they still seek a family history that says their parents wanted them. They want happy memories of their childhood. Their sense of self can be badly damaged by a parent's offhand comment such as, "We had to get married because I was pregnant with you."

ALERT!

Teenagers without rules tend to get into trouble or drop out of school. Even though they pretend otherwise, they want their parents to provide a structure within which they can operate, resentfully sometimes, but safely. Parents need to be on the same page so that teenagers know what the rules are and that they will be enforced.

Even teenagers may have a hard time with a shared parenting arrangement. With so many demands on their lives—activities, friends, dating—they seek a secure home base. They need rules. Some parents go through a second adolescence after divorce, trying to experience things they think they missed the first time around. They may eliminate rules for themselves and their children, too.

Parents need to respect the many activities that compete for time with their teenagers. They need to work very hard at saying good things about the other parent. Teens are very aware that they are part-Mom and part-Dad. They need to believe this is a good thing.

Parental Alienation

Parental alienation is a term that can have different meanings to different people and in different settings. Basically it describes a systematic process by which one parent engages in behavior that alienates the children from the other parent. Sadly, children are often used as pawns in a divorce. A parent will sometimes do anything to get children on their side and use that to hurt the other parent. Any tactics you use to alienate your children from your spouse are problematic.

In some cases, children may come to have negative feelings about a parent because of what they have seen and heard while living in the household. Children develop feelings of their own toward parents as a result of their experiences and how they are treated. Negative feelings toward one parent or the other are not necessarily a result of brainwashing; rather, they are normal emotions in the context of a family going through divorce. Children's normal feelings should never be ignored or confused with parental alienation.

If your spouse alleges parental alienation, you should seek legal advice immediately and seriously consider hiring a lawyer. This is a serious allegation that has resulted in the removal of children from the accused parent's custody on many occasions. Do not take it lightly.

While the idea originally received a lot of attention in the context of child custody disputes, it has more frequently been labeled junk science in court. As a result, many courts will not even hear the allegation. Even as recently as 2005, the American Psychological Association stated that it did not have an official position on parental alienation syndrome, further calling into question its usefulness in the context of custody.

CHAPTER 4

Deciding Whether to Hire a Lawyer

Whether you decide to represent yourself or obtain an attorney, you should start the process by doing some research. Once you have a basic understanding of the process, you should obtain legal advice even if you decide to go it alone. There are many decisions to make regarding children, support, property, and assets that should not be made without knowing the laws of your state and how they are applied. It is critical that you understand your rights before you navigate the emotional and complex waters of a divorce action.

4

Can You Do It Yourself?

A person who decides to represent himself in a legal action is called a *pro se* litigant. Deciding whether to appear *pro se* or hire an attorney can be a difficult decision. Sometimes it is tempting to appear *pro se* to save the money you will spend hiring an attorney. Do not let this be the deciding factor. Remember that a divorce will impact the things you hold most dear, including the time you spend with your children and the division of your property and assets. The outcome will decidedly impact your future plans.

Before you decide whether you can do it yourself, you should gather information about your state's divorce laws and consult with an attorney. Find a local law library. A law library is a special kind of library that contains only legal resources. Law libraries can be found at most law schools and in some court facilities. To find your nearest law school, look on the Internet or call your local university. To find out if the court has a law library open to the public, call the local county, supreme, superior, or appeals court and ask. The Internet is another great source of information. Just make sure the information you are reading is for your state.

Once you find a law library, go and ask a librarian for a copy of your state's divorce laws. Make sure you obtain the laws of the state where you will file for divorce because laws vary from state to state. These are typically found in a statute or treatise book. In some states, you may have to look at several different books to get a good overview. Start reading. Do you notice anything? You should notice pretty quickly that laws are written in legalese, a form of archaic language that many nonlawyers find confusing.

If that weren't enough to make you nervous, you should know that laws may differ from what's in the statute book because appellate courts have issued decisions changing them. The legislature writes the laws, and the courts interpret them. After a case is tried, one or both of the parties may challenge the trial court's decision by appealing it. The appellate court reviews the trial and the trial judge's decision and then issues a decision that may agree or disagree with the trial court. In the process of agreeing and disagreeing, the appellate court will decide what the law really means. Their decision becomes what is known as case law. Case law provides further interpretation of a law and helps predict how an issue in your case might be settled by a trial judge.

Case law can be jurisdiction-specific depending on which court has decided the case. What this means is that courts in one area of the state may have a slightly different interpretation of a law than courts in a different area of the state. When learning the laws that apply to your case, make sure you are reading cases in your jurisdiction. As you read, write down any questions you have regarding how certain laws may apply to aspects of your own case. Read as much as you can about divorce. Once you have a basic understanding of the law, you should seek legal advice about your case.

ALERT!

While the Internet is always a good source of information, you must be very careful that the information you find applies to your particular jurisdiction. Don't rely on information that has been posted by other people who may have gone through the divorce process in your jurisdiction. Make sure that the information comes from a reliable source!

Why You Need Legal Advice

Even if you have already decided that you want to go it alone, you should spend the money for a consultation with a good divorce lawyer. No amount of research on your part can substitute for an hour with a good divorce lawyer. Not only can a lawyer provide you with information about your case, she can point out pitfalls that you may not have identified in your research. Make this time count and prepare in advance for your consultation. It will help if you prepare a list of the issues you have identified as important before you meet with the attorney. Remember that you are paying for an hour of someone's time to provide the information that you want. Before an attorney will answer any questions, you will have to provide an overview of your situation. Prepare a summary in advance so you can present it as quickly as possible, leaving you time to ask questions that you have formed from your research.

In English, Please

Good lawyers understand the statutes and the case law, or judicial decisions, that modify those statutes. They will read the weekly decisions of the appellate courts and stay up-to-date on all aspects of the law.

A good divorce lawyer will know the divorce law of your state as it applies to you and translate the law into language you can understand. The lawyer will read the history of the marriage you have written and quickly pull out the most legally important facts. He will explain why some facts are legally important and some are not. The lawyer will explain your rights and responsibilities and tell you how the law will affect your divorce.

The Divorce Process

The lawyer will tell you about preparing and serving the summons and complaint and probably ask you how you think your spouse will react. A good divorce lawyer will know whether the papers need to be served right away to protect you, the children, and your assets. The lawyer then will explain the process, from preparing these initial papers to collecting information from your spouse and others. The lawyer will explain how and where settlement negotiations fit into the picture and under what circumstances you may consider going to trial before a judge.

Divorce Behavior

You need to know the rules of divorce behavior. A good divorce lawyer will explain how certain behaviors can help or hurt you during the divorce. The lawyer can give you advice about the wisdom of getting involved with a new person, about losing your temper with your spouse or your children, and about how to behave during a custody evaluation. The lawyer will tell you how judges expect you to act in a courtroom or in a judge's office.

Not Any Lawyer Will Do

Have you noticed the phrase "good divorce lawyer" in this discussion? It's essential that you find a lawyer who really knows divorce law. Most of us wouldn't ask our dermatologist to pull a tooth. Likewise, you don't want a personal injury attorney to handle your divorce. Some lawyers think divorce law is a no-brainer and anyone can do it. That's not the case. Beware the lawyer who does only one or two divorces a year because divorce law changes, and you want a lawyer who keeps up with the changes.

FACT

Divorce law is complex and difficult. It requires a lawyer who does this kind of work all the time. Do not hire or consult with a lawyer whose practice is less than 50 percent family law. Also make sure that the lawyer's goals are the same as your goals. This will ensure a shorter and more cost effective relationship with your attorney.

After meeting with a lawyer, you may be rethinking your decision to go it alone. If you have any doubts, err on the side of caution and hire an attorney. If you have children, property, or assets and expect a disagreement with your spouse, you should strongly consider hiring an attorney.

Finding Resources to Help the Pro Se Litigant

If you are still considering representing yourself, chances are you are making this decision because of financial reasons. Before committing to this choice, explore the available resources in your community for obtaining a pro bono or free lawyer. If you are financially eligible, you may qualify for a legal aid attorney or, in some states, the court can appoint a *pro bono* attorney to represent you at no cost. You should exhaust all possible resources to obtain an attorney before deciding to appear *pro se*.

Still committed to being a *pro se* litigant? You will now need to explore community resources that can help. Many states have uncontested divorce packets that are available through the county clerk's office or even on the Internet for free or at a low cost. This packet will provide you with copies of all the forms you will need to complete an uncontested divorce and directions about the process. If not, you can obtain forms and other necessary information from your local law library. If you are not afraid of paperwork, have little or no assets, and are in agreement with your spouse about how to divide your property and assets, this may be an option worth considering.

If you are looking for a little more help, contact your local legal aid office, law school, or nonprofit legal services provider to ask what resources they may have for *pro se* litigants. Many of these programs offer clinics that *pro se* litigants can attend. At a clinic, several attorneys will answer questions or help you complete the paperwork associated with a divorce.

In recent years, the divorce self-help center has sprouted up in many locations. Many of these centers can be a good resource for obtaining forms, directions, and answers to simple questions. Use these self-help centers cautiously as they may be operated by nonattorneys. Make sure the information applies to your jurisdiction and the facts of your case.

You can get legal services without paying a fortune. Call or visit your local bar association and ask for a list of free or reduced-cost service providers and attorneys. Check the Internet for other free or low-cost legal resources that may be available in your community.

The divorce process and filing requirements vary from state to state, which is why it is important for you to understand the requirements of your particular jurisdiction. In some states all you need to do is fill out the required papers, sign them before a notary public, pay your filing fee, and file your papers. Your divorce will be made final through an administrative process. When the decree has been signed, you'll be notified by mail that your divorce is final, or that it will be final a specific number of days after the decree was entered into the court system.

In other states, you'll need to go to court for a final hearing. You bring your judgment and decree, which you have prepared ahead of time, for the judge to approve and sign. If you have to go to court and have no idea what to do when you get there, call the judge's clerk and ask. Don't be afraid to ask the judge's staff! Court staff can be very helpful and will usually provide basic information about the process of a court appearance, but they will not be able to offer legal advice. Always be courteous in dealing with court staff even if they are unable to answer your questions.

Finding a Good Divorce Lawyer

If you've decided to hire a divorce lawyer, you need to think of this process as a marathon, not a sprint. Do not settle on the first attorney you call and do not assume that a higher billing rate means a better lawyer. Take your time if you can. Ask friends and family if they know any good divorce lawyers. If they've gone through a divorce, get the names of lawyers they believe did a good job. Don't be surprised if they give you the name of their spouse's lawyer. If you have a friend who's a lawyer, ask your friend who he would hire for a divorce lawyer, and why.

Ask other professionals who work with families. Do you know any therapists or social workers? Anyone who works at the courthouse? Check with your local bar association. It often has a lawyer referral service. Don't be afraid to ask questions. Don't be intimidated or feel pressured. Don't make the mistake of confusing competence with experience.

Try not to pick an attorney out of the Yellow Pages unless there is no other alternative. If you have to use this method, be sure you interview the attorney and find out about her background. Look in the Yellow Pages under "Attorneys—Divorce and Family" or under "Lawyers." Check the listings for the lawyers who limit their practice to family and matrimonial or divorce law.

Family Law Practitioners Differ

Within the practice of family law, lawyers differ in their methods and beliefs. They have a variety of personalities, both in and out of the courtroom. They will use their expertise to tell you how they think the law applies to your case and how they will use the law to try the case or to settle it. If you talk to five different family law practitioners, you could get five slightly different responses as to how they will handle your case. Finding a divorce lawyer is like buying a new pair of shoes. You have to try them on to see which one fits best.

What You Want Steers Your Choice

What do you want your lawyer to do for you? What are your objectives? The answers to these questions will have an important effect on whom you select to represent you. For example, suppose you and your spouse get along reasonably well. You've been married more than ten years and have two children. You own a house, two cars, retirement assets, and a time-share. You need a divorce attorney because you need to protect your children and your property, but you're confident you can work out a settlement. You don't want to fight with your spouse; you just don't want to be married any longer. You want an attorney who is willing to negotiate, consider alternative dispute techniques, and most importantly, respect your desire to engage in a civil and amicable divorce process.

Maybe you're pretty emotionally charged. You surprised your spouse in bed with someone else, and now you want to tell the judge and anyone else who will listen how you've been done wrong. You want the toughest, meanest divorce litigator in your community. The first lawyer you talk to says judges aren't that interested in hearing your sob story. You ignore that lawyer's advice and continue looking until you find a divorce lawyer who agrees to your wishes. You've now selected a lawyer using your emotions instead of your intelligence. This choice will not only cost you a lot of money but will create hostility with your spouse that may take years to overcome and cause your children endless heartache as they watch the two of you battle it out every time you see each other.

Like Your Lawyer

You want to choose a lawyer you can trust, someone who's smart. You want someone who really listens to you and is honest about what will happen. You want someone who answers your calls, keeps you informed, and is on your side. You don't want someone who is going to run up your bill by allowing you to chat about things that are not important to your legal case.

You'll probably end up spending a fair amount of time with this person, so listen to your gut as well as your brain. It's extremely important that you trust your lawyer and feel comfortable asking questions. You're under no obligation to hire a lawyer just because you met with him. If you're intimidated or uncomfortable with him, look for someone else. You'll have to ask your lawyer a lot of questions and work closely with him during the divorce. Make sure you're compatible. Also remember that every contact with your lawyer is billed to you. In order to reduce the cost of your consultation or divorce, focus on your legal issues, not on making polite conversation.

Interviewing Lawyers

You've gotten a list of names from friends, family, your therapist, and the Yellow Pages. Now you're ready to interview some lawyers. How do you start? First of all, call the office for an appointment. Ask whether the lawyer you want to interview charges for an initial consultation. If there's a charge, find out how much. Is it a flat fee? Is it an hourly rate? Most attorneys charge by the hour, which is why it's important to prepare for the interview in advance. Ask some background questions before making the appointment. Find out if the lawyer limits her practice to family law; if not, ask what percentage of the practice is dedicated to divorce cases, how many years the practice has been open, and how often the attorney practices in your jurisdiction. The answers to these simple questions may prompt you to call a different lawyer.

Conflict of Interest

A lawyer can't represent you in your divorce if he has had previous dealings with your family or your spouse. However, it's okay for the lawyer to represent you if previous contact was with you alone and if that contact did not involve the issues of your marriage.

Some divorcing people meet with certain lawyers in the community just to try to prevent these lawyers from representing their spouses. Ethically, once a lawyer has discussed a divorce with one spouse, she is disqualified from representing the other spouse. Here's how it works. There's a local divorce lawyer known for tough tactics and making divorce cases long and painful. You don't want to hire that lawyer, but you also don't want your spouse to hire her, either. You meet with her and give her some information about your marriage. You don't hire the lawyer. Now that lawyer may be disqualified from representing your spouse unless he can show that you and the lawyer didn't discuss the substance of your case. While this tactic doesn't always prevent the barracuda lawyer from representing your spouse, it may work.

Sometimes a lawyer can't represent you because you and your spouse have worked with another lawyer in the firm. For example, you and your spouse had one of the divorce lawyer's partners draft your wills. This lawyer has obtained information about your assets; therefore, she can't represent you unless your spouse says it's okay.

ALERT!

Be sure to ask how you will be billed. If you do not receive a bill, call your lawyer immediately because you should closely monitor how your money is being spent. Compare the bill against your own records so you can settle any discrepancies as soon as possible.

Busy Lawyers

When you call the lawyer's office to schedule an initial consultation, ask to speak with the lawyer directly. If the lawyer is too busy to talk with you, this is probably a bad sign. It may be a warning that the lawyer will be too busy to talk with you after you've hired him. You want to speak directly with the lawyer so you can briefly outline your case before scheduling a meeting and confirm that the lawyer handles your kind of case. For example, if you have a custody issue, you need to know whether the lawyer handles custody cases, and whether he has the time to take one on at this time. You save yourself time and money by finding this out by telephone.

If the lawyer can't take your case, ask for a referral. If he asks whether you're considering other lawyers, give their names and see if he knows the attorneys on your list. Lawyers rarely say bad things about other lawyers. They tend to be more subtle, so try to pick up on the message. If the lawyer knows the attorneys on your list but suggests names other than the ones you have, he is telling you he doesn't think too highly of the people on your list. However, don't select a lawyer based solely on the referral of another lawyer.

Prepare Questions

Review your objectives again as you prepare to interview prospective lawyers. You should plan to interview at least two or three lawyers.

Prepare a list of questions to include the following:

- **What is your lawyering style?** You want to know how a lawyer sees herself. You want to know if the lawyer is proud of her trial work, the ability to help negotiate a settlement, or perhaps a combination of these skills.
- **What are your credentials?** You want to know how long this lawyer has practiced family law and what his range of experience is. In particular, you want to know how much experience he has with cases like yours.
- **How many cases like mine have you taken to trial?** You want to know if the attorney often takes cases to trial as opposed to settling. In addition, you want to know if she has trial experience should your case go to trial.
- **How busy are you?** You want to know whether the lawyer will be available to answer your telephone calls. You want to be sure he will be the person you talk to and the person who comes to court with you for all matters, not just the trial.
- **Will any part of my case be handled by other staff in the office?** You want to know who is actually going to be working on your case. Many attorneys have associates, paralegals, or legal assistants who also work on cases. This can help reduce the overall cost of the legal services provided. You want to make sure that all work is overseen by the attorney you are hiring and that she will be the one appearing with you in court.
- **Will you take the initiative to seek a settlement?** It's important that your lawyer stay current with the facts of your case and take positive steps to get your issues resolved.
- **How much do you charge?** You need to know how the lawyer charges for his work. You want him to explain the fee agreement clearly and in language you can understand. If he has indicated that other staff from his office will work on your case, make sure he tells you if and how the fee will change. If the lawyer is offering a flat fee for his representation, make sure you know what that flat fee includes and particularly what it does not include.

- **How much do you think my case will cost?** It is difficult if not impossible to predict how much you will spend on a divorce. This is because there are so many unknown factors. If the case settles, it will be cheaper. If the parties can agree on the value of an asset rather than hire an appraiser, it will be cheaper. Beware of the practitioner who tells you that your case will cost a certain amount unless she is offering to represent you for a flat fee rather than an hourly rate. At best, a lawyer can offer you a ballpark figure of what your case will cost based on her hourly rate and whether your case settles or goes to trial.
- **Who makes final decisions as to tactics and objectives?** It's important to know that you will have the final say on tactics and objectives.

Custody Issues

If you anticipate you'll be dealing with a custody disagreement, you need to find out what experience the lawyer has in this area. When your children's future is at stake, you want a lawyer who has significant experience working with the courts and the experts who work with families. You need a lawyer who can evaluate your chances of obtaining the result you want and who will tell you when you aren't being realistic. Custody litigation is the single most effective way to create a war between you and your spouse where one does not currently exist. When interviewing a lawyer regarding custody issues, be honest about the situation and don't exaggerate facts and circumstances. Be cautious regarding promises that you will be awarded custody, particularly if the plan the attorney proposes involves drastic measures.

For example, let's say you've been a working father and your spouse has been a stay at home mother who has primarily cared for your children. The lawyer you visit suggests that your wife will probably be awarded custody unless you can prove she is unfit. To do this, he suggests you should hire a private investigator to follow her and photograph her in her daily activities with the children. The attorney assures you that everyone has something to hide, including your spouse! Think carefully about this course of action. If you have concerns then it may be a reasonable suggestion. However, if you know deep down that your spouse is a good parent, don't let a lawyer convince you she's not.

Big Money Cases

If you have significant assets, you need to find out whether the lawyer has handled big money cases in the past. Is yours the biggest to ever walk into his office? Maybe he doesn't have enough experience in handling complex asset issues to handle your marital estate. You don't want him to develop expertise at your expense. Rather, you want someone who knows the money experts in town and how to work with them to get an understanding of your situation.

Should You Hire the Hotshot?

Should you select a hotshot big-city lawyer? Your case is in another county, but you're attracted by this lawyer's reputation. Consider using an attorney who lives in your county. A local lawyer knows the judges, the other lawyers, and any quirks of the local practice. Big-city hotshots often aren't well received in the country. Ms. Local Lawyer probably will enjoy beating up on Mr. Big City Hotshot. If you're paying your fancy lawyer's travel costs at a significant hourly rate, your spouse may take advantage of this by setting lots of hearings that will eventually wear you down financially and lead you to settle for less.

Does Gender Matter?

In a metropolitan area, gender isn't an issue because as many good men as good women practice family law. In that locale the real issues for you are competence and personality of your lawyer. However, in some rural jurisdictions a "good old boy" mentality that women should be at home with the kids may still exist, so check this out if your case will be heard in a rural court. By the same token, hiring a woman probably won't give you an edge in a custody case, nor will it make you look better if you are a male and your spouse has accused you of domestic abuse. Good lawyers are good lawyers, regardless of gender.

It's a Small World

Good divorce lawyers in a community know each another. They're a tightly knit group: They see each another often in court, they belong to the local family law section of the bar association, they attend continuing education courses together, and they may have a drink together after court to talk about cases and the stresses of their profession. Not only do the lawyers know each other, they also know the family court judges.

QUESTION?

Can the same lawyer represent me and my spouse?
A single lawyer cannot represent the interests of both spouses; it's just that simple. Don't believe any lawyer who says she can. Rather than a single lawyer for both parties, you may want to consider a mediator who will act as a neutral party for the negotiation stage of the divorce.

You want your lawyer to know the judge who will decide your divorce. This doesn't mean the judge will be biased in your favor. It means your lawyer will be able to tell you what to expect and how to present issues in the way most likely to get the results you want. Don't be alarmed if the lawyers greet each other or the judge by first names. The fact these folks are friends doesn't mean collusion or bias will occur. It simply reflects the practice of this specialized area of the law.

Buyer Beware

A few words of caution: Beware of the lawyer who promises you all the things you ask for because it's unlikely you'll get everything. You want a lawyer who helps you develop realistic expectations. The lawyer who promises more than he can deliver often will end up being evasive and difficult to reach by telephone when the day of reckoning arrives.

Beware the lawyer who tries to talk you out of a well-reasoned position, saying things like, "I can get you way more than that" or "You're entitled to permanent alimony" when you don't even want alimony. After all, this is your divorce.

While you do want the lawyer to explain your options, you should be the one who decides which ones to pursue. You want to stay in charge. Remember, you hired the lawyer to work for you. Don't let yourself stray from your own carefully thought-out choices.

You need to use great care in selecting a lawyer who is an expert in divorce. You should be able to trust your lawyer and be able to talk to her. You need to feel that she listens to you and has your best interests in mind. You'll be working closely with your lawyer over the course of your divorce, so you need to feel comfortable and protected by the lawyer you choose.

CHAPTER 5

Hiring and Working with Your Lawyer

You've interviewed several lawyers and decided to hire one. Now it's time to meet with him and sign a retainer agreement which will govern how you work together. Now is the time to start to form goals and objectives for resolving your divorce. You will need to find out all of your possible options and the different strategies the lawyer might use to help achieve your goals. By knowing what to expect and how to work together, you can have a positive and productive experience.

5

Money Talk

It's time to talk money. Lawyers charge by the hour, and no doubt fees will vary among the lawyers you interview. Cheaper isn't necessarily less good, and expensive isn't necessarily better. You should hire the expertise you need for your situation, so if your case is simple and straightforward, you don't need the local custody expert or the big-estate guy. An experienced family law lawyer whose practice is primarily the uncomplicated divorce will serve you ably. If you do have a tough case, then by all means hire the expertise you need, and be ready to pay for it.

Lawyers usually ask for a retainer—a down payment—to be applied to the hours put in on your case. Divorce lawyers will normally ask you to sign a retainer agreement, which is a document that outlines the rules you and your attorney will follow in handling your divorce. In most states this is required by law.

ALERT!

If your attorney asks you to sign a retainer agreement, read it carefully. If you don't understand something, ask for an explanation. During your divorce, it's important that you never sign something you don't understand.

The agreement should clearly state the lawyer's hourly rate and the rates of paralegals and secretarial staff. Many lawyers charge in quarter-hour increments. This means that a five-minute task or telephone call will be billed as fifteen minutes. Some lawyers also charge double or triple for telephone calls taken at their homes or after hours. The agreement should be clear about how the lawyer bills for telephone calls, travel to court, copies, and faxes. A provision stating the lawyer will fire you as a client if you don't keep your bill current probably will be included.

Sample Fee/Retainer Agreement

Here is what a fee/retainer agreement looks like. Obviously, the dollar amounts will correspond with what the lawyer you're hiring charges.

1. Purpose

By this agreement I hire <u>Excellent Law Firm</u> to represent me and to be my lawyers in my marriage dissolution proceeding. I understand that <u>Lawyer's Name</u> will be my primary attorney and that she may use other attorneys in the firm to assist her.

2. Fees

(A) Hourly and per-occurrence fees

Legal work done on my file by <u>Lawyer's Name</u> will be billed at <u>$300</u> per hour. Other lawyers who work on my case will bill at their normal hourly rate. Legal assistants who work on my case will bill at <u>$75</u> per hour. Law clerks will bill at <u>$75</u> per hour. Secretarial work will be billed at <u>$20</u> an hour or will not be billed. Fees will be updated annually, and I will be notified of any rate changes. Billing is done in quarter-hour segments.

I also will be billed for any copying and faxing done for my case.

The hourly fees include the time my attorney and staff spend traveling to and from court, depositions, meeting with experts, etc.

I will be responsible for all filing fees.

I will be billed for all telephone calls generated by my case.

I have ten (10) days to object to items on my monthly bill. If I do not object, I will waive any subsequent objection to the fees on the statement.

This means you need to review your bill as soon as you get it and raise any objections right away. Otherwise, you'll be deemed to have agreed to all charges.

(B) Retainer

The following are four variations of the retainer. Your lawyer may use one or more of these, so read the retainer provisions carefully.

Variation 1: I will pay you a retainer of <u>$5,000</u> when I sign this contract. You will use these funds as an advance to be applied to the time spent on my case.

When the retainer is exhausted, you will bill me monthly, and I will pay the monthly statement in full within thirty (30) days of receiving it.

If there is money remaining from the retainer when our attorney/client relationship ends, you will refund any balance to me.

This retainer is the least beneficial to the lawyer because once the money is used up, the lawyer has no recourse but to bill for his time.

Variation 2: I will pay you a retainer of $5,000 when I sign this contract. You will use these funds as an advance to be applied to the time spent on my case. Excellent will send me an itemized bill each month. When the retainer balance has been depleted to $1,000, I will be expected to renew the retainer to the starting figure of $5,000.

If I do not renew the retainer in full and on time and my retainer balance falls to $0, Excellent has the right to refuse to provide future legal services on my case and to withdraw as my lawyer. If there is money remaining from the retainer when our attorney/client relationship ends, you will refund any balance to me.

Variation 3: I agree to pay Excellent Law Firm $5,000 in advance, which will be held by the law firm in its trust account to secure my payments.

Excellent will send me an itemized bill each month. I will pay the bill in full each month within thirty (30) days of receipt. If I do not pay in full and on time, Excellent has the right to refuse to provide future legal services on my case and to withdraw as my lawyer.

Should Excellent withdraw, it may pay itself any outstanding amounts I owe for services up to the date of withdrawal. If the $5,000 advance payment exceeds what I owe, Excellent will return any surplus.

The fact that the law firm has $5,000 of your money in its account may encourage you to use your lawyer's time well and to pay your bills. Your lawyer can withdraw if you don't pay, and he may take what you owe from the money in the lawyer's account, so you're not ahead if you don't pay. You lose your lawyer and your money.

Variation 4: In addition to the hourly fees, I will pay a nonrefundable retainer fee of $5,000 that, when paid, immediately becomes a fee that has been earned by my attorney. This is a minimum fee. It is paid in consideration of my attorney reserving and committing time to be available in representing me, thereby precluding my attorney from accepting other clients and employment, including potentially conflicting interests. If more time is spent on this case than this fee would cover at the stated hourly rates, <u>Excellent</u> will bill me monthly, and I will pay in full within thirty (30) days of receipt.

Even if your case settles after your lawyer has put in three hours of time, or $900 worth of her time, she keeps your $5,000. This may not be as bad as it looks. Maybe this lawyer is an expert in an area in which you had issues. Maybe hiring this expert lawyer helped get the case settled faster. Your lawyer still will have to participate in drafting the final documents, so maybe it was a good idea to hire the expert attorney after all.

(C) Premium fee

The final fee may include such an additional fee as justified by the complexity, difficulty, and results of the case.

It's unethical for divorce lawyers to charge a contingency fee, that is, a fee based on a percentage of whatever money is awarded to you. To get around this, some lawyers charge a performance bonus—extra money to them if they get you an outstanding result. If the attorney is going to charge such a fee, it must be included in the retainer agreement.

3. Decisions

I reserve the right to make all important decisions regarding my case. <u>Excellent Law Firm</u> cannot settle the case without my permission.

The law firm is obligated to disclose any settlement offers to you.

4. Communications

<u>Excellent</u> will keep me informed about what is happening in my case and will send me copies of papers it sends out or receives. When I have to make an important decision, <u>Excellent</u> will explain my choices and offer me advice.

I will inform <u>Excellent Law Firm</u> of any change in my address, telephone number, e-mail address, employment, and circumstances. I will not withhold information from my attorneys.

5. Problems

If I am unhappy with the manner in which <u>Excellent Law Firm</u> is handling my case, I will first explain the problem to <u>Excellent</u>. If we cannot resolve our differences, I can terminate this agreement and a) hire another lawyer, b) represent myself, or c) choose not to pursue the case.

In a divorce, you can't stop the case unilaterally unless you're the plaintiff/petitioner—the instigator—and no answer has been filed by your spouse. In reality, you're limited to hiring another lawyer or representing yourself.

If we terminate our relationship for any reason, I owe the fees generated to that point.

6. Responsibility for and Collection of Fees

I am ultimately responsible for my fees. The court may order the other side to pay all or part of my fees, and, if they do so, I will receive credit for same. If they don't pay, I can either pay my attorney to try to collect them, or pay them myself.

You are responsible for paying your lawyer, no matter that the court ordered your spouse to pay.

I grant to my attorney a lien on all property, money, assets, spousal maintenance, or things of value that are recovered, obtained, preserved, or protected for me in the lawsuit. Any amounts I owe shall be payable from them.

If your lawyer places a lien on your homestead real estate (the marital residence), he can't foreclose the lien and force you to sell your house. However, when the house is sold, you must pay the lawyer from the sale proceeds.

7. Capacity

I am of sound mind and body. I am not under the influence of alcohol or mind-altering drugs. I have read this agreement and understand it. I have had any parts that I did not initially understand explained to me.

Make sure you ask for explanations if you need them. Don't worry about looking dumb. You are probably not used to reading documents with language like this, so it is understandable that you may need some clarification.

I approve and accept this contract. I agree to be bound by its terms.

Dated _____   Client Signature _____

If a nonrefundable retainer is used, a second signature like the one following probably will be required.

I understand that the retainer fee paid herein will not be held in a trust account, and I will not receive a refund if I terminate the services of <u>Excellent Law Firm</u>.

Dated _____   Client Signature _____

After you've drawn a huge breath and signed the retainer agreement, you're officially your lawyer's client. Now that you've agreed to pay your lawyer huge sums of money, you need to do everything possible to use his time well.

Tell the Truth

It's of the utmost importance that you tell your lawyer the truth, the whole truth, and nothing but the truth—no matter how ugly it may be. This often is hard to do, but it's the only way your lawyer can competently represent you. Your lawyer has to have all the facts. Nothing hurts your case more than for your lawyer to be surprised by information the other side produces. If your attorney is caught off guard and unprepared, your credibility with your lawyer will be permanently damaged. If you have skeletons in your closet, it's better to tell your lawyer before you have dealings with the other side. Your lawyer also can give you better advice with all the facts.

Write a complete history of the relationship with your spouse, including any relevant time before marriage. Today many people live together or begin to commingle their assets before they marry. For example, it's not uncommon for an unmarried couple to buy a house together, which may affect the characterization of their marriage assets. Give a complete history to your lawyer and review it with her, leaving nothing out. Have your lawyer explain which are the legally important parts of the relationship as opposed to the emotional highlights.

ALERT!

Do not lie to your lawyer, ever. Do not "forget" important information. Do not try to blame your spouse for something you did. No matter how well you think you've covered your tracks, lies almost always come out. If your case goes to trial, your credibility may be the determining factor in whether you get what you want. To many judges, once a liar, always a liar!

Limit Your Calls

Limit telephone calls to your lawyer. Try not to call when you're angry or upset because you'll have a hard time focusing on issues. Make a written list of the things you want to discuss before you call so you remember to ask all your questions. Write down your lawyer's answer so you don't have to ask the same questions again.

It's best to keep a record of your phone calls to and from your lawyer. Compare your records to the monthly bills you receive. Though it's not likely that your lawyer will intentionally try to rip you off, mistakes are made.

When your lawyer tells you how the law will affect a certain issue, you may respond, "but that's not fair." Don't confuse fairness with the law because the two are very different. Remember, your lawyer is the messenger. Don't shoot the messenger who brings bad news.

Be Courteous and Keep Your Lawyer Informed

Be cordial to your lawyer's staff. They're the ones who put your calls through, so you want them on your side. Lawyers talk to their staff members and they'll hear about it if you're nasty to someone. This advice applies when you go to court, too. You and your lawyer should always be courteous to the judge's staff because they'll be quick to tell the judge who has been unpleasant or arrogant.

Do as much of the legwork as possible; it costs a lot of money for your lawyer and legal staff to collect data that you can easily get yourself. Even though you may be operating at less than full efficiency, you can call your tax preparer for tax returns. You can get your credit card records. You can pull all your investment account statements. It will keep you busy with some nonintellectual tasks. Pay your lawyer to interpret documents, not merely collect them.

Keep your lawyer up to date. Notify your lawyer if you move, change telephone or fax numbers, or e-mail addresses. Your lawyer needs to stay in touch with you, so don't make him take extra time (that you'll end up paying for) to hunt you down. Keep the lawyer up to speed about important developments in your life, such as a change in your employment or a change in where your child lives. Keeping your lawyer up to date will help him represent you well.

Can't Get Any Satisfaction?

If you're dissatisfied with the way your lawyer is handling your case, first take a look at the problems. Not returning telephone calls? Maybe you're calling too often or trying to address issues that should be discussed with a therapist. You don't like the answers to your questions? Your lawyer has no plan of action? This is indeed worrisome. If you and you lawyer can't agree on a plan and begin to implement it, perhaps you need to look elsewhere.

Getting a Second (or Third) Opinion

Perhaps this would be a good time to get a second opinion. You always can talk to another lawyer about your case.

FACT

You should be treated with respect. If you're uncomfortable with the way your lawyer talks to or treats you, you ought to consider looking elsewhere. A divorce can be a long and trying process, so you should have someone on your side that you are comfortable with and can trust.

It may be that your lawyer is giving you legally correct answers to your questions, and you don't like the content of those answers. It may be the plan you want to adopt is impossible or unrealistic. If two lawyers tell you so, they probably have a point, but it may be worth it to get a second opinion for your own peace of mind.

Firing Your Lawyer

You can, of course, fire your lawyer at any time. You probably won't have too much trouble finding a second lawyer. However, if you've run through three lawyers, a fourth is going to think long and hard before agreeing to represent you. Nevertheless, timing is a consideration. For example, it's not a good idea to fire your lawyer the week before you're scheduled to go to trial. Your new lawyer may not be able to get a continuance (an adjournment to a future date) from the court for time to prepare.

Report Unethical Behavior

If your lawyer proposes a course of action you believe is unethical, you can report her to the board or committee in your state that reviews attorney conduct. You can find the name and contact information of this organization from your local bar association. This board is made up of lawyers who oversee the behavior of practicing lawyers in your state. They review complaints from clients, other lawyers, judges, and citizens about the behavior of licensed attorneys, and they have the authority to discipline lawyers.

They can also recommend that a lawyer lose her license—be disbarred—for unethical behavior.

ALERT!

Be sure the behavior you complain about warrants discipline. Just because you didn't get the results your lawyer promised isn't enough to file a complaint. Unless your lawyer came to court unprepared or under the influence of drugs or alcohol, you probably don't have case. Reviewing complaints and writing the responses are very time consuming. Make sure your complaint is real.

More ethics complaints come out of family law cases than from any others—probably because divorce cases are highly emotional. Most complaints are probably made because lawyers have a hard time telling clients bad news, so clients' expectations are not met. Some lawyers do behave unethically. Fortunately, it's a small minority, and you'll be doing everyone a favor by reporting them.

Disputing Fees

You can challenge your lawyer's bill. Most states have a fee arbitration program where you and your lawyer present your arguments about the bill. If you use fee arbitration, you both agree to abide by the arbitrators' decision.

You can also challenge the fees in court. If your attorney has kept good records and you signed a fee agreement, especially one in which you have to object within a few days or deem that you approve the bill, the court will probably award the lawyer fees that he can document. Especially in divorce cases, fees aren't adjusted by results obtained. This means you can't get a reduced fee if your lawyer didn't get you custody of your children.

If you chose your lawyer well, you probably won't have problems with communication or strategy. And if you do your share of the work, you'll keep your lawyer's fees manageable and won't have to fight over them. If you listen to your lawyer and accept his advice, you'll have reasonable expectations and be able to negotiate with the other side. Working with your lawyer can be a good experience.

CHAPTER 6

What Courts Can
and Can't Do

Many divorcing couples are mistaken about what
courts can do for them. They expect a judge to right
the wrongs of the marriage, see only their point of
view, give them the kids and the assets, and make
it clear to the other spouse just how awfully he
behaved during the marriage. Courts provide a great
way to resolve issues when you can't agree with your
spouse. However, you forfeit some control over your
situation when you put your life in the hands of a
judge.

What Is a Divorce, Anyway?

A secular divorce—as opposed to a religious divorce—is the legal ending of a marriage. Many states now call divorce a "marriage dissolution," which is probably even more accurate.

For the couple who has been married only a short time and has no children, divorce usually means cutting the ties that bind and moving on. The couple has some regrets, some sadness and, perhaps, some anger. Mostly, the couple decides the marriage isn't working and isn't healthy for either of them, so they divide their possessions, draft their papers, and begin a new life. If these people meet again in later months or years, it's usually by chance and usually feels okay.

Children Complicate Divorce

For people with children, divorce is more complex. The role of a parent is for a lifetime, and for that reason, divorce for a family with children can't be simply an ending of the adult relationship because the family will need to have contact for years to come.

Children see divorce as redesigning their relationship with their parents: "On Tuesdays I'm with Mom; on Wednesdays I'm with Dad." Regardless, they expect to continue relationships with both of their parents. Even so, children worry a lot about losing a parent through divorce. Sometimes one parent tries to punish the other by undermining the ex-spouse's relationship with the children, perhaps by refusing to let the children spend time with the other parent or by saying ugly things about her to the children. Some children lose years of knowing a parent, and vice versa. Sometimes a relationship is lost forever, a devastating loss to both parent and child.

ALERT!

Courts can't make parents behave in a cooperative, supportive way. Only the parents themselves can choose to do this. When parents behave badly, the only option left to the court is to impose a structure on the parents for sharing the responsibility for the children. How the parents behave within that structure is beyond the power of the court.

Even though it may be tempting to use children as a weapon against your spouse, it is critical to remember that while you may be hurting your spouse, you will also be hurting your children. Children who have been used in this way often require therapy in order to resolve the psychological problems they incur as a result of these tactics. Some children never recover and grow into adults with severe relationship issues. Judges who become aware of parents using these tactics will typically impose harsh penalties against them.

Regardless of how hostile you feel toward your spouse or your spouse feels toward you, it is best for you, your spouse, and your children to develop a plan for rearing the children in a cooperative, supportive way. This includes an ongoing financial arrangement that divides assets in a way that eases financial worries. If there aren't enough assets to overcome financial worries, the burden at least should be shared. That way, your energy can go to living your life and raising your children.

Ending a Long-Term Marriage

Couples ending a long-term marriage need to balance many competing considerations. They may have adult children who are outside the authority of a divorce court, but law does not mirror life here. Adult children are staying in the nest longer and return to live with their parents more often than they did in the past.

In some states, parents are required to support children until they reach eighteen years of age; in other states the requirement ends at twenty-one years of age. Past this age, the court lacks the ability to require parents to support their children. This means children of the marriage may not be able to attend or continue attending college or trade school, even when this was clearly a part of the marital plan.

A long-term marriage will more likely have the traditional roles of breadwinner and homemaker. For the homemaker, the prospect of old age without money is very scary, especially because people are living longer. If you are in your forties or fifties, it may be very difficult for you to get a job that pays reasonably well if you don't have any work experience. Even then, you'll have only a few years to generate retirement savings.

Couples with adult children still living at home are faced with providing support, even though these children are legally adults. They need to finance two homes. They need to make arrangements for retirement. They need to set up separate, coordinated estate plans that operate for the benefit of their children and grandchildren. Older divorcing couples have issues that are different from couples whose children are under eighteen.

Parents Should Behave Respectfully

All parents need to divorce in a respectful, dignified way because they still will have to deal with one another as parents and grandparents. Their children will experience milestones when they graduate from college, marry, and have their own children. The family still will celebrate birthdays and holidays—events children will want to be festive, not clouded by their parents' anger or bitterness over the past.

FACT

The court is limited to setting a visitation schedule and ordering financial support, and it can only respond to violations of these orders. The judge cannot control the subtle sniping and irreparable damage it causes children when parents do not behave respectfully toward one another.

Your children will want both of you to participate. Presumably, most parents don't really want to spoil their children's big moments or expend negative energy every time they have to deal with their ex-spouse. Families need to get through the divorce and get on with their lives.

Reality Rear-Ends Expectations

People end up frustrated and upset with the divorce process because they have expectations about the process that bear little semblance to the reality of going to court. People going through a divorce often use words like fair, win, and punish. It wasn't fair that the marriage failed. Why should the divorce be fair? Perhaps the words fair and just get confused. What about winning or losing? Nobody wins in court!

A Closer Look

Let's take a closer look at these unmet expectations. First of all, what is a court, really? It's a place where an elected or appointed person, the judge, makes decisions when you can't make them for yourselves. A judge makes decisions by applying the laws governing the issues in each case. Legislatures and appellate courts devise these laws, and many of the laws put limits on the trial judge's decision-making power. Even so, the judge's decisions will have a tremendous impact on your lives.

See You in Court

Couples often decide their marriage is over in the context of significant conflict. For many people it's not easy to have a rational discussion about ending a relationship. The relationship has hit the rocks because of factors that generate bad feelings: unmanageable debt, addictions to substances, gambling, spending, extramarital affairs, and clashing philosophies. On top of these, people often feel an agonizing sense of failure or a sense of worthlessness. People beginning a divorce are angry, upset, and often irrational.

The reality you must come to accept is that you're better off staying out of court. Court can be draining, both emotionally and financially. If it's at all possible for you to negotiate with your spouse, do so instead of trying to punish her with a court battle.

"I'll see you in court!" is often used as a parting shot from one party to the other. What expectations lie behind this challenge? Many people believe courts will fix what is broken, shape up the wrongdoer, understand the issues, and see fairness as they do. Not likely. Regardless of how right you think you are in your cause, you are more than likely to lose on at least a few of your issues when you go to court. In addition, you may completely destroy any chances you had to develop a postdivorce relationship with your spouse.

Reality Check

The judge is there to enforce the laws of the state, not provide a supportive and therapeutic environment for divorcing couples. It's important to know that the laws of divorce don't deal with the feelings of the people who are getting divorced. There are no provisions in the divorce laws to help you cope with your sadness or anger that the marriage is ending.

Second, laws governing divorce limit what judges can do. Divorce laws are specific in most states, and most now have no-fault divorce laws that cite irretrievable breakdown or irreconcilable differences as the basis for the divorce. State laws spell out what factors judges should use in deciding custody of children and visitation, in determining what is marital property and how it should be divided, and in awarding spousal maintenance—also called alimony—and child support. The judge has to follow your state's rules unless he can show a good reason not to. The laws are one size fits all even though each divorce has its own particular set of problems that requires its own set of solutions.

The trouble is, the divorcing couple doesn't know about these limitations when they hurl that "see you in court" challenge. As a rule, divorcing couples expect a judge to right the wrongs of the marriage using laws and the legal system. The result? Expectations and reality don't fit.

A Judge Can't Fix Your Spouse

Let's take a look at how fairness, winning, and punishment fit into a system of courts and law. Fairness and winning are two of the most abused words in divorce court. Most of the time when someone says "It's not fair" that person really means "I didn't win," because most people define fairness as getting the results they want. However, courts deal with justice and with decisions. Justice means properly applying the law to the facts before the court; a court decision means resolving the issues you and your spouse presented in your papers. Nobody wins in divorce court. Beware those who tell you otherwise! There is no more fairness in court than there is in life.

At the Beginning

Suppose you go to see a lawyer to begin the divorce process. You tell her you've been through hell in your marriage and now you want out. You want a fair result—and by "fair" you really mean you want to win, and you want to punish your spouse for all you have suffered. You want the lawyer to draft court papers that will make your spouse feel bad, look bad, get his deserved punishment, and be forced to reform.

You may well be able to make your spouse feel bad. After all, you'll feel pretty bad yourself, remembering and reliving all the ugly pieces of the marriage. Plus, your spouse can respond to your papers with his version of the marriage, which, in turn, probably won't make you feel very good. It will probably make you darned mad, and you'll want to file more papers with the court in response to your spouse's papers. Then your spouse will respond. Then you'll respond. On and on you go, generating more legal fees and hostility with each exchange.

Paper Merry-Go-Round

The papers you and your lawyer prepare and file with the court may well make your spouse look bad, but a judge doesn't care much. The judge's job is to implement the law, and the law has little to say about good and bad. So what you've gained, after expending a significant amount of energy—all negative—taking paper potshots at your spouse is a massive pile of paper for the judge. You've run up large legal fees, made yourself good and mad, and destroyed any possibility of having a civil relationship with your spouse following your divorce.

Remember, you're hoping this paper mountain will lead to a judge shaping up your spouse. The judge has your papers, but she also has your spouse's papers, denying he is a louse and pointing out that you're no angel, either. The judge doesn't know you two. And if she did, she couldn't ethically hear the case. All the judge knows about you is what's in your papers. The law doesn't empower the judge to shape anybody up. Besides, if you weren't able to do it, why do you think anyone else will be successful?

Judge from Another Planet

The judge issues an order based upon the papers in the file, setting the rules to be followed while the divorce is in process. When you read it, you wonder what planet the judge lives on. The order bears absolutely no relationship to the reality of your life. Furthermore, no one is motivated to reform, and the possibility of reasonable negotiation between you and your spouse has become extremely unlikely.

"It's not fair!" you cry.

Unrealistic Expectations

Think about the papers you and your spouse filed with the court. What was in those papers? They contained selective information about your lives and character designed to persuade the judge to make certain decisions. You compiled your list of complaints about your spouse, carefully editing out any information that might be construed in a positive light. Your spouse responded with another list of horrors.

ALERT!

> The judge can't make good decisions without accurate information. If you allow your anger to dictate the information in your papers, the facts will be twisted. If your case goes to trial, you may end up looking like a liar; at the very least, you could be perceived as someone who is prone to over-reacting. This could result in an unfavorable decision.

Suppose you have children and one of the issues before the court is a temporary arrangement for their care. After you and your spouse have told the judge all the terrible things about each other you can remember (or create), the judge has precious little information to devise a workable parenting plan. The parents, who have all the information, give the judge—a stranger—only selected bits and pieces. The judge can't fill in the blanks that you left. The judge can't always determine who's lying and who's telling the truth. As a consequence, the judge's order often doesn't work and increases your frustration and misery. That means you've just spent a lot of money to obtain this unworkable order.

Separating the Law from Your Emotions

Too often divorcing couples have mistaken expectations of what the court process is about. The court process deals only with the legal part of a divorce, that is, the part addressed in laws. But divorcing couples are often much more concerned with the emotional part of the divorce. The emotional part of the divorce is just as important as the legal part, to be sure. However, the legal system is the wrong place to address emotional issues. Judges and attorneys work with the laws enacted by the legislature. They don't have the skills and training to do therapy and should not be entrusted with this important piece of the uncoupling process. Most communities have skilled therapists who truly can help the parties address the emotional issues of the divorce. They, not the court, should deal with the psychological impact of getting divorced.

The Court's Perspective

Look at it from the court's perspective. Angry, divorcing people in significant conflict bring issues to court because they want judges to solve their problems. At the very least they want judges to be the tiebreaker on issues they can't resolve by themselves.

Selective Information

Divorcing people spend a lot of money, time, and energy preparing court papers with their lawyers. They provide selective information about themselves and the other side. Some of that information may be either wholly or partially untrue. Sometimes when both parties tell the court about an incident, the only way a judge knows they're talking about the same thing is that they have the same date, time, and location!

The court—the stranger—reads the papers. Sometimes a judge will form doubts about the ability of both spouses to be good parents. He may ask the state's child protection agency to investigate the family and make a report back to him. Should the judge find that neither you nor your spouse is a fit parent, your children could be placed in foster care.

Relying on a Stranger

When you ask a judge to settle any issue in a divorce, you are asking a stranger, who knows nothing about your life except the bad things you and your spouse have said about each other, to settle the issue. It's challenging for a stranger to make a useful decision about other people's lives using information that was provided in a litigation setting. The couple that litigates ends up angrier, poorer, and often forced to live with an unworkable court order. Once again, divorcing parties have unreasonable and inaccurate expectations about the court process, and they are bitterly disappointed by the end result.

Not only do you lose significant amounts of control when taking your divorce to court, but you also pay for that loss of control. If you absolutely must go to trial, you may want to do some of the clerical work for your case to save a little money. Talk to your lawyer about the possibilities.

This same kind of scenario can play out at any stage of the divorce. While the divorce is pending under that unworkable order, you may come back to the court to get the order changed or to enforce it. You may bring another matter before the court. You may seek a final resolution of all issues from the court. Every time you bring your issues to court, you're turning over the decision-making authority to a stranger who has to rely on your information to make the decisions.

Taking a Different Route

There is light at the end of the tunnel. Now that you know a judge can't fix what's broken, you need to take a different approach. After all, you're an intelligent person who knows more than you think about this divorce thing. For sure, you know lots more about your family than the judge does. Why can't you, your spouse, and the lawyers negotiate a resolution of the issues at hand?

The advantages of negotiating a settlement are significant: You don't run up huge bills. You don't get your blood pressure up to dangerous levels. You do stay in control. You do end up with a document based on the reality of your situation. You do end up with a plan that works. Most importantly, you have not scorched the earth when it comes to your spouse.

Picking Your Court Battles

Some divorces never use the courts, except to get the final judgment and decree signed. Some divorces have minimal involvement with the courts, maybe a temporary hearing, a pretrial hearing, or a settlement conference in which an agreement is reached and put on the record. Putting an agreement on the record is legalese for reciting the agreement in front of a judge and a court reporter, usually in a courtroom. Both parties agree under oath that this is, in fact, their agreement and they will be bound by it.

Once the agreement is presented, agreed to by the parties, and approved by the court, one of the lawyers prepares the judgment and decree incorporating that agreement. Usually the lawyer representing the petitioner/plaintiff will do this, or maybe it will be the one who has the information in his computer. Once it is approved by both parties and their lawyers, the judge signs it. Once you've made your agreement in front of the judge, you don't have to go back to court again, because the lawyers will take care of the paperwork. Your lawyer will let you know that the decree has been entered and when the divorce is final.

Back and Forth to Court

Other divorce cases are in court almost monthly for years. She brings him to court for paying support a few days late. He takes her to court for claiming the children are sick on his visitation days. Her lawyer hauls him into court because he hasn't answered the interrogatories that were due two days ago. She sells her car and he brings a motion for half the money.

On and on and on it goes. These repeated trips to the courthouse often are symptoms of the parties' inability to let go of their relationship. These litigious folks really haven't finished the marriage. Their frequent court appearances are one way to guarantee seeing each other on a regular basis. What an expensive—and negative—way to continue a relationship.

The Courts as a Battering Ram

Some people use the courts as a battering ram. They want to repeatedly tell the judge, and anyone else who will listen, that their spouse is a loser. Maybe they want to exhaust their spouse emotionally and financially, so he finally caves in and accepts an unfavorable settlement. In some cases the primary wage earner of the relationship may try and use up all of the marital resources on litigation, knowing that she has a good job and can start over while the other spouse, who has primarily stayed home and foregone job advancement, is left to rely on some limited maintenance payments and his minimum wage job. When one of the parties uses the courts in this way, she also uses financial resources that could be better used to take care of the family. If you have such a spouse, make sure you point it out to your lawyer and if possible the judge in your case.

Think Before You Act

As you may have heard in other contexts, pick your battles. Some things are way more important than others. For example, protecting your kids is paramount, so going to court may be the only way to protect them. If you can't make the mortgage payment because your spouse is behind in his support payments, this is another reason you need to go to court.

Some couples use the courts as a way to threaten or punish one another. Unfortunately, most learn too late that they have hurt themselves as well—both financially and emotionally. If you're determined to take your issues to court, first stop to consider why. Make sure you've exhausted all your other options before making this decision.

Don't make hasty decisions about bringing your issues to court. Determine if your choice is going to be cost effective. For example, if you want to try to get spousal maintenance reduced by $20 a month, you may be better off waiting until you have other issues to present to the court. A motion will probably cost you $1,000 or more in lawyer fees. You'd have to save that $20 a month for more than four years just to pay your lawyer. Saving your court battles for the things that really matter will save you money and promote a better relationship between you and your spouse.

Judges Differ

You'll benefit by understanding the terminology used in court, the jobs of the people you'll come in contact with, and some of the procedures that you must follow when filing for divorce. Most of all, you should know different judges have different opinions and the resolution of your divorce can vary depending who renders the final judgment.

Judicial Officers

Judicial officers are judgelike people that courts hire to help judges handle the caseload. They're called different names in different jurisdictions, although the most common names are referee, commissioner, magistrate, and hearing examiner. They hear cases and issue orders just like judges. Sometimes their orders have to be countersigned by a "real" judge but not always. If the order doesn't have to be countersigned, you can appeal the decision to the judge who oversees their work.

FACT

If you want to contest a court order, you may not get the same judge and might have to start all over again. Whether you get the same judge varies from state to state and county to county. Some courts have a special family court, and once your case is filed it stays with the same judge or judicial officer.

While judicial officers are a step lower on the power ladder, they're usually very capable and knowledgeable. Many are retired judges or lawyers who have practiced in the field for years. Most of them have had lots of experience in family court and really know the law.

Notice to Remove

When a case is filed with the court, the court administrator working in family court will assign the case to a judge. You or your lawyer may be unhappy about the assignment based on past experiences or things you have heard about the judge. In some cases, your lawyer may suggest that you try to have the case assigned to a different judge. This is not a decision your lawyer makes lightly, because there are often repercussions to the lawyer if the judge is insulted by the request. Therefore, you should accept your lawyer's recommendation, knowing that your lawyer is willing to risk the downside of the judge's reaction in order to get a better result for your case.

QUESTION?

What if you are assigned a judge and he makes a decision you think is unfair?
It still doesn't matter. If this happens to you, you can only appeal the judge's decision, not ask for a different judge. Laws provide certain reasons for seeking to remove a judge, but they are limited. Check with your lawyer to see what your state allows.

Jurisdictions vary in terms of your ability to request another judge. In some states, you have one chance to say you want another judge to hear your case. You don't have to give any reasons, but you do have to exercise this right quickly, usually within ten days of getting notice of a judge's assignment. In most systems this is called a Notice to Remove. The other side gets one free shot, too. Of course, when you remove the judge assigned to your case, you may get another who is just as worrisome, given the facts of your case.

If you don't use the Notice to Remove and at some later time you want a different judge—for instance, after you get your first order from the judge—you will have to exercise a Removal for Cause to show that the judge assigned to your case has shown actual bias toward you or your spouse. This is very hard to do, especially because the judge you're trying to get rid of is usually the one who will hear your motion to remove for cause.

The Judges' Reputations

Judges develop reputations for delivering certain kinds of opinions most of the time. Some seem to award high alimony/maintenance. Some always give children to their mothers. Some are pretty wishy-washy about enforcing orders. Some are not good listeners. Some make decisions based on what happened to them in their divorces.

Lawyers talk with each other about judges, and they know the reputations of the judges in their courts. Your lawyer will advise you about a judge and whether it's worth trying to get a different one. While you should make the final decision, you probably will have to rely on your lawyer's advice pretty heavily. A judge with a known bias who also has a reputation for fairness and for listening to the facts may be persuaded to abandon his bias in a specific case—maybe yours. Only your lawyer can tell you the risks and options here.

Circumstances Do Change

At any time during the divorce process, you may learn new information that could change the process or outcome of your divorce. You may find out your spouse has gotten a second job or is working under the table at the local bar. Now, your spouse earns as much as you do or even more. This might be a reason to go back to court to get your support obligation reduced if you're paying your spouse support or if you have joint custody of children. Don't underestimate the value of a change in circumstances.

FACT

Even if you have already received temporary orders from the court, they can be modified as circumstances change or as new information is learned. Not every change of circumstances warrants a change in the temporary order. To be sure the change warrants going back to court, consult your lawyer.

Regardless of whether you think it is a small change or not enough to make a difference, mention it to your lawyer and let her be the judge. Things that seem insignificant to you could make a big difference in court. Even if one change doesn't make a difference, over time many small changes will add up and could mean the difference in custody, support payments, or the distribution of assets.

You might learn that your spouse has been involved in some worrisome activities or hasn't been taking parental responsibilities very seriously. You may want to ask the judge to change a temporary custody order and give the children to you. Ask your lawyer.

If a child moves from one parent's household to the other, this change will affect child support and custody. You may want to have this change reflected in a new court order. In fact, you may feel that you need a new court order to protect the child. Your lawyer can help you decide whether to take this matter back to court.

Use the courts effectively. Provide the court with clear and helpful information so it understands your position. Focus on the long-term result and don't let emotions get in the way of good decision making.

CHAPTER 7

Alternative Dispute Resolution

Alternative dispute resolution is a great way to divorce with dignity and control and with a minimum of emotional upset and cost. You and your spouse can resolve your issues outside of court, because you're the ones who have the information needed to make the decisions. Committed and knowledgeable professionals will help you along the way, but you and your spouse will maintain control. If you make the decisions, you'll put your energies into making those decisions work. Plus, you'll stay out of court.

You Have Alternatives

It's very important to know what you want from a divorce. You need to decide two things: the result (parenting, property, financial support) and the resolution process to get that result. After you've read this chapter, you'll be able to compare and contrast two dispute resolution processes—alternative dispute resolution and litigation. Think of dispute resolution as a range of possibilities, from being totally in charge of decision making to putting the decisions completely in the hands of a judge.

You've got three choices for how to resolve your disputes while staying in control of the decision making.

- **Negotiation.** If you and your spouse negotiate an agreement on how to divide your assets, parent your children, and support two households, you are totally in charge.
- **Negotiation with lawyers.** If you add lawyers to the process, you and your lawyers will try to resolve the issues, but you'll still be mostly in charge, although the lawyers may influence your decisions.
- **Mediation.** If your lawyers suggest mediation, you'll add another player—a mediator—who will meet with you, your spouse, and sometimes your lawyers to try to resolve your issues.

In all three cases, you and your spouse will still be the decision makers, but in two cases you'll be helped by professionals.

ALERT!

When you're making the decision of how to proceed with the divorce, try to keep your emotions out of the process. Sometimes swallowing your pride is the best course of action. If you're hurt or angry, you'll most likely want to punish your spouse by taking her to trial, but this may not be in your best interests.

If you're unable to resolve your issues using negotiation or mediation, you'll have to give up your decision-making authority and look to someone else to do the job. Here you've got two choices:

- **Arbitration.** This means you, your spouse, and the lawyers select an arbitrator to resolve the issues you're unable to resolve yourselves. While you do choose the arbitrator, this person makes the decisions, so you don't have final say.
- **Court trial.** If you don't want to use arbitration, your last choice is to turn the case over to a judge who will decide the issues. You don't get to choose the judge, so the decision making is totally out of your hands.

Negotiation

The three negotiation options allow you more control than leaving the final decisions to an arbitrator or a judge. This section outlines the differences between the different forms of negotiation.

Negotiating Directly with Your Spouse

The main advantages to negotiation are that you avoid stress, end up with an agreement that works, and lay the foundation for working together in the future if you have children.

In dispute resolution by negotiation you and your spouse sit down and work out your settlement together; then you take your agreement to your lawyers for their input. Each of you should have a lawyer unless your marriage has been very short, you have minimal assets, and you have no kids. The lawyers may tell you some of your agreements are not in your long-term best interests and the law would provide a different result. They also may point out you're missing some important information, such as the value of certain assets.

Armed with new information, you and your spouse meet again, determine just what additional information you need, set a schedule to get it, and set a date to meet again. You meet again with your documents and negotiate some more. Finally, you reach an agreement that you and your lawyers agree is acceptable. Your lawyers put the deal into a written agreement, which ultimately becomes the final divorce decree. Sound impossible? Lots of divorcing couples do this successfully.

Negotiations with Lawyers

If you and your spouse can't work it out at the kitchen table, each of you will need to hire a lawyer and detail what each of you wants from the divorce. The two of you and your lawyers will then meet to decide how to proceed and what information each of you needs to provide in order to discuss settlement. You set a date for another meeting, by which time everyone should have had a chance to review the information exchanged. At this meeting, the four of you sit around the conference table in one of the lawyer's offices and negotiate a deal.

Negotiation works best when you and your spouse still have some trust, you both know what your assets are, and the power balance is pretty equal. If you can communicate and are willing to exchange relevant and reliable information, you can probably come up with creative solutions to various issues that enable both of you to get what you want.

This process usually takes several meetings because you often don't have all the information you need by the second meeting, or a new issue comes up that requires additional information. If you have an emotional reaction to your spouse's settlement proposal, step away from your emotions and look at the proposal objectively—it's the bottom line that matters. This simple negotiation process is used successfully in many divorces.

Negotiations by Lawyers

If you and your spouse can't sit at the same table without taking cheap shots at each other, put your lawyers at the conference table to negotiate while you and your spouse are separated in other rooms. Again, these negotiations require the exchange of information about your assets and income before agreements can be made. Your lawyer will talk with you periodically as he and the other lawyer work out the issues to make sure you're in agreement.

Finally, a settlement will be reached, but as you can imagine, this process is somewhat cumbersome. The message has to travel from lawyer to client back to lawyer and back to the negotiating table. The message may get lost or distorted moving from person to person, so sometimes it has to be done all over again.

FACT

Keeping clients separated keeps the parties calm, and it keeps the lawyers in charge. While you have to give up most of the control, sometimes this is the only possible alternative to going to trial. Although you have less control, you'll still decide the terms of the final agreement.

Levels of Control

You're definitely in charge when you negotiate face-to-face with your spouse. You have less control when you bring lawyers into the picture. In fact, your lawyers may straight out tell you to do certain things or to hold out for certain results that you may not even want. Be careful here. Remember, this is your divorce.

Negotiation is probably the most common process used in getting divorced. The more complicated your assets, the more people will be involved in the negotiations. You may need to have your accountant (who should be certified), a business appraiser, a residential real estate appraiser, a vocational evaluator, and a child custody expert participate in negotiations. You can't reach agreements without information—information about your children's needs, your assets, and the law—but the greater the number of players in the negotiations, the higher the cost of the process. Even so, the negotiation process involving experts will still cost less than going to court.

Collaborative Law

Collaborative law is a form of negotiation with lawyers, but it differs from traditional forms. Collaborative lawyers are committed to assisting clients to reach a settlement without going to court. In fact, they're so committed to this concept they require all players to sign a contract stating they will withdraw from representation if the case cannot be settled or if one of the parties doesn't play by the rules of collaborative practice.

FACT

The underlying tenet of collaborative law is that it takes away the threat of going to court—the ultimate hammer. If the parties agree to stay out of court, they will need to put all of their energies into the settlement process.

Collaborative lawyers describe the process as making a commitment to a principled, negotiated settlement without the threat or use of power.

The Parties Agree

In collaborative law, parties agree that if an expert is needed, they will select a qualified neutral expert, and that any neutral expert used in collaboration can't be called as a witness if the case ultimately goes to trial. This means that you can use the expert to help you develop a settlement plan without fearing the expert might later be called to testify in a way that could be harmful to you or to your spouse. There's a greater sense of informality and freedom in working with this expert.

The parties and the lawyers also agree that anything said in sessions is confidential and can't be used in a trial unless the parties agree to use it. This means you can agree to values or a parenting plan for settlement purposes knowing that if you can't settle and have to go to trial the lawyers can't tell the court what went on during the negotiations.

The parties also agree to provide any relevant information and documents requested by the other side. Ordinarily, the parties also agree that the documents exchanged during this process won't be considered confidential and can be produced at a trial if the dispute can't be settled out of court. If you don't make this agreement, all the documents exchanged in negotiations will be shredded and you'll have to start all over with a formal discovery process. This would be unnecessarily time-consuming and expensive.

A Variation on Collaboration

A variation of the collaborative approach requires the divorcing couple to hire a male-female coaching team of two licensed mental health professionals, a child specialist, and a financial specialist if the amount of assets of the marriage is great enough. The coaching team helps the parties stay focused on interest-based negotiating, rather than posturing to try to gain a superior position or sniping at one another about the emotional stuff.

QUESTION?

What is interest-based negotiating?
Interest-based negotiating focuses on the bottom line: for example, what ends up in your pocket when the dust settles or what kind of parenting plan works for you. The idea is to get what you want without worrying so much about what your spouse gets. Ideally, you both get what you want.

The idea here is to promote a sense of everyone working together to resolve the issues. Sometimes this can be challenging because you and your spouse may want the same thing—for example, primary physical custody of the children. Even so, the professionals will help you and your spouse examine each issue to help determine what would be best for all of the parties concerned.

Collaborative Law Is Becoming Common

Collaborative law is growing in popularity. It arose because many family law practitioners believe the legal system is poorly adapted to the needs of people getting divorced. These lawyers have decided the legal system promotes hostilities rather than helping families develop new structures that let everyone get on with their lives. Collaborative law puts the parties in charge and gives them the responsibility for making decisions. Lawyers provide legal advice and explain potential legal consequences of the parties' decisions. Parties can focus on their children's needs instead of on their animosity toward each other. When the divorcing parties reach a settlement using the collaborative process, they spend less money getting divorced and probably won't need to use the courts in the future. Sometimes they even like each other better!

You May Be a Groundbreaker

Collaborative law is a relatively new concept, but more and more lawyers are becoming familiar with the process. Some jurisdictions may even have collaborative law centers where you can locate attorneys who have been trained in the process. If you'd like to try this approach to your divorce, you'll need to look for lawyers who advertise themselves as collaborative.

Collaborative lawyers have a number of websites where you can learn more about them. Search for "collaborative law" on your favorite Internet search engine or contact your local bar association or court and ask if there are any collaborative law centers or attorneys in your area.

Once you've located an attorney, make sure to ask the lawyer about her training in collaborative law and her experience with the process. Since it's a relatively new concept, you probably won't be able to find someone who has been doing it very long. Try to find someone who has had both specialized training and a few cases under her belt. The last thing you need is to be a test case!

The Downside of Collaborative Law

When collaborative law works, it works very well. But when one side refuses to play by the rules, it does not work at all. Then both of you have to hire new lawyers and start almost from scratch. This can be frustrating, time consuming, and expensive.

Mediation

Mediation, which is used for many kinds of disputes, is a form of resolution that uses a third person—a mediator—to help parties resolve issues. The basic idea is that the parties make the decisions, and the mediator is a facilitator. The mediator's job is to clarify positions and suggest alternative and creative ways to resolve the issues. It's possible to have two people serve as co-mediators, so, for example, if each of you wants a person of your gender to be the mediator, you can hire a man and a woman to work together.

You Still Need a Lawyer

Although it's important that the mediator understands divorce law, most mediators want spouses to have their own attorneys because it's not the mediator's job to tell you about the law. When you and your spouse reach agreements in mediation, you will run them past your lawyers, who will make sure you're making informed agreements. Sometimes lawyers and experts, such as certified public accountants or appraisers, attend the mediation sessions with you. They can bring useful information that you may need to resolve your issues.

The Mediation Process

When you make an appointment with a mediator, expect to receive a detailed questionnaire to be filled out and returned to the mediator prior to the session. At the first session, the mediator will explain the process and will probably ask you to sign a contract that includes rules and an agreement to pay for the mediation. You may want to review the contract with your lawyer before agreeing to mediate.

Once you agree to mediate, the real sessions begin. You, your spouse, and the mediator will decide what issue needs to be addressed first. Suppose the top item on your agenda is how to survive financially while the divorce is going on. Your and your spouse can present your budgets and together take a look at the money available to support two households. Maybe there isn't enough money to support two households, in which case you may negotiate a way to continue to live in the same household. Or you may agree that one of you will pay the other temporary support, so each of you can live in separate locations during the divorce. If you make the agreement, you'll make the effort to make it work.

When you reach an agreement, the mediator prepares a memorandum of agreement. You will need to bring this to a lawyer, who will then prepare the necessary legal documents to complete your divorce. While one lawyer can draft the agreement, keep in mind that one lawyer cannot represent both you and your spouse, even if he says he can. To best protect your interests, you should have any final documents reviewed by a lawyer who you have retained to represent your interests.

Finding a Mediator

Every community has excellent mediators—the trick is finding them. The first step is to hire your lawyer, and then have your lawyer help you find a competent mediator. Most states have a list of certified mediators, which means the mediator has completed state-approved mediation training. Successful completion of such a course means only that. Although mediators may or may not be lawyers themselves, mediators are not licensed to practice mediation. No state has a governing body that keeps mediators toeing the line. This is why it is important for you to have your own lawyer review any final documents before you give your final consent.

Remember, it's not the mediator's job to come up with the solution to the problem. That's your job. The mediator can give you helpful information and push the parties toward a compromise, but ultimately you make the decisions.

Advantages of Mediation

Mediation has several advantages over going to court:

- Mediation is voluntary and nonbinding. If you don't reach an agreement, you're free to try another avenue, such as arbitration or going to trial.
- You're in charge of the process, and you make the decisions.
- Mediation is usually a quick way to resolve disputes.
- The process is private and mediation sessions are confidential.

- In most states, you can meet with a mediator much more quickly than you can get your case heard in court.
- You'll probably be able to talk to your ex-spouse after the divorce. This is good for your mental health, your kids' mental health, and your financial health.
- You're more likely to comply with an agreement of your own making.
- The techniques you learn in mediation can be used to resolve disputes in the future.

If you can make it work, you'll be satisfied with the mediation process and the results. An added bonus will be the bundle of money you will save by avoiding litigation.

Some Cautionary Notes

Mediation doesn't work if one party goes into it with the wrong attitude.

Even though you may want mediation to work, it simply may not. If you're not making headway in trying to mediate a settlement, your best plan is to get on the court calendar as quickly as possible, help your lawyer present your position well, and let the judge decide.

Mediation also doesn't work when one of the parties is afraid of the other. If domestic violence has occurred in the marriage, the power imbalance is often too great to successfully mediate a settlement. The mere process of mediation can also put the victim of domestic violence in greater danger. Finally, mediation doesn't work when one of the parties hides or transfers marital assets. Of course, when any of these conditions are present, no process works very well. Then the only alternative is to go to court and give control over the decision making to a judge.

Arbitration

In arbitration, you and your lawyers meet with a neutral arbitrator whom you select at a hearing that is less formal than a court proceeding. However, the hearing follows the rules of evidence used by courts, and the arbitrator's decision is normally binding and final.

Arbitration has a number of advantages:

- It's voluntary; it happens only if you choose it.
- It's informal, simple, and less stressful than going to court.
- You can select your own arbitrator, usually an expert in divorce law, and often a retired family court judge.
- The focus is on cooperation and maintaining good relations.
- Like mediation, it's a private process, and the information provided at the hearing is confidential.
- No lengthy and expensive appeals are needed.
- Arbitration is a lot less expensive than trial.

However, arbitration also has disadvantages:

- You may have your arbitration hearing without doing complete discovery (the gathering of information), because the arbitrator, unlike a judge, can make a decision based on incomplete evidence if she deems the evidence to date is conclusive.
- The arbitrator may not explain the reasoning in her opinion and order.
- You can't appeal. (This also may be an advantage depending on how you feel about the decision.)

As you can see, arbitration isn't a cure-all, but it can still outweigh the disadvantages of giving a judge the power to make all your decisions.

New Trends in Alternative Dispute Resolution

The area of alternative dispute resolution is constantly being fine-tuned, and you may want to take advantage of some growing trends. You may not be able to come to an agreement using negotiation, mediation, or arbitration, but some slightly different options offer you privacy, a quick timeline, and a relatively low cost.

Mediation-Arbitration Hybrid

It's possible to combine forms of alternative dispute resolution. The most common hybrid is using mediation and arbitration in tandem, often referred to as "med-arb." For example, you and your spouse mediate and resolve all your issues except spousal maintenance; you then agree to submit this issue to arbitration. The beauty of this concept is that you exercise control over all the decisions that you can agree on, then let a third person resolve issues you can't resolve.

When you choose med-arb, you should have your lawyers prepare a written agreement stating that you'll mediate all issues you can, and if you're unable to mediate an issue, you'll submit that issue to arbitration. It's critical to be clear about whether this arbitration is binding or nonbinding. If it's binding, the arbitrator's decision is final. No appeal is possible and your divorce is done. This is cheaper and faster than going to court, and you'll be happier with the outcome. If it's nonbinding, you can decide you don't like the decision and go to trial.

The Special Master

In some states, you and your spouse can agree to hire a private sector expert, called a special master, or a special magistrate, to be your judge. This is similar to binding arbitration, except that your agreement will state you have the right to appeal the decision of the special master. That is, you give this person the authority to decide your case as if he were a trial court judge, and, just as if you were in a trial court, you reserve the right to appeal. A special master will charge for his time; it will be expensive, but you get your case heard by an expert in the field, and you get it heard now. Avoiding delay may save you money in the long run. It will certainly mitigate the emotional stress of having the case drag on and on and on. Your divorce will be as legal and final as if a judge had heard it.

CHAPTER 8

Beginning the Divorce Process

You've decided divorce is the only option and now you're wondering how a divorce begins. What happens next? Who will pay which expenses? Where will your kids live? Will you have to move? When it comes to finding out about divorce, don't ask your best friend who went through it or rely on information from an Internet website or some other source. You should take your million questions to the lawyer you have carefully selected.

Getting Started

First you'll interview several lawyers and select one that feels right to you. Let's assume you've found a good divorce lawyer and are ready to begin the process. Your lawyer will probably send you a form to complete on the history of your family and your marriage. You'll fill out the form and mail it to him so he can review it before your next meeting. Some lawyers prefer to meet with you in person first so they can get a sense of your case.

Your Marriage History

When you get together, you and your lawyer will first review and sign a retainer agreement. Then you'll review the marital history together. Your lawyer will help you understand what parts of your marriage history are important to the divorce process and what parts are not legally important. For example, it's important that you inherited some property from your aunt during the marriage. It's probably not important that your spouse seemed to prefer reading a book in the evening to talking to you. Your lawyer will also want to know what aspects of your divorce are most important to you so he can begin to think about settlement options.

ALERT!

After that first meeting with your lawyer, it's a good idea to rethink your objectives. Objectives need to be reasonable, obtainable, and based on reality. Revenge should not be an objective. It's a visceral response that may produce short-term results but long-term harm.

Listen to Advice, But Stay in Control

You will tell your lawyer what you hope to accomplish in your divorce, and he, being a good divorce lawyer, will tell you what parts of your plan are reasonable and what parts are not. For example, if you tell your lawyer you want custody of your children, but you work sixty hours a week and your spouse stays home with the children, he will tell you that unless something is seriously wrong with your spouse, you're unlikely to get custody.

You need to listen to this advice. Many people spend a lot of money pursuing goals they can't obtain, usually because they're too wrapped up emotionally in the issue to see the reality of the situation.

Your lawyer may say you're entitled to more than you want. Think hard about this advice. Be sure you're the one who decides what you want. Sometimes pushing for more is what turns a divorce from friendly to hostile.

Financial Documents

You and your lawyer will make a list of the documents you need to develop an understanding of your financial situation. You will possess some of the documents, which you can provide easily, and your spouse will have some of the documents, which may or may not be easily obtained. Other papers are held by the bank or other institutions. You and your lawyer will develop a plan for getting all the documents, but remember that anything you can do to help collect the required documents will save your lawyer time—and save you money. If you think your spouse may take or destroy important documents when she learns of your plans to divorce, you may want to make copies and put them in a safe place.

If your lawyer says you need to round up certain financial information before you begin the divorce, get the documents right away. When you respond quickly to your lawyer's requests, you help move the process along. Your lawyer can prepare better, clearer papers if he has the necessary information.

Here's a list of basic financial information needed for a family with modest assets, including a house and retirement accounts:

- Recent paycheck stubs, at least for the past four weeks, but the more the better.
- Recent bank statements showing checking and savings account balances and activities, whether individual, joint, or for the parties' children.

- Recent mortgage statement on all property owned by the parties, whether individual or joint, showing amount owed and interest rate.
- Recent credit card statements, whether individual or joint, showing balance information.
- Recent retirement account statements showing contributions and present values.
- Recent statements on all financial investment accounts including IRAs, stocks, bonds, or other similar accounts, including present balance and interest rate.
- Recent statements or appraisals of any other property or investment, whether individual or joint, such as art, jewelry, coins, boats, or other similar items.
- Time share agreements, whether individual or joint.
- Lease agreements, whether individual or joint.
- Current real estate tax bills.
- Documents from recent home transactions (refinancing or appraisal).

Providing your lawyer with a copy of these documents will help him evaluate your case and give you a more realistic idea of what you can expect in a settlement or an order after trial.

Commencing the Divorce: The Summons

To begin the divorce and set the process in motion, your lawyer will draft the required papers, which could be called a Summons with Notice, Summons and Petition, Summons and Complaint, or sometimes simply a Complaint. This document tells your spouse he has a set number of days to respond to the paperwork, usually twenty or thirty days. If your spouse does not respond, he could be found in default. Default means you can proceed with the divorce without your spouse's participation. In some jurisdictions, the summons can also contain restraining provisions such as directives that neither party is to hide or dispose of assets while the divorce is pending. In some states, a summons restrains parties from harassing or otherwise bothering each other. It may require the parties to keep all presently existing insurance in full effect and not to change beneficiaries.

The Petition or Complaint

The petition or complaint tells the court basic facts about your marriage, why the court has jurisdiction, and why you want a divorce. Each state has specific requirements about what must be in the petition or complaint, which your lawyer will know. The petition or complaint will typically include most of the following information:

- Names, addresses, and birth dates of the parties.
- Date and place of the marriage.
- Children's names and birth dates.
- Employment and income of the parties.
- Statement that the jurisdictional requirements of the state have been met, which means one or both parties have lived in the state long enough.
- Statement that the marriage is over, usually irretrievably broken or irreconcilable differences in no-fault states
- Finding of fault in states that require it or where it is beneficial to the distribution of property.
- Amount of time parties have been separated. (Some states require a minimum period of separation before divorce.)
- Real estate owned by the parties.
- Other property owned by the parties (cars, boats, retirement plans, insurance).
- If applicable, orders from other courts, like family court, which have already been obtained.
- If applicable, notice of any existing orders of protection.
- A statement that no other action for divorce is pending in another state.

After the petition or complaint sets out the facts, it then describes what the petitioner is asking for. This part of the petition or complaint is called the "prayer for relief." It usually asks that the marriage be dissolved, that the children live with one or both parents, that one of the parties supports the other, and that the property be divided fairly and equitably. Sometimes the relief is a short, numbered list at the end of the petition or complaint, and sometimes a detailed explanation for the requested relief is included in the body of the petition or complaint.

The petitioner (sometimes called the plaintiff) and her lawyer sign the petition or complaint. By signing the document, you indicate that you believe the information to be true, and the lawyer recognizes his obligation to be ethical in drafting papers and in representing you. The signatures are then notarized.

Never sign anything you haven't read or don't understand. This is a life lesson, but it holds especially true in matters of divorce. Also, never sign your name to documents containing false information—you will likely be found out and the price you pay could be quite high.

Make sure the petition or complaint is accurate in every way. If there are facts that your lawyer has included that are not quite right, tell him before he files the petition or complaint. It is worth paying the extra money to have your lawyer change the petition or complaint rather than to go forward with it containing inaccuracies or false information. The petition or complaint is a sworn document, meaning that when you sign it you are swearing to its truth and accuracy. You never want to have to say to the court later that you made a mistake because you may look like you were lying.

Serving the Papers

Service is the legal term used when legal papers are delivered from one side to another in a case. Usually a summons must be personally served, that is, the papers must be handed to your spouse. Your lawyer will probably hire a process server—a civilian who works for a company that serves and delivers legal documents—to serve the papers to your spouse. There will be a fee associated with hiring a process server that will vary depending on how difficult it is for the process server to find your spouse. A spouse who is trying to evade service can cause you to run up quite a bill if the process server has to make multiple attempts to serve the paperwork.

If this is to be an amicable divorce, at least for now, your spouse may prefer to pick up the papers at your lawyer's office rather than risk being served in a public place. Your spouse's attorney may also be able to complete service. You may also be able to get a mutual friend to serve the papers. These methods are far more cost effective than hiring a process server.

A Notice of Motion and Affidavit

You may want a court order giving you custody and child support or the use of your home, a car, a bank account, or some other relief during the divorce. Unless you and your spouse can negotiate the terms of this order, you'll need to prepare a motion asking for these things and explaining why you need them. A Notice of Motion is a legal document, prepared by your lawyer, that says to the court and your spouse that you are going to ask for certain relief from the court on a specified day and time. If you need immediate relief, your lawyer will file an Order to Show Cause (discussed later in this chapter), which can include a request for temporary orders that govern the parties' behavior until the time of the hearing.

You must attach an affidavit to your Notice of Motion, which is a sworn statement your lawyer will prepare based on the facts you provide. The affidavit tells the court why you need the relief you're seeking. Your lawyer may also prepare an affidavit, sometimes called an affirmation, if there is information the lawyer has obtained or certain law that the court should be aware of that supports your request.

Persuading the Judge

You'll want to tell the judge the things you believe will persuade him to do what you want. For instance, if you have school-age children, you might tell the court you want them to live with you in the family home to minimize the disruption to their lives and allow them to attend the same school, play with their friends, and participate in their neighborhood activities. You might say you need the newer, bigger car to transport them safely and you need the bank account to pay the monthly household expenses.

If you and your spouse disagree about a parenting arrangement—temporary or permanent—you'll need to make a motion asking a judge to decide. You'll need to prepare an affidavit explaining why your proposed arrangement is best for the children.

FACT

In making your proposal, be sure to think of what will be best and least disruptive for the children. If you and your spouse live far apart, the judge will probably try to avoid sentencing the children to life as commuters and minimize the number of exchanges during the school week.

It's important to tell the judge in this affidavit how the children have been cared for up to this point, because judges tend to maintain the status quo for children. If you've been their major caregiver, say so; if you haven't been, then you need to present a very strong case for making the change. Be reasonable. If your spouse has always been the primary caregiver for the children, don't try to change that now just to upset your spouse. Changes will also upset your children. If your spouse has been more of an occasional parent because of her work schedule, don't try to force her into taking on more than she can manage just because "it's about time" she took an interest. Your children will be the ones to suffer having to deal with an exhausted parent who is unfamiliar with their routines.

Restraining Orders

Is your spouse likely to behave badly when served with the divorce papers? Will he try to hide marital assets? Will she spend like crazy, running up big credit card debt? Might he run from the state with the children? If any of these are possibilities, maybe you need to ask the court to issue some restraining orders, which you can serve on your spouse with the summons and petition.

A restraining order is an order issued by a court that tells one or both parties they are not allowed to do a particular thing. For example, a restraining order could tell the parties they cannot sell or dispose of any of their property. Another example of a restraining order, also called an order of protection, tells one spouse to stay away from the other or limits contact in some way. If you decide you need restraining orders right from the beginning, you've also committed to going to court. You can request that the court issue an *ex parte* order, meaning the judge has only heard one side of things, but a hearing will likely be scheduled as quickly as possible so the judge can hear from both sides. Judges only issue *ex parte* orders in extreme situations, so if you really think you need one, be very specific about your reasons in the papers you submit to the court.

If your lawyer believes it's possible to get such an order, you'll need to prepare all the paperwork, plus a plea for emergency relief that sets out why the judge should grant it. Your lawyer will prepare an *ex parte* order or an Order to Show Cause, which she will take to the judge for signature before the papers are served on your spouse. These orders contain hearing dates at which time both sides can speak on the issues. Once signed, a temporary order directs one or both of the parties to do certain things.

FACT

Judges usually don't like *ex parte* orders unless they are absolutely necessary. Judges are especially cautious about issuing orders that throw someone out of his house. You must really need such an order and be able to justify that need. Seek this extraordinary relief only if you must, and make sure an emergency really exists.

The *ex parte* order is a temporary order, justified because an emergency exists, and is usually valid only until the hearing. In addition to those provisions that apply to both of you, depending on the circumstances, the order may give you temporary use and occupancy of the house, use of a car, or temporary custody of the children. It may also order your spouse to pay you temporary child or spousal support.

If the court issues an *ex parte* order, a hearing will also be scheduled, usually within a couple of weeks, so both parties can attend and present their version of the situation. *Ex parte* orders can apply to one or both spouses depending on the situation. There is no limit to the type of relief that can be requested in an *ex parte* order, but what a court will order varies greatly from jurisdiction to jurisdiction.

Order to Show Cause

An Order to Show Cause is usually the legal document that accompanies a request for emergency orders. It is similar to a Notice of Motion except there is no waiting period between the time you file your papers and the receipt of a temporary order. This document, along with your affidavits, is presented to the judge, *ex parte*. The Order to Show Cause can contain specific orders that if signed by the judge have the full force of temporary orders. The Order to Show Cause demands that your spouse appear in court and show cause as to why your requested relief should not be granted. For example, the Order to Show Cause may contain a provision ordering your spouse to pay you a specified amount of temporary support, and your spouse will need to explain why this shouldn't be necessary.

If you obtained an *ex parte* restraining order or your spouse is too angry and upset to meet and negotiate, you'll need a temporary court order that will stay in place until another temporary order replaces it or until the final judgment and decree is issued. To get that temporary order from the judge, you'll need to bring a motion.

Depending on the laws of your state, your lawyer may or may not have to provide your spouse's lawyer with a copy of the Order to Show Cause before taking it to the judge. Not all courts in all states will issue such an order, but if your court will do so, it will provide you with some temporary relief until a hearing can be held. Once the Order to Show Cause is signed, the papers get served on your spouse.

To Court or Not to Court

Even if you don't need the *ex parte* restraining orders, you and your lawyer might decide you need some rules to govern behavior during the divorce. Say you're afraid your spouse will try to keep you from seeing the children, and you're also concerned your spouse will continue to spend money you don't have staying in a house you can't afford. You know your spouse will be really angry when the divorce papers are served, but you tried discussing your situation before going to a lawyer and it didn't work out. What can you do?

Temporary Orders

You can try to negotiate rules that will govern your family's behavior during the divorce. If your spouse hires a lawyer, the four of you can meet to discuss a temporary arrangement. The lawyers can also develop a plan and present it to you and your spouse. You'll want to decide who will live in the marital home, when the children will be with each of you, how you'll pay for two homes, what funds can be used, what documents need to be exchanged, and what property needs to be valued by a third person.

ALERT!

Rather than a gazillion affidavits, find a positive way to take out your frustration and anger. For every angry statement, retort, or sarcastic criticism you want to level at your spouse, do a lap around the track or an extra lap at the pool. Exercise is a great stress reliever and a way to relieve your frustration outside the courts.

If it's possible to negotiate a temporary arrangement, one of the lawyers will draft a document called a stipulation for temporary relief, stipulation and temporary order, or interim agreement, which is then signed by the judge. You, your spouse, and the two lawyers will sign the document. If you need a court order incorporating the terms of the agreement, one of the lawyers will get the order signed by a judge.

Motions

The minimum amount of paperwork consists of the motion and affidavit. If you have issues that involve children, you will probably seek affidavits from friends and family who know about your skills and attributes as a parent. Given these issues and others you might have, your motion and affidavit may grow into a thick pile of papers very quickly. These papers have to be served on your spouse or your spouse's attorney, and the other side will probably respond with a motion and affidavits of its own.

Your affidavits will probably upset your spouse, just as you'll probably be upset when you get your spouse's responsive papers, including responsive affidavits. Now you have to respond to your spouse's papers with new affidavits. Then maybe your spouse responds to your responses.

At some point, the exchange of papers has to stop, so most courts set a deadline for filing papers. Some states limit the amount of exchanges that can take place on a single motion. Deadlines vary from jurisdiction to jurisdiction, but your lawyer should know what is required. Some courts will resolve motions on the papers without the need for a temporary hearing, but others will require one.

The Temporary Hearing

If you've chosen to go to court, at some point you'll actually have to go to the courthouse for your first hearing before a judge.

FACT

Sometimes both sides show up unprepared at the temporary hearing, which is a bad idea in most courts. The judge can assess fines and court costs to anyone who shows up unprepared. And the judge has a long memory, so you don't want to annoy the person who will ultimately decide your case.

Before the Hearing

You and your lawyer will go to the courtroom where your motion is to be heard. Your spouse and lawyer will be there, too, and maybe your spouse's parent (for moral support) or your spouse's new love interest (just to get you upset). This ploy usually works. It's not uncommon for people waiting outside the court to lose control during this time of high stress and emotional volatility, so court administration usually assigns a number of deputy sheriffs to the family court. The presence of uniformed officers helps to keep things calm, and the officers are trained to respond quickly if folks get out of control.

It's best to come to court with only your lawyer and any expert who may present information at the hearing. Family and friends may increase the tension and be a distraction.

During the Hearing

Say your hearing is scheduled for 2 P.M. At 2:45 the judge's clerk pokes his nose out to tell you the judge will see you shortly, which turns out to be another half an hour. Finally, it really is time for your motion to be heard. You and your lawyer sit at one table before the judge's bench; your spouse and lawyer sit at the other. The judge appears, and everyone stands until told to sit. After that the clerk may announce the case so the judge knows which file to look at.

ALERT!

Never bring children to a court hearing unless the judge has specifically asked to see them. Divorce is stressful enough for children without making them active participants in your war with their other parent. Courts do not look kindly on parents who bring their children to court

The lawyers introduce themselves, and then your lawyer argues on behalf of your motions. Your spouse's lawyer responds. Maybe each lawyer responds to the other's arguments. After the judge has heard both sides, she can make a ruling from the bench or tell everyone that she will take the matter under advisement and issue an order within a specified time period. You're dismissed and leave the courtroom.

In some jurisdictions, the temporary hearing may be much less formal. It may begin with the judge speaking only with the attorneys. Each side presents their case and the judge may decide to issue a temporary order or set down one or more issues for a hearing where she will take testimony from the parties. After discussing things with the attorneys, you and your spouse will be called into the courtroom and be told about the decision and the need for a hearing. In some cases, the judge may want to ask you or your spouse a question to gather more information before making a decision. Your lawyer should talk to you ahead of time to let you know how the court in your jurisdiction usually handles temporary hearings.

After the Hearing

Well, how about that! Your heart was beating a mile a minute, your future was on the line, and you didn't get to say a word. Not only that, your lawyer didn't point out all the lies in your spouse's affidavit and didn't even argue some of the points you thought were important. And the judge has a specified time period to issue an order? What are you supposed to do in the meantime?

Your lawyer assures you the hearing went well and tells you to be patient and wait for the judge's order.

The Judge Issues a Temporary Order

Eighty-eight days after your court hearing your lawyer calls to say the judge has issued an order, and suggests you come to his office to review it. With a sinking feeling, you drop everything. The order is a disaster. It feels like the judge never read your papers or heard your lawyer's arguments. You never got to say anything to the judge. You feel it is not fair and there is no justice.

FACT

The productivity of wage earners tends to decline during the divorce process. Some judges and lawyers attribute this to the wage earner's desire to pay less support, and sometimes this is the explanation. However, the process of divorce and reduced productivity really can be connected.

Because you have to move out of the house and pay most of your income to your spouse, you'll have to temporarily move in with your parents or a buddy. How long is temporarily? You'll have to drive about an hour to your former home to see your children for two hours twice a week. You'll have to work as much overtime as you can to have some spending money for your visits with the children and to pay some rent. After reading the order, you don't feel much like working at all, let alone working overtime.

The ability to appeal a temporary order varies from state to state, so check with your lawyer if you really believe you can't live with the order. Absent an appeal, you'll have to live with the judge's order unless you bring another motion that results in a different order. If you choose to live with the order, at least you have a framework within which to operate until the divorce is done.

CHAPTER 9

The Discovery Process

When you went to see your lawyer at the beginning
of the divorce process, you talked about the information needed to work out the details of your divorce.
Discovery is the process lawyers use to get information from the other side. There are many different
kinds of discovery and different ways it can be used
to your benefit and detriment. This will be a very
important part of the divorce process, so you will
need to work closely with your lawyer to make sure
you gather all the necessary information.

What's Included in Discovery?

Discovery is the process by which your lawyer obtains information that will allow him to tell you what you're entitled to under the laws of your state. You will also be required to supply information to your spouse. The kind of information that will be exchanged depends on the facts of your case. It could include all kinds of records that address custody, support, or property division. Here are some examples of information you may need to supply or want your spouse to supply:

- Current employment and income, including bonuses, stock options, and other benefits.
- Employment history, including past income, bonuses, stock options, and retirement benefits.
- Business tax returns and other records for several years if either of you are self-employed.
- Value of businesses if available.
- Personal tax returns for three to five years.
- Checks and check registers for three to five years.
- Credit card statements for three to five years.
- Documents for all real estate purchased and sold before and during the marriage.
- Value of real estate.
- Retirement benefits and assets.
- Life insurance owned by the parties.
- Value of special personal property, such as antiques.
- Value of boats, cars, snowmobiles, and other vehicles.
- Value of the animals, crops, seed and fertilizer, equipment, etc., if a farm is involved.
- Monthly expenses claimed by both parties.
- Mental health and other health histories.
- Inheritances, gifts, and claims of nonmarital assets.
- Marriage debts.

Not everyone has all the stuff on this list, and not everyone needs to have all this information to make a reasonable settlement. But this will give you some idea of the type of information that might be requested.

Discovery When You're Both Cooperating

Getting information from the other side can take several forms. In a cooperative divorce, your lawyer can simply call or write your spouse's lawyer and ask for the information you need. Your spouse and her lawyer will then provide the information they have in their possession. Likewise, you and your lawyer will provide whatever information you have in your possession. If either of you are missing any of the information the lawyers say they need, you can work together to get it.

FACT

Sharing information is the least expensive way of getting the complete picture of your marital estate. The more information you and your spouse collect and exchange, the less you have to pay someone else to collect it. This means you spend less of the marital estate trying to figure out what it is, leaving more for the both of you.

Suppose you need the records for the last year on your spouse's American Express account. Your spouse can get the records or sign an authorization permitting you to get the records. Suppose your spouse wants your medical records for the last five years, but your doctor won't provide them to anyone except you. Either you'll have to get them, or you'll have to sign a release permitting your doctor to give the records to your spouse. If you don't want the hassle of getting certain information, you can sign a release or authorization permitting the other side to obtain it.

Discovery When You Can't Cooperate

If you and your spouse can't work together to collect the information, your lawyer will need to use the muscle provided by court rules to get it. When parties are angry and hostile, they often try to keep information from each other. But if you play hard to get with information the other side is entitled to have, you end up paying your lawyer to delay the inevitable. This is not in your best interests.

If necessary, there are a number of tools your lawyer can use to obtain information. They are as follows:

1. **Interrogatories.** These are a series of questions your lawyer sends to the other side that must be answered under oath within a specified time period, usually twenty or thirty days. The questions ask for information about income, assets, parenting attributes, and other things you and your lawyer want to know.

2. **Request for admissions.** This is a list of statements that, if not denied within twenty or thirty days, are taken to be true. Your lawyer can send a series of statements to your spouse's lawyer, along with a notice that says, "If you don't respond within thirty days, these statements will be deemed to be admitted to the court as fact." These statements can be something like: "I will be able to get a good job within three months, and I will be able to support myself."

   In reality, it's unlikely a court will deem the statements admitted if a spouse fails to respond in the time period allotted, partly because this failure is very common. Most judges extend the time to respond, but some judges are tough and strictly follow the rules. You'll need to rely on your lawyer's information about your judge. To be safe, answer all discovery requests on time.

3. **Request for production of documents, also known as a discovery demand.** This is a legal demand for documents you want within twenty or thirty days. It means just what it says—your spouse must get you the documents you listed in your request if they are in his possession. These documents can range from the checkbooks of his closely held corporation to verification of Aunt Molly's cash gift in 1978 to your children's medical records. Failure to answer in the allotted time is a reason to go back to court. The good news is that the threat of seeking a court order is usually enough to get the documents.

4. **Depositions.** These are face-to-face sessions in which your lawyer asks questions of your spouse, your spouse's expert, or any other person

your lawyer thinks may have information useful to your case. The person answering the questions has been sworn to reply truthfully. A court reporter records everything and later provides a written transcript.

5. **The witness list for trial.** Depending on the jurisdiction, you may or may not be required by law to submit a list of witnesses you intend to call. The other side can always demand a list and most judges will order the parties to exchange lists. If demanded by the other side or ordered by the court, you must submit a witness list. If you fail to submit your witness list to the court and the other lawyer by a certain day before the trial, you won't be able to call your witnesses at all.

6. **The exhibit list for trial.** This is the same deal. If the other side has made a demand or the court has ordered it, if you don't give the other side your list of exhibits by a certain date, you can't introduce the exhibits.

7. **Subpoena or judicial subpoena.** This is a document completed by your lawyer that is served on the holder of a particular record. A subpoena requires the holder of a record to provide copies to the requesting party. Certain records can only be obtained with a judicial subpoena, meaning a judge needs to sign the subpoena. For example, most states require that a subpoena for mental health records be signed by a judge.

Interrogatories

In a contested process, one of the most common forms of discovery is through interrogatories. Your lawyer probably has a set of standard interrogatories, which she pulls out and adapts for each case. Lawyers call these boilerplate interrogatories. You and your lawyer should review the proposed interrogatories together to make sure they focus on information that is likely to be helpful to you in preparing your case. Preparing the interrogatories and reviewing the answers you get takes your attorney time. You pay for this time.

Sometimes, interrogatory questions are not answered in the time period allotted. Failure to answer interrogatories can be a basis for bringing a motion before the court demanding the questions be answered or the violating side be fined or found in contempt. Before your lawyer files a motion, she should try and resolve the issue with the other side. Sometimes an extension of time to reply can solve the problem without the need for costly litigation.

When you fudge the truth, you have to remember just how you fudged for future reference—not an easy task, especially when you're under the stress of a divorce. You don't gain anything by playing fast and loose with the truth when the outcome has so much impact on your future.

If your spouse serves interrogatories on you through your lawyer, take some time to prepare your answers carefully. The information can be used at trial to impeach (show the witness is lying) the answering party. For this reason it is important that you answer carefully and truthfully, even if the truth hurts. If you don't know the answer, say so. Don't guess. If you answer the interrogatories one way and further discovery provides different information, you will look as if you weren't being truthful.

Depositions

Depositions are another common form of discovery in the divorce process. Your lawyer prepares a list of questions for your spouse. Then your lawyer sends a notice to your spouse's lawyer saying, in effect: "You are to show up on March 1 at 10 A.M. at my office for your deposition to be taken." Usually lawyers have already set the date by agreement, but the notice is required by court rules. Depositions can also be used to obtain information from a potential witness, such as a person who performed a custody evaluation or valued your business.

Sometimes if lawyers haven't set the date in advance, they do the lawyers' deposition dance. One lawyer serves the other with the Notice for Taking Deposition. Then the other lawyer sends a letter saying the chosen date won't work. After a series of letters, a date is finally selected. You pay for your lawyer's time, so try to encourage him to set the date by agreement to avoid the costly back-and-forth dance.

When your spouse's deposition is taken, your spouse, your spouse's lawyer, your lawyer, and a court reporter are present. You can be present, too, if you choose. Your spouse is sworn, and she answers your lawyer's questions. Sometimes your spouse's lawyer objects to your lawyer's question and then proceeds to make a legal argument. The lawyer does this to preserve his objection. If the transcript is later used in court, that lawyer may ask the judge to rule on the objection, with the purpose of keeping that particular question and answer out of court. Everything said at the deposition is taken down by the court reporter and later transcribed for both sides and for the court.

Reasons for a Deposition

A deposition is a very useful tool because it not only allows your attorney to gather information but also affords an opportunity to see how you and your spouse act under the pressure of questioning. Many lawyers use depositions as a way to preview you or your spouse's capability (or lack thereof) as a witness. For this reason, the attorney's goal may be to see how easily you become angry or anxious under questioning. In a deposition, you are required to answer questions posed to you even if they don't seem relevant or require you to disclose personal and embarrassing information. If you are being deposed, it is critical that you stay calm and present a cool demeanor. If you cannot control your behavior at a deposition, it is unlikely you will be able to control your behavior at a trial. Many cases have been settled after a deposition because it becomes clear that one spouse is going to disintegrate on the witness stand.

Your spouse's lawyer may try to use the emotional stress of divorce against you by tempting you to argue or make outbursts that could hurt you. If your temper is flaring, take a moment to breathe deeply and think about what you're going to say before responding to a question.

Some chronic liars are exposed by the deposition; on the other hand, some good, honest folk are scared into saying things they don't mean.

Handling a Deposition

If your spouse's lawyer takes your deposition, answer the questions clearly and concisely. If you don't know the answer, say so. If you don't understand the question, ask for it to be repeated or restated. Answer only the question that's asked, and pause briefly before giving your answer to give your lawyer time to object. Do not volunteer information. Do not give narrative explanations that provide more information than needed. This may seem simple, but it can be very difficult. You may feel like you have to explain an answer. Don't! If you stick to the questions, your lawyer can give you guidance and object to questions she believes to be improper. Your lawyer can advise you not to answer a question, but your lawyer can't protect you if you blurt something out.

Discovery Can Be Costly

Discovery, or preparing for trial, is a necessary part of the divorce process, but it's also costly. Look at the number of players involved: your lawyer, your spouse's lawyer, the experts for both sides, the court reporter. All of these folks expect to be paid for their time. How much help do you need and how much can you afford? You should work closely with your lawyer to learn about the discovery tools available to you, how much each will cost and what will provide you with the most valuable information. If you are working with limited resources, make sure your attorney knows what you can afford so he can help you make the best choices. Most importantly, find out what will happen if the other side doesn't comply with your discovery demands. Forcing compliance could cost additional money that you may have to include in your budget before making a decision.

Using Experts

Some information needed to settle your divorce might not be readily available. For instance, if you need the value of your home or business, you'll need to hire an expert to figure it out. Ordinarily, you wouldn't have this value available unless you had recently done some refinancing or sold or purchased the home or business. Or maybe you need an expert to help you come up with the best parenting plan for your children. Maybe you need an expert because your spouse hasn't worked more than part time for several years, and the two of you need to know what your spouse's earning potential is and how to achieve it. Or maybe you need someone to figure out your stock options or the investment you made in rental properties with inherited money.

All these areas call for the opinion of an expert: a certified public accountant, a Realtor, a psychologist, a business evaluator, or a vocational rehabilitation counselor. In short, you need a person who has expertise in areas where you need help. Experts are expensive, so make sure you really need one before you hire his services.

Working Cooperatively Is Best

If you and your spouse work cooperatively, you can agree on the experts to use. If you can select one in each area where you need outside expertise and can agree to accept the report of that expert, you can save a ton of money. First of all, you pay only one person rather than two. Second, you will get a neutral opinion—one not favoring either side—on which to base your settlement. Third, you don't get the court involved, thereby avoiding a possible third opinion.

FACT

Divorce lawyers often use the same experts over and over because they are recognized in their field and can be trusted as independent neutrals in cooperative divorce situations. These neutrals can be of immense help to you in valuing your assets.

If you decide to work cooperatively, make sure you hire an expert that is not known to either party. The last thing you want is your spouse's best buddy from college performing the evaluation.

Valuing a Professional Practice

Let's assume you and your spouse agree to work with one expert—often called an independent neutral—to come up with a value for your spouse's dental practice. You tell your lawyers you want to hire an expert with knowledge of dental practices, and each lawyer produces the names of two or three experts. You may ask for the experts' credentials, so you have some basis on which to choose.

You and your spouse pick the expert. You tell the expert what you want, and you provide the expert with the information she asks for. The expert gives you her best opinion, and you plug it into the balance sheet you're preparing. This may sound too good to be true, but it really does happen.

Dueling Experts

Contrast this with the litigation approach to using experts: You tell the expert you "know" the practice is worth a bazillion dollars, your spouse cooks the books, and your spouse has intentionally cut back on working over the last year to reduce the practice's value. You give the expert a bottom line from which to work. "The practice must be worth at least $500,000," you say. Since you're the one paying the expert, is it any surprise that the expert comes up with a value of $550,000?

Well, your spouse hires an expert as well. Your spouse tells the expert the economy has slowed and demand for his specialty, orthodontics, is down because it's elective. The practice really is worth only the value of the used equipment, your spouse says, and the business can't be worth more than $50,000. It may even have a negative value. Since your spouse pays the expert, is it any wonder his expert develops a value of $34,000 for the practice?

ALERT!

What numbers are ringing in your mental cash register at this point? Fees for the experts, fees for the lawyers, fees for the court reporter. Valuation is very expensive, so it's important to evaluate what you are spending for the service compared to what the practice is actually worth.

At this point, you have some options. Your lawyer can take the deposition of your spouse's expert to see if there are any weaknesses in the expert's analysis. Your lawyer may well want your expert to be present at the deposition to help ask the right questions. This, by the way, is a legitimate use of a deposition. You and your lawyer want to know what the other side's expert will say at trial and whether the expert's opinion can be challenged.

Your side and your spouse's side may decide to hire a third expert, chosen by the first two experts. You may even take the issue to the court. The judge may decide a third opinion is needed from an independent neutral.

A Contested Court Hearing

At some point you bring competing experts and their reports to court for a contested hearing on the value of your spouse's dental practice. It's fair to assume the judge knows nothing about dental practices, beyond what's involved in getting her teeth cleaned on a fairly regular basis. On top of that, neither expert is a scintillating speaker, and your lawyer doesn't do much to make your expert interesting, so the judge pretty much snoozes through the daylong argument.

When the dust settles, the judge determines a value somewhere between $34,000 and $550,000. As long as the judge can come up with a reasonable explanation for the value, it will pass muster with the appellate courts. But chances are, the value will not match your expectations—or your spouse's.

After all that, here's what you end up with: expert reports costing anywhere from $5,000 to $15,000 each, a day in court for two experts and two lawyers costing anywhere from $3,000 to $15,000 each, and a stress level measuring off the charts. If you use an independent neutral from the beginning you can get the information you need for a lot less time, money, and stress. Most important, you'll end up with a real number that can contribute to a workable settlement.

Vocational Rehabilitation Counselor

Suppose your spouse has been unemployed or working only a few hours each week since your first child was born. It's clear from family expenses he will need to work full-time to generate income to support two households. Or, while you can afford to support your spouse and children now, you feel at some point he should become financially independent of you.

What if your spouse has a college degree in some esoteric field like art history and has never used this education for employment. What are his skills and interests? If neither of you can answer these questions, you may want to hire a vocational rehabilitation counselor.

You and your spouse can choose to use a vocational counselor as an independent neutral and put your energies into implementing the recommendations. Of course, you also can each hire a vocational counselor and fight about what career your spouse should pursue and how long it should take him to become self-supporting.

These experts usually work in the unemployment field, but some have expanded their practice to divorce. They usually administer a battery of tests to learn interests and skills, and they apply what they learn to what they know about the current job market. They use their analysis to make recommendations, which often include getting training or additional education. This process is sometimes called a vocational assessment.

Financial Evaluators

If you need to get a handle on your cash flow, you may want to use a certified public accountant (CPA) or other financial expert. A CPA can show how tax implications of certain actions can cost or save you money. If you and your spouse can work together in this area, you really can do yourselves a favor. So much money is spent arguing over net income, the tax consequences of paying spousal maintenance, the proper 401(k) deduction, and so on, that there's not much left over to actually live on. If the same money and energy can go into putting together a workable plan, everyone loses less.

Real Estate Professionals

Realtors can give you a good idea of what your real estate is worth, and so can real estate appraisers. While a realtor will give you a market analysis for free, an appraiser can cost hundreds or even thousands of dollars depending on your location and the size of your property. Most appraisers' values tend to be on the conservative side because appraisers usually start out with a lending institution, which generally wants to conserve its risk obligation. Realtors, on the other hand, may give your property a higher value, hoping you'll choose to work with them in selling your house. Realtors can also give you a bottom-line cash-to-seller analysis. This will tell you what you could realistically expect to receive if you sold your property immediately. This information may help you decide whether your property should be sold, but isn't always helpful in determining its value.

Experts and Children

You can use experts a number of ways to resolve custody issues. Your lawyer will know the skills and reputations of many psychologists and social workers with expertise in helping divorcing families create workable parenting arrangements. Your lawyer can assist you in hiring the person best qualified to help you accomplish your goals.

Determining Your Goals

For starters, you need to decide whether you want to negotiate a plan with your spouse or whether you want to decide what's best for the children yourself. Do you want an expert assessment of your skills and strengths as a parent? Would you rather take your spouse to court and fight over custody? What you want will influence whom you hire.

ALERT!

Use the information you get from the expert to help resolve divorce issues rather than having the expert testify before a judge who probably has little or no knowledge about the issue and is likely to make a decision you won't like. This costs you in time, money, and frustration.

Obviously, if you and your spouse can sit down and rationally work out a plan, you don't need an expert. If you agree in principle but are bogged down in details, you might want to work with an expert who is experienced in developing parenting plans.

Psychologists and Family Services

If you and your spouse want to do the right thing for your kids but are too angry and hurt to sit down and talk it through, you can hire a psychologist with expertise in parenting and children's needs, sometimes called a co-parenting counselor. The professional can be a buffer between the two of you, helping put your ideas into words that are constructive rather than destructive.

Where can you get help? Catholic Charities, Lutheran Social Service, and Jewish Family and Children's Services have social workers and psychologists on staff. Larger communities often have a family services arm of the court system to help with parenting plans and custody evaluations. Your lawyer may also be familiar with other resources in your community that offer similar services.

FACT

 need to consider costs. Will your insurance cover any of the professional's fees? Rarely. Public agencies cost less and may be able to provide all the help you need. Experts with the best reputations don't come cheap, so their use should be reserved for really difficult parents with high conflict and dysfunction.

Sometimes, these people move into private practice after gaining experience in the public sector. Lawyers who work with these folks on a daily basis come to know their strengths and weaknesses. When hiring an expert to help with parenting, you'll want to use the same approach as hiring your lawyer or personal therapist.

An Independent Neutral

Let's suppose you and your spouse can't reach an agreement about parenting after the divorce, and you can't sit down and discuss the issue. At the same time, you both really want to do the right thing for your kids.

So you wisely decide to hire an independent neutral expert to conduct a custody evaluation.

This person will probably meet with the two of you to get basic information about you and the family. The custody evaluator may ask you to fill out and return a questionnaire that may contain a section asking for your custody proposal. In addition, she may ask each of you to take a psychological evaluation or other diagnostic test to check out your mental health. She will also meet with your children to get a sense of who they are, how well they're adjusting to the divorce, and any special physical or emotional needs they may have. She will talk to friends and family, too.

The discovery process is intended to give you and your spouse information that will enable you to resolve your issues. If you ask the right questions, hire experts you trust, and listen to your lawyers, you should be able to reach a reasonable resolution without a trial.

Custody evaluations can be the final straw in maintaining civil communications with your spouse. By their nature, custody evaluations inspire hostility because you have to share with a complete stranger the intimate details of your strengths and weaknesses in parenting. A custody expert will ask you tough questions, evaluate your credibility, and even ask you negative questions in order to see your reaction. For example, an expert might say, "Your husband says you drink a six pack of beer every day, you hardly ever spend time with the children, and you yell at them when you do." Your initial response is probably going to be "how can he say those things about me?" and maybe some other choice words. What the expert is really looking for is not the truth of those statements, but rather how you react to an attack on your character. If you take each criticism and respond calmly, you will make a much better impression on the expert than if you start reciting all of your spouse's shortcomings.

When the custody evaluator has collected the needed information, she will write a report. In some states the report is given to the court, while in other states the expert will meet with the parties and deliver the recommendations. If the recommendations are not in your favor, your attorney may decide to take the expert's deposition to see whether the report can be challenged or whether to hire a second expert. This is much more time consuming, and this means it will be more expensive.

Going to War

If you and your spouse choose the ultimate custody war, you'll each hire an expert and duke it out before a judge at some point. This is the more expensive and stressful option—and it is more likely to have a negative effect on your children. In addition, after a week of bashing each other in court, you'll still be expected to somehow make the judge's decision work.

CHAPTER 10

Custody and Visitation

Custody and visitation are the traditional words used to describe parenting during and after the divorce. These words sound unpleasant and inappropriate for talking about raising children. The word "custody" carries the connotation of ownership or incarceration, and "visitation" is what you do at a funeral home. Nevertheless, these are the words found in the statutes across the nation. Try to think of these as legal terms that simply provide guidelines about how you and your spouse will share your children once you are no longer living as one family.

10

Parenting Agreements

Parenting agreements or parenting plans describe how you will care for your children after the divorce. These plans come in as many variations as there are creative parents to develop them. If parents can work together to come up with a reasonable parenting plan, a judge will typically defer to the judgment of the parents and not alter the plan. Parents working together can formulate flexible, creative, and comfortable schedules that will work best for their children. However, when parents can't agree and courts are forced to make parenting decisions, they often follow traditional patterns that do not allow for much flexibility or creativity. Courts do not do much creative work. Their job is to resolve disputes, not try to second-guess parents in conflict.

Understanding Custody

There are two separate aspects of custody, physical and legal. Physical custody refers to the actual time a child spends with each parent. Legal custody refers to major decision making about your children, including their education, religion, and health care. Decisions about where the children will go to school, what church they will attend, and who will provide medical and dental care are some examples of legal decisions. Whether your children wear braces, play soccer, or have certain friends are also examples of legal decisions.

You don't have to like your ex-spouse, but for the children's sake, try to show respect for her. It is always in the best interests of your children when you and your spouse can get along and present a united front.

If you do not have some form of legal custody, you will not be able to make decisions about your children's activities and future. You will have to submit and comply with the decisions made by the parent who does have legal custody. If you are a parent who is denied custody, make sure you ask for the right to have access to medical and educational records. Although this doesn't give you the ability to make decisions, it will allow you to monitor your child's progress.

At some point in the future, you may want to try to regain legal custody, and it will be important for you to demonstrate that you have taken an interest in your child's life. Sometimes, a court will give one parent sole legal custody but require that parent to solicit and consider the input of the other parent prior to making decisions. Regardless of your parenting agreement or what is ordered by the court, co-parenting cooperatively will be a lot easier if you can maintain a respectful relationship.

From one jurisdiction to another, courts use varying terms to describe custodial relationships between parents. There are typically seven ways custody is described.

1. **Sole custody:** This means that one parent has both legal and physical custody.
2. **Joint or shared custody:** This means that the parents share equally in both legal and physical custody.
3. **Sole legal custody:** This means that one parent makes all major decisions about the children.
4. **Joint or shared legal custody:** This means parents make major decisions about their children together.
5. **Primary physical custody:** This means the children live with one parent most or all of the time. The other parent may still have visitation.
6. **Joint or shared physical custody:** This means the children spend roughly half their time with each parent.
7. **Joint or shared physical and legal custody:** This means that parents make major decisions about their children together and the children spend roughly half their time with each parent.

Legal Custody

Parents with similar values usually can agree on major decisions for their children if they can put their hurt and anger aside and focus on the children. However, parents involved in major power struggles usually can't make these decisions together. Also, in families where domestic violence has occurred, most states' laws prohibit imposing joint legal custody on parents. Some states have a presumption in their laws that joint legal custody will be awarded, unless a good reason for sole legal custody exists. There are many good reasons why you might need to have sole legal custody. Courts have found that an award of sole legal custody is warranted where one parent is abusive, uninvolved, or absent, has untreated mental illness, or is addicted to drugs or alcohol.

Information about the Children

Most states' laws provide that both parents are entitled to information about their children unless a court has decided that it could endanger the child. Typically, parents have the right to know where the children go to school; where they worship; and the names of their doctor, dentist, and orthodontist. Both parents have the right to get school notices, attend parent-teacher conferences (not necessarily together), and participate in school activities. They are entitled to copies of their children's report cards. Both parents are entitled to see their children's medical and dental records and to talk to the health care providers. Information about the children might be withheld from an abusive or very angry parent who has made threats to take the children or has a history of interference with the children's care.

FACT

Allegations or evidence of abuse may cause the court to issue restraining orders that prevent the abusive parent from going to the child's home, school, or place of worship. However, in many cases even abusive parents are entitled to see their children's medical, school, and therapy records.

Developing a Workable Parenting Plan

If you are parents, developing a workable parenting plan is likely the most important part of your divorce. The children of divorce suffer the most serious and long-lasting consequences from conflict between their parents. Parents can do a much better job than the judge in putting together a workable parenting plan, because parents know, deep down, what's best for their children.

FACT

When parents work together, the children benefit. For example, the visiting parent is often unwilling to contribute funds over and above the court-ordered child support. However, research shows that when parents decide together to send kids to private schools or camp or music lessons, they often agree to share the costs of these enriching childhood experiences.

When parents can see past their anger, hurt, and pride, they can create a workable plan because they have all the facts. The judge almost never has all the facts. No matter how much you dislike or even hate your spouse, put it behind you for the sake of your children. Pick your battles. When you can, bite your tongue for the sake of coming to an agreement.

Physical Custody and Visitation

A parent who has sole physical custody has the children most of the time. The other parent has visitation. In some jurisdictions, the term "visitation" is being replaced by the terms "access" or "parenting time." These newer terms more accurately define the time a parent spends with a child.

Parenting Time

Parenting time comes in many different shapes and sizes. Children often spend every other weekend and one evening each week with the noncustodial parent. Sometimes they spend less time with one parent during the school year and a chunk of time with that parent during the summer. When parents live in different states or far apart in the same state, they may choose a schedule that minimizes the complications of getting from one home to the other. The children may spend the school year in one home, the summer in the other, and half the school holidays with each parent. When a parent and a child share a special interest, they can participate in an activity together and have their time together determined by the activity schedule.

While your energy may be focused on working out a co-parenting arrangement that works for everyone, you shouldn't forget about the former in-laws. Grandparents, aunts, and uncles will want to visit with the children as well.

Parents with emotional problems that make them unstable, parents who have abused their spouse or their children, and parents who have threatened to run away with the children may have their visitation supervised by a third party to protect the children and the spouse. Sometimes the supervisor is a family member; sometimes an agency in the community provides supervision.

Joint Physical Custody

Joint or shared physical custody can take many forms. Some children spend alternate weeks with each parent. Some spend Monday and Tuesday in one home, Wednesday and Thursday in the other, and alternate the weekends. Some divorced parents have the children stay in the family home, and they—the parents—move in and out on an agreed-upon schedule.

When parents live within blocks of each other, get along well, and have well-adjusted children, joint custody works well. However, it can also work under less than optimum circumstances when the parents are motivated to put the interests of their children first.

Shared parenting plans work only when the parents can put their animosities aside and focus on what's best for their children. Obviously, these parents will have frequent contact with each other and will have to work cooperatively to coordinate schedules, locate lost book bags, and make sure one of them picks up the children from activities. They will also need to live fairly close to each other. Obviously, joint custody is not for all parents.

Joint custody is not for all children, either. The children are in emotional turmoil because of the divorce. They may have a hard time remembering a complex parenting schedule and sometimes go to the wrong house, a very traumatic experience. Joint physical custody is usually not a good plan for babies and very young children. Babies and small children are generally bonded to a primary caregiver. This doesn't mean that they don't love both parents, but they usually rely on one more than another. Frequent or lengthy separations from their primary caregiver can lead to all sorts of emotional problems in young children.

Children's Preferences

Children's preferences differ with respect to how much time they spend with each parent. Many prefer joint physical custody. Interviews conducted with adults who were children of divorcing parents are clear in their preference for joint custody. By joint custody, they mean equal time with each parent. The complications created by the logistics of joint custody are much less important to the children than maintaining parental contact. Obviously, if one parent is unfit to provide care to the children, joint custody is not possible even if it would be the children's preference.

FACT

Children of divorce who grew up in a traditional custody arrangement where Mom had custody and Dad had visitation often report that they would have liked more time with their fathers. Children appear to have strong relationships with their mothers regardless of the custody arrangement, but they have a need for more contact with their fathers.

For other children, the quantity of time is less important than the quality of time. Many children will thrive and be happy in situations where they see one parent less often than the other. It very much depends on the child and the type of relationships a noncustodial parent is able to forge with her children.

Negotiate or Litigate?

As with all aspects of a divorce, you'll end up with a more workable parenting plan if you negotiate with your spouse and come up with a mutually acceptable agreement. You can take into account your schedules, your children's special needs, and the strengths each of you bring to your role as a parent. Negotiating a parenting plan means you have to be willing to compromise and reasonably evaluate your particular circumstances. Parents who develop their own parenting plan put their energies into implementing it. This means your plan has a higher likelihood of success than one imposed on you by the court.

When you litigate, you turn decision making over to a judge, who is a stranger. It's kind of like gambling—you could win big or lose big. The problem with litigation is proving what you say. Many issues come down to a "he said, she said" situation and the judge doesn't know who to believe. For this reason it is critical that you think about your situation rationally and reasonably and allege only the truth. This means that you should not exaggerate facts and details. Exaggeration is often misinterpreted as lying by the court.

ALERT!

Since a lawyer will be preparing the paperwork that you submit to the court, it is important to read all documents very carefully. Lawyers often write very dramatically to get their points across. While this is important, facts can easily be exaggerated or misinterpreted. If any information is incorrect or misleading, ask that it be changed.

It's also important to be fair. If your spouse goes out with friends occasionally, don't say it happens all the time. It is easy to exaggerate the truth in the heat of anger, so make sure to carefully read all papers you submit to the court to make sure they say what you mean.

Hypothetical Custody Litigation

Let's look at one piece of custody litigation by examining a set of opposing affidavits. Suppose the parents, Jack B. Nimble and Suzie B. Qwik, have two children, Julie, age 1, and Jack Jr., age 12. Suzie has announced she wants a divorce, and she and Jack have a huge argument. Jack leaves the house and moves in with a female coworker who lives across town, a forty-five-minute trip during light traffic. Suzie serves Jack with divorce papers. Jack responds by scheduling a court hearing to get custody of the children. (Remember, you have to prepare an affidavit to go with a motion.) Typically, motion papers filed early in a divorce action would address a multitude of issues, but the following affidavits focus only on custody.

Take a look at the two sample affidavits that follow, one from Jack and one from Suzie. These are composites of affidavits and do not represent a complete filing. Since Suzie filed for divorce, she is referred to as the plaintiff. Jack is referred to as the defendant.

After you read these, try to put yourself in a judge's shoes. What would you do with this information if you were the judge? Next, look at the "translation"—the judge's probable interpretation—of these affidavits. With any luck, you'll figure out what information is helpful and what will come back to bite you. Then you'll know what to put into an affidavit if you ever have to prepare one.

Dad's Affidavit

STATE OF MIND   DISTRICT COURT
COUNTY OF CONFUSION   FAMILY COURT DIVISION
Jack B. Nimble, being duly sworn, on oath deposes and says,

1. I am the Defendant in this divorce proceeding.

2. I make this affidavit in support of my motion for custody of my children, Julie and Jack Jr.

3 Plaintiff and I have been married for thirteen years. Julie is one and Jack is twelve.

4. Since the children were born, I have been their primary caregiver. I have been responsible for preparing their meals, getting them dressed, keeping them clean, and making sure that they receive necessary medical and dental care. When they were infants, I got up with them in the night. Now I get up with them in the morning and make our son's breakfast before I leave for work. I read them stories before I tuck them in at night. I stay at home with them when they are sick. I have been the coach of Jack's baseball team for four years. I have always been available for the children and they are closely bonded to me.

5. Plaintiff has been an inconsistent and unstable mother. Although she does not work and stays home during the day, this is the only time she spends with the children. Our son is in school all day, so he really only sees his mother for a couple of hours each afternoon before I get home from work. Plaintiff does take care of the baby while I am at work, but as soon as I get home she relies on me to provide care. Most days she leaves as soon as I get home to go party with her friends, and she is rarely home on weekends.

6. Plaintiff has never gotten up with the children when they woke during the night. She likes to sleep in, so she never made breakfast, either. One reason she likes to sleep late is that she spends a lot of her evenings out with friends, bar hopping and partying. I usually go to bed by midnight, and often she hasn't come home by the time I turn in.

7. I have been the parent who has made our house into a home for our children. Although my spouse doesn't work, she does not believe it is her job to clean the house or do the laundry. Although I work full time, I am left to do all the household chores. If it weren't for me, our children would never have clean clothes or a clean house. I have resorted to asking Plaintiff to use paper plates and cups to reduce the amount of dirty dishes that are left in the sink for me to clean up when I get home.

8. As if it's not bad enough that Plaintiff is never home, she is also setting a very bad moral example for our children. Plaintiff drinks, smokes, and

has had several affairs. Sometimes she goes to the casinos, where she drinks, smokes, meets men, and gambles. Now Plaintiff is involved with our next-door neighbor's twenty-year-old son. This is very embarrassing for our son as well as humiliating to me.

9. My spouse really isn't much interested in the children. She has her own life and just wants to be free to fool around and do her thing.

10. As a result of the aforementioned facts and circumstances, I am the parent most suitable to provide care for the children and it would be in their best interests if I were awarded temporary legal and physical custody.

Signed, Jack B. Nimble

Mom's Affidavit in Response

STATE OF MIND   DISTRICT COURT
COUNTY OF CONFUSION   FAMILY COURT DIVISION
Suzie B. Qwik, being duly sworn, on oath deposes and says,

1. I am the Plaintiff in this divorce, and I submit this affidavit in response to my husband's affidavit and in support of my motion for custody of our children.

2. First of all, I would like to say my husband must be living on another planet with another family. His affidavit is an incredible distortion of reality.

3. Defendant states that he has been the primary caregiver to our children, but nothing could be further from the truth. I have been a stay-at-home mother who has always cared for the children and the home. It is simply not possible for Defendant to provide much care for the children or take care of the house because of his work schedule. Defendant works sixty to eighty hours a week, including Saturdays. When he is at home, he is often too tired or too drunk to do anything but watch television or sleep.

4. While it is true that Defendant regularly prepares breakfast and puts the children to bed at night, this is his only contact with the children on a day-to-day basis. Since he works most Saturdays, the only other time he sees the children is on Sunday. Even then, he usually only spends a

couple of hours playing games or watching television, and then mostly with our son.

5. Defendant alleges he got up with the kids when they were babies. While he did on occasion get up and bring a baby to me to nurse, that was the limit of his participation. He likewise does not provide care when they are sick or take them to the doctor.

6. Defendant accuses me of partying, staying out late, and having a boy-friend. In the last year I have gone out in the evenings because our marriage is in such bad shape I need to spend time with friends. The kid next door mows our lawn and helps me with heavier tasks around the house because Jack can't find the time. The only reason Defendant accuses me of having an affair is because he is jealous and controlling. In fact, Defendant accuses me of having an affair with any man who as much as says hello to me, including the postman, bank attendant, and grocery store clerk.

7. Defendant alleges he provides care for the children after work and on weekends. While this is true to some extent, he neglects to mention that he works sixty to eighty hours a week, including Saturday. Defendant does make breakfast for our twelve-year-old son before he leaves for work in the morning but doesn't get home until 7 or 8 P.M. most nights. When he comes home, he does read to the kids but then usually goes to his study to work some more.

8. Defendant provides the money to run our household. I provide everything else. He never has anything nice to say to the kids and me. He is forever putting me down. If I don't do things his way, he can be very nasty. Most recently, he told me not to load the dishwasher because I didn't do it properly and the dishes don't get clean.

9. Defendant was always controlling and possessive, but lately he has become threatening and scary. He has threatened to hurt me more than once and even pushed me out of his way on several occasions when we were arguing and he wanted to leave.

10. Defendant has a serious drinking problem. Often when he comes home at night, he reeks of alcohol. About a year ago, he was arrested for drunk driving on his way home from work.

11. Jack also has never taken the children to the doctor or the dentist. I drive them to their appointments. I make sure they have appropriate

clothes and get regular haircuts, and I make sure our son does his homework. Jack has no clue about the children's lives.

12. Jack has moved in with a woman he knows from work. He has been trying to insinuate her into our children's lives. He accuses me of setting a bad moral example. Talk about the pot calling the kettle black!

13. I should have custody of our children. Jack should pay enough support to me and the children so we can stay in the house. This is the only house the children know, and they need some stability during this stressful time.

14. I am sure Jack loves our children. He should spend time with them and get to know them better.

Signed, Suzie B. Qwik

What the Judge Hears

Now try to put yourself in the judge's robe for a few minutes. What information do these affidavits provide? What information is missing? If you had to issue a temporary parenting plan, what additional information would be helpful? The judge will probably interpret these affidavits—based on considerable experience with divorcing parents—something like the following.

The Judge's Assessment

The parties are clearly angry. Dad has used his affidavit to take shots at Mom by attacking her skills as a homemaker and a mother. Mom's response shows she is stung by his criticism.

The parties have very different perspectives about their marriage. Taking their affidavits at face value, it sounds as if the children are on their own most of the time. Dad's working long hours and Mom's out partying. It's more likely that the events both parties describe as everyday occurrences happen once in a while, not all the time. It's likely that Dad works some long hours because he is the primary wage earner, and that Mom goes out with her friends now and then because she is lonely.

Mom has raised the issue of alcohol abuse. While she has provided no hard evidence, it would be a good idea to address this issue immediately. A chemical dependency evaluation of both parties will either confirm Mom's claim and, perhaps, get the abuser into treatment or put it to rest so it doesn't keep showing up in later affidavits.

If your ex-spouse or former in-laws badmouth you to your children, resist the urge to do the same. If your children witness a name-calling battle, they may feel as though they should choose sides. If the badmouthing doesn't subside, try to talk it out with your spouse or former in-laws.

Both Suzie B. Qwik and Jack B. Nimble want to be involved with their children. This is good. Dad is just realizing how important his children are to him, and it would not be surprising if he decided to cut back on his work hours to spend more time with the children. While the children will certainly benefit from more time with their father, the resulting income reduction may make finances precarious. If Dad's salary is reduced, Mom will probably have to go to work, which will mean she'll be less available to the children.

The parties have not provided useful information about the real routine in their household before the separation. The only way to get this information may be to get a custody evaluator involved. In this case, the judge may issue an order maintaining the status quo until the evaluator provides more information about the family and recommends an ongoing parenting plan.

The parties have provided little financial information. However, it's clear that somehow they've managed to survive financially until the hearing. The judge may issue an order designed to keep the mortgage paid and food on the table until a custody evaluation is completed. The judge will probably order the parents to provide specific financial information at the next hearing.

Miles Apart

What the parties thought they said and what the judge heard is miles apart. It was clearly very important to Dad to tell the judge his spouse is behaving badly, that she was not fulfilling her role as spouse. It was important to Mom to tell the judge her husband was not fulfilling his role as parent and companion. But neither party told the judge what he needed to know. How do they really parent their children? What kind of schedule would work for the family, taking into account everyone's activities, the distances between the parents' homes, and the demands of work and school?

Decisions That Please No One

The judge now has the impossible task of forming a schedule with no useful information. Many judges sidestep this task by sending families to an arm of the court. Depending on the state, it may be called court services, family services, or social services. Courts in counties with small populations probably won't have these services available, so the parties will have to hire someone in the private sector to work with them.

ALERT!

While this order may be called a temporary order, do not be deceived. Unless circumstances change dramatically, a judge may not change a temporary order after trial, particularly if the children are doing well. The temporary order has a good chance of becoming permanent.

If a judge can't avoid making a decision, the judge will probably do one of two things: Either give Mom sole legal custody of the kids with an every other weekend visitation schedule for Dad, or give the parents joint legal and joint physical custody. This would be a temporary order until trial.

Mom and Dad didn't want either one of these options, but now they're stuck with the judge's decision unless they can persuade the judge to change his mind. The kinds of things that make a judge change an order are primarily negative, for instance if one parent abuses the other or the children. Without some dramatic change, the order will stand for the duration of the divorce, unless the parents themselves can agree to a different arrangement.

How Courts Decide Custody

Suppose Jack and Suzie didn't learn the importance of making their own decisions about how they will rear their children. They've been unable to work out a plan and now they've taken their case to the judge.

It is difficult for a court to determine a child's preference. Psychologists tell us not to ask a child which parent she wants to live with, as this is putting too much pressure on a child who is already stressed out because her parents are getting a divorce. Usually preference is explored indirectly, by asking the child about her activities, favorite things to do with each parent, and similar questions.

Factors to Consider

The custody statutes of each state give the judge a set of factors to consider in deciding custody cases, including the following:

- Determining who is the primary parent, meaning the parent who was more responsible for the day-to-day child care
- The plan the parents want
- Reasonable preference of the child, if the child is mature enough to express a preference
- Relationship between the child, siblings, parents, or other significant person
- Child's adjustment to home; community, and school
- Permanence of the parents' respective living arrangements
- Nature of the family ambience in each proposed home
- Mental and physical health of the parents and children
- Length of time the child has lived where she is now living and the importance of maintaining that continuity
- Child's cultural background
- Impact of abuse on the child, if domestic abuse has occurred

In addition, if parents are seeking joint legal or physical custody, the judge needs to know how well the parents can cooperate, what methods for resolving disputes they will use, and whether it would be harmful to the child if one parent had sole custody. This latter factor deals with whether a sole custodian would support and encourage the relationship of the child with the other parent.

Interviewing the Children

In a custody trial, each parent presents evidence on the factors the judge is to consider. The judge may request an interview with the children in the judge's office to get input from them. Some states even mandate that a judge interview the children. The parents are not present at the interview, but their lawyers may be present if they so request and the judge agrees. The lawyers may submit questions to the judge that they want the judge to ask the children. The judge makes a record of the meeting. It may be used to clear up a misunderstanding about what took place during the interview; however, the record will be made available only to the attorneys, not the parents.

FACT

Sometimes the judge makes decisions about children without ever seeing them if he is strongly influenced by the parenting arrangement that has been in place since the divorce began. If the children are doing well in school and reports from counselors are favorable, a judge will want to continue a custodial arrangement to ensure the children's continued success.

Moving with Your Children

Concern that your spouse may want to relocate to another state with the children may be a strong motivator in seeking a shared parenting arrangement. Suppose you and your family live in Oregon and your spouse has family in Kansas. Your spouse is having trouble finding a decent job, and you don't make enough to support two households. Your spouse may be strongly tempted to return to Kansas under such circumstances. The laws about moving, or removal, vary from state to state, but it's harder for one parent to move a significant distance with the children when the other parent has a major role in their lives.

To Move . . .

Again, laws vary from state to state. In some states, the parent who wants to move has to show the court the move is in the child's best interests. This means the parent who wants to move has a legitimate need to move; for example, an employer makes relocation a condition of keeping a job, the custodial parent has an extended family and support system in a distant state, or the custodial parent is having a hard time making ends meet in the state where the divorce is taking place. The parent seeking the move will need to show she has done research on housing and schools and, most important, that the moving parent has a plan for the child to maintain contact with the other parent.

If you're concerned that a move may be a possibility, you may want to seek at least joint physical custody to make it harder for your spouse to take the children to a distant location. Be sure to discuss this concern with your lawyer.

Or Not To Move?

Other states put the burden on the parent who is not moving. This parent will have to show the court why the move is not in the child's best interests. The parent who is remaining will need to show that the child is integrated into the community, that the child has a close and important relationship with the parent who is not moving, that the move will be harmful to the child's stability, or that the other parent doesn't really have to move.

Not Sure the Child Is Yours?

Sometimes a question arises about the parentage of one or more of the children. Mom gets mad at Dad and tells him he's not the father. While Dad may take this with a grain of salt, given that Mom made the accusation when she was angry, the seed of doubt has been planted. What can be done?

Today, sophisticated DNA testing can determine parentage of children to a 99.99 percent probability of paternity. While blood testing still is used, most agencies that test for paternity collect a saliva sample from the mother, the child, and the putative father. From these samples it is possible to determine whether Dad is really, biologically, Dad.

The question of what you do when you discover your three-year-old isn't your biological child is a tough one. If you're the only father this child has ever known, you still may want to be Dad because you have a strong psychological bond. Courts are divided on how to handle this issue, so you'll need to discuss it with your lawyer.

CHAPTER 11

Child Support and Spousal Maintenance

Divorce means that you are going to create two households with two sets of rent or mortgage payments, two sets of utility bills, and on and on. Figuring out how to pay for all of these additional expenses is going to prove challenging as you move through the divorce process. Child support and spousal support are the two methods that help equalize the division of income and hopefully make it possible for everyone in the family to continue living at approximately the same standard as before the divorce.

Child Support

If you have children, you have a responsibility to support them. In most states this obligation continues until the children marry, die, join the military, finish high school, obtain full-time employment, or otherwise become emancipated. Some states end the obligation at age eighteen; others extend it to age twenty-one. Ask your lawyer about the law in your state.

Historically, child support orders varied widely from state to state and from county to county. Child support was based on the reasonable needs of the child and the payor's ability to pay. This arrangement gave judges a lot of discretion in determining child support awards. Often the spouse ordered to pay child support didn't pay, so households with children experienced significant reductions in living standard.

Creating Guidelines

In the 1980s, Congress responded to growing concerns about the impoverishment of children of divorce and the increasing number of single-parent families on welfare. Congress passed child support enforcement amendments that required all states to develop guidelines by October 1, 1987, or risk losing the federal contribution to their welfare programs. States responded, and today all states have child support guidelines. Even though these guidelines have improved the process for obtaining child support, there are still many people who don't pay their support regularly or on time.

Three Primary Approaches

At present, there are three primary approaches implemented by different states to determine the amount of child support. The first approach is based on percentage of income and only considers the income of the noncustodial parent. States that use this approach have developed a chart that includes the income of the payor, the number of children, and percentage to be paid. Percentages vary based on income, number of children, and in some cases the age of children. This approach, which makes certain assumptions about the payor's ability to pay child support, is based on a formula rather than on the child's needs. It does not take into consideration the custodial parent's income.

The second and most common approach is the income shares model. The idea here is that the child should receive the same percentage of parental income as if the parties were living together. The incomes of both the custodial and noncustodial parent are considered in this model. Using both incomes and a chart that determines the percentage of parental income to be paid per number of children, the court will calculate the amount of support the child should receive from both parents. That amount will then be divided between parents based on their proportion of earnings to the total income. The noncustodial parent will then pay his share to the custodial parent.

The third and least common approach, called the Melson formula, requires the court to determine the basic needs of each parent and then set the child support. But because the majority of states use a percentage of income approach, most of the current child support discussion is focused on determining the income of the payor.

FACT

Parents can't waive child support. The law says that child support is a child's right, and no parent can take this right away. In some cases, child support can be suspended, that is, not paid for a period of time because of overall financial circumstances or because of the parenting arrangement.

All three approaches generally fix an amount called the self-support reserve. The self-support reserve is an amount of money that the state has determined is the minimum amount needed by a person to live. If the amount of child support you are supposed to pay leaves you with income that falls below the self-support reserve, the Court will usually reduce the child support amount. If your income is below the self-support reserve before the court even calculates child support, most states provide for a minimum amount of support to be paid like $25 or $50 per month. In all three approaches, a provision is usually made for deviation from the formula if you are the parents of a child with special needs. If you have extraordinary expenses, make the court aware and be prepared to show proof of these expenses when you go to court.

What Is Income?

Income can come from many sources. Most employed people are paid a salary, while some self-employed persons pay themselves only when their business makes enough money to do so, thereby controlling the timing and amount of their income. Some people receive investment income, either from dividends paid by stocks or from profits made by investing in the stock market. Some people own investment property, such as an apartment building, and receive rental income. Some people had a good job last year but quit when the marriage fell apart. The court may impute income to them (ascribe a certain amount to them as if they were still working).

Reading Your Pay Stub

If you work for wages, you get paychecks with a pay stub, which provides a lot of information. It shows your gross income before anything is deducted. It shows your deductions and your rate of withholding. For example: M-3 means "married with three exemptions." Your pay stub shows what you get paid per hour for regular and overtime, how often you get paid, and how many hours you worked the last pay period. It will show whether you are paying for health and dental insurance, and whether you've invested in a plan that enables you to set aside pretax dollars for paying medical and dental bills. Your pay stub also shows how much from each paycheck goes into your retirement plan.

If you're self-employed or otherwise unable to predict your income due to commissions, bonuses, or other factors, you may need to look at tax returns or paycheck stubs for several years to develop realistic income figures. Sometimes the court will take an average of your earnings over the past few years to determine a number for your income.

All of this information is important. First of all, it tells you how much money you earn each pay period. If you're paid weekly, you can multiply your net pay by fifty-two and divide by twelve to get your monthly income. If you're paid every two weeks, multiply by twenty-six and divide by twelve to get your monthly income. Because most budgets are computed on a monthly basis, it's helpful to compare monthly income to monthly expenses.

Your spouse gets to see your paycheck stubs, too. If you're socking away a large percentage of your pay into retirement or over-withholding so that you get a tax refund at year's end, you can be sure your spouse or your spouse's lawyer will notice this right away. If you operate a business, your spouse's lawyer will be able to look over your books and see what you are deducting as business expenses. While these deductions may be valid for IRS purposes, they may not be for child support purposes.

Other Income

If you have investments, they may generate income. (If they don't, you may need to make some changes!) Stocks pay dividends and bonds mature. Some people buy and sell stocks, and others buy and sell real estate. If you invest in a new venture, you might lose money the first few years, which you can take as a deduction on your taxes. Understandably, your spouse will want to keep an eye on this venture, but it's unlikely you'd invest in a business if you didn't expect it to make money at some point.

If you receive allowances from your employer for food, a car, or housing, this too can be counted as income. If you own a small business and deduct expenses from your income taxes for these items, the amounts could be added back into your income for the purpose of child support calculation. Amounts you deduct for depreciation on equipment or business assets can also be added back into your income for child support purposes.

Social Security

If you or your spouse are near retirement age, you'll want to figure out your eligibility for Social Security benefits. When people have been married for more than ten years, a spouse who doesn't work is allowed to collect on the earner's Social Security record and is usually eligible to receive up to half the earner's Social Security. The age of eligibility will depend on when the earner entered the job market. As society ages, the age of eligibility goes up.

If you or your spouse becomes disabled and eligible for Social Security disability benefits, your children may be eligible for benefits, too. While most courts take the position that these benefits are not a substitute for child support, this money is available to help take care of the kids. You are not exempt from child support requirements because you are receiving social security disability. The court will still evaluate your income and determine what amount you will have to pay. Even though your income will probably be less than the self-support reserve, you will still have to pay the minimum amount that your state allows.

Imputed Income

Say your spouse had a good job during the marriage. Angry now, your spouse quits and refuses to look for a new job. If you take her to court for child support, the court may well determine that because your spouse earned $20 an hour on that job, she has the ability to earn $20 an hour. The court imputes this income to your spouse and orders child support accordingly. Or, say you decide to change jobs and take one that pays less and provides no overtime. The court may use your previous earnings as the basis for the support order, imputing to you the ability to earn the amount you earned before.

FACT

Supporting two households after divorce is complicated. You need a lawyer who knows your state's laws and can help you develop a support plan that stretches the dollars. Divorce lawyers know how to analyze your financial situation and will help pinpoint optimum levels for child support and spousal maintenance.

The court can also impute income if it appears that you have hidden income or failed to disclose an asset. Let's say for example that you are a sole proprietor and you produce an income tax return that shows you make $50,000 a year. However, the way you live suggests that you make a lot more. For example, you drive an expensive car, have an expensive apartment, and take fancy vacations. If your spouse can prove that you are spending more money than it looks like you're making, the court may decide you are hiding money. Under these circumstances, the court can impute earnings to you. Any time the court imputes income, it must set forth in its decision the exact reasoning by which the amount to be imputed has been calculated.

Imputing income can create a financial mess. When orders are based on what the court believes you can do rather than what you're actually doing, you can quickly fall behind in your support obligation. As a result, the spouse relying on the support order will not have the money needed to pay bills.

One purpose of imputing income is to encourage the unemployed or underemployed payor to find a good job and to discourage a dishonest spouse from hiding income and assets. Another is to maintain a consistent child support obligation, so that when the payor does get a decent job the accumulated back payments, called arrears, can be collected for the benefit of the children.

Deviating from Guidelines

Most judges treat child support guidelines as if they were carved in stone, but there are circumstances that warrant a deviation. Many states have established certain factors to be considered by the court in deciding whether a deviation from the guidelines is necessary. Judges are reluctant to deviate from the guidelines because they have to make written findings in support of any deviation. Making findings is a lot of work.

Going Up

If you want the court to issue a support order that is higher than the guidelines, you will have to give a reason. Perhaps you have a special needs child who requires twenty-four-hour care. Maybe throughout the marriage you and your spouse were able to send the children to private schools and summer camps. Circumstances should not change for the children unless there isn't enough money to maintain past benefits.

Coming Down

If you need to ask a court to deviate downward from the guidelines, you must show a very good reason why it is necessary. You may be supporting a child from a prior marriage. Ordinarily that support obligation would be subtracted from your income before applying the guidelines. However, this is only going to be true if your obligation is set forth in a court order. Perhaps you have a new child with another person, born during your separation from your spouse. Courts take the position that your first family comes first, that you took on this new obligation with knowledge of your existing one. Rarely will the court reduce your support to enable you to take care of a new child. Another good reason to request a deviation is if you are unemployed through no fault of your own, for example, if you were laid off. During the time you are looking for a job, the court may reduce your obligation. Once you find work, your obligation will usually be reinstated to the proper amount under the guidelines.

Joint Custody and Child Support

Child support guidelines assume one parent has primary physical custody of the children. When parents share physical custody equally and have comparable incomes, child support is often reserved, meaning neither pays support to the other. The parents share the costs of health insurance, uncovered medical expenses, child care, college, and extracurricular activities.

FACT

Statistics show that visitation and custody influences the payment of child support. Those parents with joint custody or who have regular and frequent visitation time with their children are more likely to pay child support than those who do not have custody or visitation rights.

If one parent earns more than the other, that parent will probably pay child support to the parent with less income. Some states have adopted formulas for determining child support in these cases. For example, the smaller income is subtracted from the larger one with the applicable percentage applied to the remainder. This formula can produce a harsh result for the lower-income parent, but it's easy to compute and, therefore, appealing to courts.

If you and your spouse choose a shared parenting arrangement, you can also decide how you will finance it. If you and your spouse make an agreement about support, you're not bound by the guidelines; however, the court will have to approve your agreement. Ideally, each household should have similar income available to meet the needs of the children. When one household is rich and the other poor, the imbalance may undermine the shared parenting plan.

Enforcing Child Support Payment

A major reason the federal government got involved in family law was to enforce court orders for child support. Prior to 1980, collection rates were abysmal, and child support orders were mere pieces of paper. Today, income withholding is used to collect child support. An employer deducts child support from the payor parent's paycheck and forwards it to the state collection agency, which then sends it to the payee. The employer is obligated to notify the state agency if the employee quits his job. The employee is obligated to notify the state when re-employed, and the new employer has an obligation to check for and honor existing support orders.

ALERT!

Whether you fail to pay the basic child support obligation, maintain health care, or pay college expenses, the court can take action against you. The court can revoke the driver's or professional license of a nonpaying ex-spouse as well as her passport. The judge can also issue a warrant for the nonpayor's arrest if she fails to show up in court.

Parents ordered to pay child support can be tracked by social security numbers from state to state and even outside the United States. The Uniform Reciprocal Enforcement of Support Act authorizes one state to enforce another state's orders. Every state has a child support enforcement agency that is dedicated to collecting and enforcing child support orders. If you are a parent who is having trouble collecting child support you can go here for help, whether or not you received public assistance. The services are available to everyone. In addition to collecting child support, this agency may be able to help you file violation petitions, figure out arrears, and monitor job changes by the payor.

Health Care and Childcare Costs

Most states require the payor parent to maintain health and dental insurance for his children and to contribute to child care costs. Other states allow for these costs by deviating from their child support formulas. Most states provide for a pro rata division of costs proportionate to the parents' respective incomes. Parents usually agree that providing quality health care for their children is of paramount importance. As a result, the best outcome occurs when parents take a look at the health care available through their respective employers and select the best coverage. They may agree to split the cost of insurance coverage and any uncovered medical expenses for their children, or to prorate costs based on their relative incomes.

If parents don't agree, the court will usually order the payor parent to maintain the health insurance. In some states, the cost of the health and dental insurance is divided pro rata between the parties so the payor will receive a credit for the nonpayor spouse's portion. The cost of uncovered medical expenses such as copays, glasses, contacts, or braces are also divided in this way.

In order for both parents to work, children are often left in day-care facilities or in before- and after-school programs, which can be very expensive. In some states, the cost of these services is divided *pro rata* between the parties in the same way that medical costs are divided. In other states, the division of these costs is considered a deviation from the basic formula. Still other states make no provision for these additional costs.

College Expenses

If you have children approaching college age or already in college, you will need to make provisions for the payment of these expenses. If you are the payor, you may think your child support payment should be reduced if you pay college expenses. While some judges will take this into consideration, the more common approach is that the payor will continue paying her monthly obligation and pay an additional amount for college expenses. The thinking here is that the custodial parent is still going to have to maintain a home for the child, even if he is away at school. In addition, the custodial parent is still responsible for buying clothes, providing spending money, and paying for all additional expenses.

Courts take different approaches in determining an appropriate division of costs and generally examine a variety of factors set forth in the law. In evaluating a request for college expenses, the court may examine certain factors, for example: whether the parents went to college, whether the parents had planned on sending the children to college before they separated, and whether the children are successful academically. If the court determines that a request for college expenses is appropriate, it will then decide how much each parent is to contribute. Sometimes the court will set forth a given dollar amount, capping payment and requiring the child to take out loans for any remainder. In other cases, the court will order a *pro rata* division of all of the college expenses based on the parents' respective incomes. In some states, the payment of college expenses is considered a deviation from the basic formula and may not be granted at all depending on the circumstances.

Heavy Hand of the Law

Courts have several weapons in their arsenal for the person who doesn't pay court-ordered support. Not only can the court revoke driver's or professional licenses, the judge may find the person in civil contempt of court. That person can be sent to jail for civil contempt, provided the judge gives the contemnor (the person who is in contempt) the ability to get out of jail by paying the support owed, or by paying part of what is owed and contracting to pay the balance.

The court can also issue a money judgment against a nonpayor spouse. A money judgment can be recorded as a lien against real property or be used to seize the contents of a bank account or other property of value.

Spousal Maintenance

Child support is largely determined by statutes that have formulas for figuring out the amount of support to be paid. Statues and case law also set the rules for spousal maintenance, or alimony, but the judge determines the amount to be paid. Spousal maintenance is a payment from one spouse to the other for the recipient's support. If the parties litigate this issue, a judge has discretion to decide the amount and duration of a spousal maintenance award.

Taxable Income

An important characteristic of spousal maintenance is that it is paid with before-tax dollars. If you're the payor, when you do your income taxes, you deduct spousal maintenance payments off the top before determining your gross taxable income. This means it's much cheaper to pay spousal maintenance than it is to pay child support, which is paid with after-tax dollars. For instance, if you're in the 40 percent tax bracket, your spousal maintenance costs you 60 percent of its face amount.

FACT

In Texas, spousal maintenance is only available when the parties have been married at least ten years, and then it is limited to a maximum of $2,500 a month for three years. Homemaker spouses try to get out of Texas for their divorces. Payor spouses try to get in.

Spousal maintenance is taxable income to the recipient. Usually a person who receives spousal maintenance has little earned income and is living in the house with the children, and thus gets a deduction for the mortgage interest and as head of household for tax purposes. The recipient spouse usually has a minimal income-tax liability; therefore, paying spousal maintenance can stretch a family's dollars. It's an important tax-planning tool.

Of course, if you are the payor spouse, you may feel that your spouse does not deserve this extra money. Even if you make $50,000 a year and your wife makes $25,000, the court could order you to pay spousal maintenance, especially if you have a long-term marriage. The court will try to equalize the income from both parties. Try to weigh all the tax and other benefits to you, your spouse, and most importantly your children prior to litigating this issue. If you work together with your spouse and are both reasonable, you will probably be able to come up with a solution that works for you both.

Some Alimony History

Before 1950, courts routinely awarded homemakers, typically female, lifetime spousal maintenance, unless the woman had misbehaved, committed adultery, or abandoned the marriage, for example. At that time, most married women were unemployed and totally dependent on their spouses for support.

After the women's liberation movement, judges' attitudes toward spousal maintenance changed, and the awards dried up. This was particularly difficult for the fifty-five-year-old woman who had never worked outside the home. A judge was likely to give her $400 a month support for ten years, even if her spouse could afford to pay substantially more. The harsh results of these court decisions led to yet another turnaround. Today courts are again awarding lifetime spousal maintenance to spouses who have been career homemakers, and the awards are usually sufficient to enable these dependent spouses to meet their financial needs.

Temporary Maintenance

Spousal maintenance can be temporary or permanent. Most states' statutes give judges some guidance here. Temporary spousal maintenance is often awarded in a shorter marriage where the homemaker spouse had a decent job before the children were born and, with some educational or vocational updating, can get back into the job market.

You may be tempted to make your spouse pay alimony for reasons other than financial need. Again, try to not let your emotions get the best of you. It's better for all of those involved if you can work on a way to become financially independent and move on with life.

Sometimes spousal maintenance is awarded for a specific number of years. The number of years is usually based on a period of time that the judge has determined will allow the spouse to become self-supporting. Sometimes it's a period of years necessary to complete a degree or master's level education program. Other times it's based on a number of years the person will need to advance to a higher paying job in their field of employment.

When the parties can't agree about temporary spousal maintenance, they may hire a rehabilitation counselor to evaluate the skills, interests, and employment opportunities of the spouse seeking maintenance. This counselor can provide guidance to the parties and, if necessary, to the court on what it will take to get this spouse back in the job market.

Permanent Maintenance

When a court is asked to decide permanent maintenance, statutes and case law usually provide guidance. Most state laws set out certain factors that should be considered—length of the marriage, or if the marriage is less than ten years, a very good reason why the homemaker spouse cannot re-enter the work force. Maybe young children are at home or the spouse has serious health issues or a disability. A judge is directed to determine whether the spouse seeking maintenance lacks enough property to generate independence or is unable to provide adequate self-support.

When a judge decides the maintenance amount, he must consider a number of factors, for example: the standard of living enjoyed by the parties during the marriage, the payor spouse's ability to pay, sacrifices made by the homemaker spouse in terms of giving up a career, and the ability to provide for retirement. The judge can also consider factors that might limit the payor's liability, such as a spouse's wrongdoing during the marriage or an intentional misuse of assets. Some laws state that if a judge can't conclude a homemaker spouse will some day be self-supporting, he should award permanent maintenance. The obligation to pay spousal maintenance usually ends when the payor dies or when the payee dies, remarries, or otherwise becomes self-supporting. Sometimes it ends when the parties reach Social Security age and the nonpayor spouse is able to collect on the earnings record of the payor spouse.

Once an award of spousal maintenance is made, it is difficult to change absent a significant change of circumstances. Either party can seek modification of spousal maintenance before that term ends if circumstances warrant an increase or reduction. Some examples would include gain or unintentional loss of employment, injury or disability, extraordinary medical expenses, and marriage by the recipient spouse.

Modifying Support Orders

Child support and spousal maintenance payment orders can be modified if the financial circumstances on which they are based change. Sometimes the order will specifically set forth what types of things constitute a change in circumstances. The payor parent may get fired—a possible basis for a temporary reduction in child support. However, if the payor got fired for cause, this may not be a basis for reduction. One of the children may run off with the circus—another reason to reduce child support. Maybe the person receiving spousal maintenance finishes a college refresher course and gets a good job, which may be a basis for reducing or reserving her spousal maintenance. The person paying spousal maintenance may retire and seek a reduction or termination of the support obligation.

It is of critical importance to be sure that your judgment contains very specific information about the financial basis for child support and spousal maintenance provisions so that changes in circumstances are clear. If many years pass between entry of the decree and a motion for modification, everyone could forget the basis for the original order.

Keep in mind that retirement benefits may be treated differently depending on the specific facts of a case. If a couple in their forties is getting divorced, retirement benefits will probably be treated as property—marital assets to be divided. If the parties are in their late sixties, they may be receiving pension benefits, which are then treated as income. The law is clear: Pension benefits are either assets or income, not both.

It is important to remember that even where a pension benefit is divided, your spouse may still be making more money than you. Say that your spouse worked the same job for forty years. The two of you were only married for twenty-five years. You are entitled to collect a pension benefit based on only the number of years you were married. Just because you are both collecting on his pension doesn't mean he won't have to pay spousal maintenance.

Preparing a Budget

You will need to prepare a household budget to help you and your spouse figure out appropriate support levels. Some people keep track of monthly expenditures with a computer program. Others have no idea what they spend each month. Those who keep records need only add up a year's worth of grocery bills and divide by twelve to get an average monthly grocery expense. Those with no clue need to start keeping track immediately or get the household check registers for the past year or two to develop a sense of household spending.

ALERT!

Even though you may be accustomed to living the high life, this doesn't mean you'll be able to continue such a lifestyle following the divorce. Nearly all divorcing couples must create budgets and alter their spending habits. This will be especially difficult if you are the custodial parent, but it can be done through careful budgeting.

Budgets are important to establish the family's standard of living during the marriage. If your family has sent the children to private schools, taken several vacations each year, or dined out often, these expenditures should be reflected in check registers and credit card bills. If you need to take the issues of child support and spousal maintenance to court, you'll want to show the court the family's standard of living during the marriage. This will have a greater impact in the area of spousal maintenance, particularly if you have been a homemaker. Since child support is largely determined by specific percentages to be applied, standard of living is assumed within the formula. The more you make, the more you will pay for child support purposes.

Use real numbers when you prepare your budget. This is not the time to put together your dream budget. When your budget exceeds your combined incomes, something is not right. Judges go to the grocery store, too. A judge will not be pleased if you pad your budget. She needs you to provide helpful information, and you will get a better result if you do so. Most people forget to include a variety of expenses in their budgets. Think very carefully about your expenses and list everything. People often forget things like cigarettes, cat litter, dog food, flea prevention products, newspaper, haircuts, car washes, and dry cleaning. Make sure you include all of your expenses because even the little things can add up to hundreds of dollars per year.

CHAPTER 12

The Marital Estate and How to Divide It

We've talked about the emotional divorce and the legal divorce, and we've considered how you'll parent your children during a divorce. Here and there you've seen references to marital and nonmarital property and equitable division of property. Now it's time to take a closer look at all of the pieces of your financial situation. At the end you'll have a much better idea of what your financial situation will look like after the divorce.

The Marital Estate

The marital estate is the property you and your spouse have accumulated during marriage. Nonmarital property is the money and property you bring into the marriage, the money and property you inherit, or the money and property given to you by someone outside the marriage.

Sounds simple, and sometimes it is. Suppose when you got married, you really didn't have much stuff. You had recently completed school and started a job, and you were renting an apartment. About the only things you had were a computer, your bicycle, some camping gear, and an old car that wasn't worth much. Your spouse had a cell phone, a bed, and a table. Family and friends gave you things as wedding presents: sheets, towels, silverware, a blender—typical wedding gifts. At this point, the sum total of your marital estate was the gifts you received as wedding presents. The items you brought into the marriage, modest as they were, were yours before the marriage and would be labeled premarital.

FACT

Some people are under the assumption that common law marriages are subject to the same laws as traditional, lawful marriages. This isn't necessarily true. While some states do recognize common law marriages, others don't. It's best to check out your state's laws to better understand your rights following the breakup of such a relationship.

If your marriage ended that first year, you would probably divide up the wedding gifts by each taking those that came from your family or friends. If your premarital stuff was still usable, you probably took it as well. Many brief marriages are this simple, so if your marriage lasted only a short time, consider going to your local self-help center and doing the divorce yourselves.

A More Complicated Situation

During your marriage you worked for a small start-up company that hit it big. Your salary increased rapidly, and soon you were making more money than you'd ever dreamed of. Your spouse had a decent job, too, but made a lot less than you do. To help you out in the beginning of your marriage, your parents gave you some money toward a down payment on a house. After you began to earn some serious money, you and your spouse also bought two new cars and a time-share in Florida. Eventually you bought new furniture and took some great trips, charging these big expenses on your credit cards.

The Good Years

After a few years of the good life you decided to add children to the picture, so you had two children, two years apart. The little company you work for continued to flourish, and you got bonuses consisting of money and stock options. Because you had the big income, you two decided your spouse would stay home with the children. Although you spent most of the money from your job, you did put some aside in retirement funds and played around in the stock market a bit. After you had been married eight years, your spouse's favorite uncle died and left her $10,000, which she invested. You bought a duplex to rent out and used the rental income to pay the mortgage and maintenance on this property. Your spouse did the hands-on managing of the property, including some repairs.

If you decide to divorce, you need to know about the potential financial consequences. For starters, what is the marriage property, the marital estate? All the things you purchased during the marriage using the money both of you earned are marital property. That would include the cars, the time-share, the duplex, the furniture, the retirement funds, and the stocks you bought with your income.

Divorce on the Horizon

While working on the duplex, your spouse developed a relationship with one of the tenants. Your spouse bought the tenant gifts and paid for them with the credit cards issued in both your names. One day you happened to open the Visa bill and discovered a charge for a watch you'd never seen. When you confronted your spouse, she admitted the affair, at which point heated words were exchanged, and she left the house.

Breakdown of Marital Assets

Staying with this hypothetical situation, the house may or may not be a total marital asset—it depends on the character of your parents' gift for the down payment. Typically, parents give money to the happy couple, but when the happy couple gets divorced, the parents sometimes remember they really gave this money to their child alone. Often the only proof of the parents' intent is to whom they wrote the check. If they wrote it to both of you, their gift will be considered a gift to both of you, and the entire house is a marital asset. On the other hand, if the check was made out to you alone, you can claim your parents gave you this gift, and this contribution to the value of the house would now be considered nonmarital property.

What about your spouse's inheritance from her uncle? It sure looks like a gift. Let's suppose your spouse actively played the stock market with that money, buying and selling on a regular basis.

ALERT!

If you bring property into the marriage or inherit property during the marriage and want it to remain yours, keep it clearly separate or keep very good records of how it's used; otherwise, it will become marital property to be divided with your spouse should you divorce.

In some states the active management of funds would define any increase in their value as marital property. But if your spouse simply bought GE stock, for example, and let it sit there, any increase in value would be characterized as passive, and the entire amount, including the original gift, would keep its nonmarital status. If your spouse put the stock into both of your names, however, the stock would change from nonmarital to marital.

Still Another Scenario

Let's change our facts a little. Suppose you owned a house before you got married, and shortly after the marriage you sold it to buy another, using the money from the sale of your house to buy a new family house. For the next eight years, you and your spouse made mortgage, tax, and insurance payments from money earned during the marriage. At the time of the divorce the house is worth a lot more than you paid for it. In such a case, many states will give you a nonmarital interest in the house from that initial investment, providing you have documents clearly showing you moved the money from your first house into the second.

How Do Courts Divide Property?

The answer is, "it depends." Many states are equitable distribution states, which means marital property is to be divided equitably. Equitable does not necessarily mean fifty-fifty, although it does often work out that way. In community property states, marital property, called the property of the community, is always divided equally. Some states still retain the concept of fault in their divorce laws, meaning that one person has committed some bad act during the marriage that has caused the divorce. Therefore, if one party in the marriage has behaved badly, he can be punished by getting less of the marital property. It's important to know your state's laws before you begin a divorce.

Create an Inventory

To divide your property, you first need to know how much you've got. Get an inventory form from your lawyer or use the Asset Summary Sheet in Appendix B, and make a list of all your property. If household goods and furniture are an issue for you, make a separate, detailed list of this property. If you're still living in the house, go to each room and itemize the things in it. If you can, photograph or make a video recording of the contents of your home just in case things start to disappear during the process.

If you're not living in the house any more and don't have your possessions committed to memory, you may need to get permission from your spouse to walk through to write your list. If you own antiques, paintings, sculpture, china, sterling silver, crystal, electronics, jewelry, coins, or other collections or items of significant value, you may need to have them appraised. In most communities, experts who mostly handle estate sales can value these items.

FACT

The furniture in your home is considered used furniture and is now worth much less than when it was new, even if you paid a lot for it. Now your furniture's value is in its usefulness. Ask for those items that will minimally furnish your new place. Let the rest go.

It's very helpful if you and your spouse can agree on a date of valuation. If all property is valued as of about the same time, you will be comparing apples with apples. If you can't agree, and your lawyers can't agree for you, the court will choose the date of valuation. This date is usually the date the divorce was commenced or the date of the pretrial hearing or the trial itself. If you've been in the divorce process for some time, the values you have may be old, so they will need to be updated to the date the judge selects. Rather than have a whole new appraisal conducted, sometimes the court will allow you to get an update from your original appraiser. This may save you some money, but if you have a lot of property, this can become an expensive process.

Asset Summary

Take a look at the following asset summary and you'll see a list of items showing your values and your spouse's. Our example puts both your and your spouse's values all on one document to make it easier to understand, but they would be two separate documents in real life. This asset summary is meant to give you an idea of what should be included and what you need to know about each item. For more detail, refer to the Asset Summary Sheet in Appendix B.

Asset Summary

Asset	Wife's Values	Husband's Values	Values Stipulated for Settlement Only
Personal Property			
Furniture	5,000	10,000	8,000
Furnishings	1,000	3,500	3,000
China, silver, crystal	12,000	18,000	15,000
Jewelry and furs	3,000	15,000	9,000
Homestead (purchase date)			
Market value	380,000	478,000	400,000
Mortgage	[213,000]	[213,000]	—
Second mortgage	[43,000]	[43,000]	—
Net equity	124,000	222,000	144,000
Apartment building (purchase date)			
Market value	609,000	463,000	528,000
Mortgage	[379,000]	[3790,000]	—
Net equity	230,000	84,000	149,000
Sweat equity	—	68,000	—
Lake cabin (purchase date)			
Market value	400,000	315,000	380,000
Mortgage	[12,000]	[12,000]	—
Net equity	388,000	303,000	368,000
Back taxes	—	—	
Boats and vehicles			
Fishing boat and trailer	7,500	6,000	6,000
2008 Nissan Maxima			
Market value	30,000	19,000	26,000
Encumbrance	[12,000]	[12,000]	—
Net value	18,000	7,000	14,000

Asset Summary (*continued*)

2007 Chevy Impala

Market value	19,000	16,000	17,00
Encumbrance	9,000]	[9,000]	
Net value	10,000	7,000	8,000

2005 Harley Davidson

Market value	18,000	18,000	—
Encumbrance	14,000	—	14,000
Net Value	4,000	4,000	

Securities

240 shares GM stock (purchase date)	—	See market quote	—

Bank accounts

Savings	minimal	minimal	—
Checking	minimal	minimal	—

Life insurance

Company/Policy number			
Face amount	25,000	125,000	—
Cash surrender value	2,000	—	—
Loan	—	—	—

Retirement accounts

Deferred comp./account number	—	319,000	319,000
Company/Plan name	—	—	—
Owned by	—	—	—
Profit sharing	—	—	—
Pensions	—	—	—
Keoghs	—	—	—
IRAs	—	—	—

Asset Summary (*continued*)

Business interests			
Name	To be determined	—	—
Type	To be determined	—	—
Ownership interest	—	—	—

Debts			
VISA	21,000	17,000	17,000
MasterCard	8,319	8,319	8,319
Discover	2,870	3,100	2,870
Sears	300	—	300
Loans to parents	15,000	—	—
Total	—	—	28,489

What does this all mean? If the parties are pretty far apart on values they've given to a number of items, it's a good bet the items on which they've placed a lower value are the items they want. For instance, if the wife wants to keep the house, she'll want it to go into the overall property division at a lower value, so she gets more of the other property.

Surprise!

The parties often learn new information by looking at the asset summaries their spouses prepare. For example, you may learn for the first time that taxes on your lake cabin haven't been paid for the last two years. You thought that your spouse had taken care of this. Or maybe this is the first time you've heard your spouse is claiming a nonmarital interest in the house. And where did this "loan to parents" come from? That was a gift, you thought. And can you believe it? He went out and bought a motorcycle.

Sweat Equity

The person who put in a lot of work on real estate that you own together may claim the property is worth more because of this work. This is probably true, but depending on the jurisdiction, the court may or may not credit a spouse who put out this effort. Sometimes a spouse will use this argument to try to create an interest in the other party's nonmarital property, which can work in some cases. Another way the sweat-equity argument arises is when one of the parties has refinished antiques and wants credit for making them more valuable. Courts are not easily persuaded by the sweat equity argument, so if you plan on making it, try to find documentation like pictures or before-and-after appraisals to support your arguments

Bring in the Experts

The parties who filled out the asset summary did not have their major assets valued by an expert. Instead, they assigned values based on guesses or what someone told them. Maybe they went to a marine store and priced new boats, or to the local gift shop and priced silver. Perhaps their Realtor buddy gave them a ballpark number for houses in their area. If values given to the items on the list are all roughly equal, then it probably won't be necessary to involve an expert. However, if the values placed on certain items are vastly different, these items should be valued by a neutral third person or, if you litigate, by two not-so-neutral experts.

Even if you are able to agree on a value of a property without professional input, be careful that you are not selling yourself short. Markets can change rapidly, affecting the value of property in big ways. If you have a valuable asset, you might want to consider hiring an expert just to make sure you know its actual value before you bargain it away.

Words about Debt

The date of valuing assets may not work as the date for establishing debt. You may have frozen your joint credit cards shortly after you decided to divorce and can use balances as of the date both of you stopped using the marital credit cards. Or, you may have both been charging up a storm since you separated and the cards are now maxed out.

You will need to take a close look at what each spouse has charged to determine if it should be a shared debt or an individual one. If you used credit during the separation because your spouse wasn't providing financial support, the reasonable debt accumulated for living expenses may be your spouse's responsibility. On the other hand, if you used your card to finance a solo trip to Vegas, that debt is yours and yours alone. Determination of the marital debt will need to be based on your particular circumstances. Just make sure you're informed about what exactly has been charged on the marital credit cards before you agree to pay.

You may be overwhelmed by the amount of debt you are left with following the divorce. Before you turn to bankruptcy, consider consumer credit counseling services or debt consolidation companies to help you get out from under the weight of money owed.

Values for Settlement Purposes Only

After you and your spouse prepare your inventories, you should schedule a four-way meeting between both of you and your lawyers. Before the meeting, each side can provide the other with documentation that has been collected—things like recent property tax statements, mortgage and rental statements, investment reports, statements from retirement accounts, life insurance, bank accounts, and any recent appraisals. If you refinanced your home recently, you may already have a house appraisal in your file along with other lender documents that might be helpful.

The First Meeting

Using the asset summary, you meet at one of the lawyer's offices and you and your spouse take a look at each other's summaries. (Remember, there will be two lists—one with your values and one with the values assigned by your spouse.) Look for areas of possible agreement. For those items that show important differences, try to find a solution. For example, you can look at Blue Book values for the vehicles and narrow your differences. You can agree to use independent neutrals to obtain values for other items, such as the real estate and the business. Set a timetable for getting these values and schedule a second meeting.

A Second Meeting

By the second meeting, the real estate appraisals and business valuation should have been completed. At this second meeting, put your energies into trying to develop that third column labeled "agreed values for settlement purposes only." This label means you're not bound by these numbers if you're unable to reach agreement and negotiate a complete property division.

More Work to Be Done

You may be able to agree on all the numbers except the business valuation done by the independent neutral. Now you'll need to hire your own expert, and your spouse will probably want to hire an expert, too. Keep in mind that every time you hire an expert, you're going to pay thousands of dollars for her initial report and thousands more for her to come and testify if your case goes to trial.

You hire the new experts and, after two or three months, they submit their reports. It's possible the two new experts have come up with a business value close enough to the first value so that you now can agree. If not, you may choose to litigate only this issue. It's not a perfect result, but it's better than taking all your property issues to court.

While money certainly matters, it isn't worth going to war over. If you and your ex-spouse spend all your resources fighting over values and settlements, you may very well have nothing left to fight over once all is said and done. Negotiate whenever possible.

Final Division of Assets

Assume you have been able to create that third column. The next step is to decide who gets what. With any luck you'll be able to negotiate a division of the major items of marital property. Take a look at the following Proposed Division of Assets form.

Proposed Division of Property

Asset	Wife	Husband
Homestead	144,000	—
Cabin	—	368,000
Apartment building	149,000	—
Furniture	—	8,000
Furnishings	—	3,000
China, silver, etc.	15,000	—
Jewelry and furs	9,000	—
Nissan	—	14,000
Chevrolet	8,000	—
Boat and trailer	—	6,000
Harley Davidson	—	4,000
Retirement Accounts	Half	Half
Debt	—	[28,489]
Business	—	—
Cash equalizer	25,000	[25,000]
Grand total	**350,000**	**349,511**

You put in the agreed-on values for the property items, according to who gets what. When you total the values in each party's column, you may find that one of you is getting significantly more than the other. If this is the case, you will need an equalizer. In the example, the husband needs to pay a cash equalizer of $25,000 to make the balance sheet come out even.

QUESTION?

What is an equalizer?
An equalizer can be a cash payment or a division of another asset, such as a retirement fund, that makes the final division close to fifty-fifty or some other figure that you have agreed is equitable. Your lawyer can adjust figures and amounts to make things come out even, but make sure you understand exactly what you're giving up and getting.

It's wise to split as few assets as possible unless they're easy to divide. You can split your stock holdings easily if they're publicly traded. Dividing the shares of a closely held corporation may be more difficult. If it's the family business, you need to think about whether it's a good idea to each retain an ownership interest after the divorce. In our example, the Proposed Division of Property sheet still doesn't show a value for the business, but it proposes alternatives for dividing it. In this example, each spouse will retain half of the stock in the business and share earnings fifty-fifty. Otherwise, they will have the business valued and set up a plan for one spouse to buy out the other over time. The cash value of the life insurance was so modest, the parties may have decided simply to maintain the insurance for the benefit of the children.

Personal Property

You may have noticed that household goods and personal property aren't addressed in detail in the asset summary and property division. Lawyers and judges hate dividing personal property. It's not uncommon for the parties to have pages and pages of inventory and to become quite irrational about getting their stuff. Too often the cost of dividing personal possessions exceeds its value. The reason? The parties aren't really fighting over stuff; they're still caught up in their power struggle and their inability to let go.

Personal property can be divided in a number of ways. If you can agree on the list, you can draw straws to see who chooses first, then select items on a rotating basis until they're divided. Or, you can have an auction: Each of you makes a list of the property you want with its value, then each of you can buy items on the other's list at the price noted.

If you have family photos you'd each like copies of, make copies and share the cost. Make sure each spouse has electronic copies of digital photos as well. The same principle applies to family videos. You can have copies made and agree to split the cost of doing so.

Do your best to divide your possessions yourselves. Only you know the underlying emotional attachments and significance of your things. To the lawyers and the judge it's just stuff that can be easily replaced. Keep in mind that an argument over these kinds of items will just make you look petty before the judge. If you have more important issues to be decided, fighting over personal belongings may distract the court from the items that are really important. Take the high road and let your spouse have that one item he can't live without.

Dividing Retirement Benefits

Many different kinds of retirement accounts exist. The most common general categories are defined benefit plans and defined contribution plans. In a defined benefit plan, the plan will pay you a specific amount per month when you retire. The amount may depend on your retirement age. For example, it may be a smaller amount if you retire before age sixty-five. Depending on the plan, you may be able to select different options. Before you agree to any proposed division, make sure you know what the plan will allow. Make sure your lawyer has obtained a plan benefit description so you will know what division will provide you the best benefits and protection.

Wherever possible, divide assets in their entirety. Splitting retirement accounts requires that additional documents be prepared after the divorce. If one of you keeps an interest in real estate awarded to the other in the form of a lien, you will have to deal with each other when that lien interest is due. A clean break makes it easier to move on with your life.

A defined contribution plan is one in which you invest a specific amount each month from your paycheck during your employment, which may or may not be matched by your employer. These funds are invested and, you hope, increase in value over the length of your employment. When you retire, you can select among various options as to how you will receive these funds. You can take a lump sum amount or elect to receive monthly payments. If you put pretax dollars into a deferred compensation plan, you'll have to pay taxes on these moneys when you receive them.

Qualified Domestic Relations Order

Some retirement accounts, such as 401(k)s, can be divided by a Domestic Relations Order (DRO) or Qualified Domestic Relations Order QDRO, (pronounced "kwadro"). Your lawyer needs to draft the QDROs after the divorce is final. These documents direct an employer to divide and later pay out the retirement funds according to your agreement. If one of you dies before the DRO or QDRO is submitted and approved, the retirement funds may be dispersed differently from your agreement.

Don't wait until after your divorce is final to figure out what benefits are actually available through the retirement plan. By then it will be too late to maximize your choices. Find out before you are divorced what options are available. For example, can your spouse choose to receive a lower monthly payment so you will continue to receive benefits if she dies first? Do you need to specify that you will share in any cost-of-living allowances that are applied after your spouse retires? Is there an option that provides for a death benefit payment? You should also make sure you know how any subsequent marriages by your spouse will affect your benefits, if at all.

ALERT!

If you agree to use a DRO or QDRO as part of your asset division, make sure it is drafted immediately after the divorce is final. You may lose money you planned to live on in your old age if your ex-spouse dies before the DRO or QDRO has been drafted and approved by his employer.

A defined benefit plan can't be divided by a DRO or QDRO, and neither can retirement funds for military personnel, federal employees, or for some people who work in the public sector. Each plan is different and some have provisions for payment of benefits to a spouse or ex-spouse, but the participant must submit the right paperwork to the retirement system to make this happen. You and your spouse will have to agree on a division of the payments when they begin and on a surviving ex-spouse provision. If retirement funds can't be divided, you may have to use other assets to make an equitable property division. Or, you may choose to divide payments when they are made. A potential danger here is that the recipient may not live until retirement or may die soon after the payments begin, leaving the ex-spouse high and dry. Collecting money from an ex-spouse can also be very challenging, particularly if she is still angry about the divorce.

Social Security Benefits

If you and your spouse have been married for more than ten years when you divorce, you are entitled to receive a percentage of your former spouse's benefits. This can be very helpful if you have been a stay-at-home spouse who has not earned a lot of wages. Check with your local social security agency to find out exactly what benefits are available. This knowledge might encourage you to stay in the marriage a few more months to make it to the ten-year mark. Don't underestimate the value of this benefit, especially if you have not worked very much. Collecting on your record and your ex-spouse's record could mean a difference between $600 and $1,500.

A Second, Third, or . . . Marriage?

If you're marrying for a subsequent time, you may want to take specific steps to protect the assets you acquired during and after your previous marriage(s). If you come into this subsequent marriage with a lot of property, you'll want to talk to a lawyer about preparing a prenuptial, or before marriage, agreement. The purpose of a prenuptial agreement is to protect assets both for yourself and for your heirs—children you have from a previous marriage, for example.

A prenuptial agreement lists your property and your beloved's property. Depending on the jurisdiction, you can make a variety of agreements in a prenuptial. You can decide who will have custody of any children, how much support will be paid, and how any assets acquired during the marriage will be divided. It makes specific provisions for how this property will be divided in the event of death or divorce. For instance, you might agree that if the marriage lasts less than three years, each of you takes back all your property, one of you pays the other a cash settlement of so many dollars, and you both move on. If the marriage lasts longer, you agree that different terms apply.

Doing a Prenup the Right Way

If you decide to use a prenuptial agreement, you need to do it right. Prenuptial agreements are often challenged when the parties divorce, and courts end up throwing them out as unfair or signed under duress. In some states, a challenge can only be made if the parties are married fewer than a certain number of years. If your agreement throws your formerly beloved out in the cold with only the clothes on his back, the court may want to avoid such a harsh result. As with any agreements made between spouses, the court can decide to change the terms if it believes the circumstances support such a change. For example, if your prenuptial says that you own various stocks and that you alone will retain them in the case of a divorce. During your seven year marriage, you did nothing with the stocks but your spouse spent hours every day playing the stock market. As a result, your stocks have quadrupled in value. A judge could find that giving you title to all of the stocks would be unfair to your spouse. Your prenuptial agreement is now found to be unconscionable and your spouse is awarded a share of your stocks. The point here is that no matter how ironclad you think your agreement is, provisions can be changed.

Other Protective Measures

If you enter into a subsequent marriage without a prenuptial agreement, you may want to take other steps to protect assets you bring into the marriage. The problem here is that when folks think about marriage, they seldom think about protecting their property. Some couples find the notion of valuing your property before the marriage insulting and inconsistent with the foundation of the institution of marriage. For these folks, dividing property is like saying your marriage is doomed from the start. Don't be fooled by these emotions. All too many couples start their marriages this way and it's the spouse with assets who always pays the price if the marriage fails.

A prenuptial agreement is like insurance. Just because you buy life insurance it doesn't mean you think you're going to die tomorrow. The same is true of protecting your assets. If the marriage ends and you're the spouse with all the assets, you'll be thanking your lucky stars you took steps to protect yourself.

ALERT!

Prenuptial agreements need to be prepared carefully. It's ideal if both parties are represented by lawyers who review the document. Both parties should fully disclose all their assets, and the terms of the agreement should be fair. The agreement should be signed as far in advance of your wedding day as possible.

In the best of all possible plans, you would have your house and any other real estate valued the month of the wedding. You would make copies of bank statements and investment or retirement account values for that month. If you owned a business, you would have its value documented at that time as well.

People almost never do this; it seems so heartless and crass. When they divorce, they have no idea what their stuff was worth when they got married, and they can't compare those values with present-day values. Remember, if you want to establish a premarital interest in anything, you have the burden of proving it to a judge. Tracing nonmarital interests gets only more complicated as you bring more assets into a marriage. If you don't keep good records, you won't be able to show where your money or property went, and you won't be able to make a nonmarital claim.

Impact of Bankruptcy

Bankruptcy law is a specialized area with rules that change frequently. Be aware that it's a potential hazard. If your spouse decides to file for bankruptcy during the divorce, you'll need to consult with an attorney who specializes in bankruptcy law if your own lawyer doesn't have this expertise. Do this right away to protect yourself and your assets. A bankruptcy proceeding puts a stay on your divorce proceeding. This means you will not be able to proceed with your divorce until the bankruptcy is resolved. If your spouse discharges the joint credit cards and other debt, the creditors can come after you, and you may need to join in the bankruptcy.

ALERT!

Child support, spousal maintenance, and other obligations "in the nature of support" are not dischargeable in bankruptcy. Be sure to have language in your divorce decree that labels the payment of certain obligations as "additional support."

If your spouse files for bankruptcy after the divorce, your property settlement may be totally undone. Again, you need to act quickly with the help of a competent bankruptcy lawyer. You'll be unable to collect your property settlement during the automatic stay of the bankruptcy. If the final divorce decree made your spouse responsible for various debts and obligations, they may fall back in your lap. Make sure your settlement agreement and/or divorce decree has language that protects you against this possibility.

Divorce attorneys sometimes overlook this area of law. Most settlement agreements contain provisions that clearly state the financial obligations of each spouse to the other are not dischargeable in bankruptcy. In addition to this protection, the agreement should contain a "hold harmless" and indemnification clause to offer further protection. A hold harmless clause says you will be held harmless from the repayment of a debt. An indemnification provision means that should a creditor come after you from a debt, you can turn around and go after your spouse. What's important to remember about these clauses is that while they do offer some protection, if your spouse has no money to pay the debt, the result is the same. You don't get what you're entitled to.

CHAPTER 13

Moving Toward Trial

At some point after you file the summons and petition to begin your divorce, the court system will decide it's time for you to come to court. Assuming you haven't already had some pretrial proceeding, the court system will take over and try and move your case along. In some states, nothing will happen unless you file something asking for a hearing, but in others you will eventually be sent a court date. You and your lawyer will need to meet and prepare for going to court.

Why Have a Pretrial Hearing?

Courts use the pretrial hearing, also referred to as a pretrial conference, to get organized for the upcoming trial. Your court will have its own set of rules and forms for the hearing. The forms must be completed, sent to the other lawyer, and filed before the hearing. The court will expect you and your spouse to have completed all discovery, lined up all witnesses, developed trial strategy, prepared a settlement proposal, and discussed settlement.

ALERT!

Lawyers like to blame courts for the perception that divorces seem to take forever. The judge's view is that lawyers are rarely ready for trial when a date is first set. It's more common for the lawyers to ask for a continuance (rescheduling) of the court date than it is for the court to need a continuance of the hearing.

When a pretrial notice arrives at your attorney's office, you probably won't be ready to go to trial. Remember our discussion about discovery? You may be waiting to receive a report from an expert, documents from your spouse, or information from outside sources. For example, suppose you've hired an expert to assess the value of your spouse's business. Your expert may have requested financial records from your spouse, but she has been slow in providing all of the requested information so your expert hasn't completed the report.

Are You Ready for Pretrial?

What if you're really not ready? Of course, you and your lawyer will need to discuss whether you should ask for a continuance, also called an adjournment, or go unprepared. In some states, a pretrial conference is simply a way of bringing the parties together to establish a trial schedule and promote settlement discussions. Complete preparation is sometimes not necessary. You should rely on the expertise of your attorney to decide whether to ask for a continuance.

This decision depends a lot on your judge, and also on whether the same judge will handle both the pretrial and the trial. There are two lines of thought here. Some judges feel they shouldn't preside over both the pretrial and the trial. They base this on the fact that settlement discussions may occur at the pretrial that might influence trial decisions.

Settlement discussions between parties are generally not admissible at trial. This is to protect the rights of the parties because if a judge knows what one party was willing to agree to before trial, it could bias the judge in his decision at trial.

Other judges feel they should handle both the pretrial and trial. In some jurisdictions, a pretrial conference may happen with the judge's law clerk, and you may not see the judge at all unless the parties come to a settlement agreement. Where a judge is involved at the pretrial conference, you and your attorney may get an idea about how a particular issue will be judged at trial. For example, if a judge tells you how he feels about spousal mainte-nance at the pretrial hearing, he sends a clear message about how he will decide at the trial. This message can help the parties settle, although many judges can be very subtle in their comments in order to protect the rights of the parties. It's also important to remember that at a pretrial conference the judge does not have all of the information and has not had the benefit of hearing the testimony and evidence that the parties will present at trial. While it is always better if you can settle your case, a trial might be neces-sary if you and your lawyer believe that the evidence is compelling and in your favor.

To Go or Not to Go

If your judge is a stickler for the rules, you should not go to the pretrial unprepared, because you don't want to make him angry and possibly nega-tively influence his later decisions. If your judge is more flexible, you could go to the pretrial and use it as an opportunity to get a feel for the judge's perspective on issues. Again, when the judge gives you his take on certain issues, he gives you tools to move toward settlement.

Deciding to Settle Your Divorce

There's some evidence that simply going to the courthouse encourages settlement. Judges like to say a chance to settle exists every time parties come to court. Pressure of the upcoming trial and fear of the unknown is strong. You could get vibes you don't like from the judge, and you may finally understand you'll be letting this person make decisions that will affect your future. You may well decide negotiating a deal is a good idea. Going to court can also make parties angrier. If you feel your partner is becoming angry and threatening, make sure to tell your lawyer.

Narrowing the Issues

Whatever your decision—going to pretrial or asking for more time—you and your lawyer may decide this would be a good time to meet with the other side. You probably don't need to have all discovery done to talk settlement. Agreements can be made about the division of assets even if you don't have the final numbers. At the very least, you may be able to reach some agreements and clarify disagreements. The more you agree on means the less you have to fight about at trial. Lawyers call this narrowing the issues.

Try not to let your emotions get in the way while trying to settle. You should always stay focused on your objectives. Present the issues in a clear manner and suggest a realistic resolution. This is not the time to anger your spouse or make her jealous, and it is definitely not the time to harass her.

A list of agreements and disagreements can help you focus on preparing good, clear information in areas of contention so you and your lawyer can prepare an organized argument for the court. It also allows you to focus your resources on gathering evidence and preparing testimony on a limited number of points. You're much more likely to persuade the judge if he understands what your side is saying. This means presenting clear testimony and supporting evidence when possible.

Partial Agreement

If you have a conference with the other side and reach some agreements, one of the lawyers will draft a partial stipulation. This document sets forth agreements made at the meeting, and is signed by both parties and their lawyers. It becomes part of the court file. Be sure you read the stipulation carefully before you sign it, because you'll have a very hard time changing agreements afterwards. Also remember that it is never too late to change agreements or go to trial before you place your name on the dotted line. Once you've signed your name, you're committed.

Most court rules require divorcing parties and their lawyers to discuss settlement before a pretrial hearing, but they often don't get around to it. Some judges will assess fines if spouses haven't gotten together to talk before pretrial. Other judges will require the parties and their lawyers to use the pretrial time to discuss settlement, then set a new pretrial date.

Lawyers write in legalese, so if you don't understand parts of the agreement, be sure your lawyer explains them. Don't settle for something that is unclear or vague just to save money. If you sign an agreement that doesn't work for you, the money you would have spent going to trial will pale in comparison to what you will probably spend trying to change it. If something in the agreement is different from what you thought you'd agreed to, discuss this new wrinkle with your lawyer. If it's not a major deal, maybe you'll want to accept it rather than jeopardize the rest of the agreements. However, if it is a major deal, don't sign the agreement until this item has been dealt with to your satisfaction.

Pretrial Paperwork

The paperwork that is required for pretrial hearings differs in each state, but there are some similarities. In general, the court wants basic information about the parties, children, and assets, including a financial statement similar to one you might fill out for a bank loan. Each state will have a form called a Statement of Net Worth, Financial Disclosure Affidavit, or another similar term. It can be another trip down the Wonderland rabbit hole to put financial statements of the divorcing parties side by side. Are these people from the same family? The same world?

When parties prepare court papers, they often develop an advocacy mindset. This means they massage data to work to their advantage. Sometimes massage turns into outright lies. A business owner puts its value at nothing; the owner's spouse says the business is worth big bucks. A spouse uses income figures from a prior job, or from before a recent raise, to minimize her income. You get the picture. While you or your spouse may even do this to some degree without realizing it, a close review of your finances and income will help. Don't forget that credibility is a huge factor in success at trial. Don't risk your credibility by taking a trip to numbers fantasyland. Chances are the evidence will prove you wrong every time, and your credibility will be destroyed.

Budgets

In addition to the financial statement, you'll need to prepare a budget. Depending on the state, a budget is sometimes included in the forms. Again, budget and wish list are not the same thing. One party's budget often exceeds the total family income. It's important to prepare a real budget based on prior spending and including changes brought about by the divorce. For instance, the family home may have been sold, so each party could afford to own a home. The monthly mortgage payments for each party are now different. Dad had been staying home with the children but has gotten a job. He now has an income, but the family now has child-care expenses as well.

Sticking with Reality

Finally, each side prepares a settlement proposal. Again, this isn't time for a wish list or the time to get your spouse upset all over again. It's time to make a realistic settlement offer based on all the information you've obtained during discovery and based on all the information in your gut.

For instance, if the custody study recommends that Mom be the primary parent because she's always been there for the kids and you works long hours away from home, you know in your gut she's a good mom and will take good care of your children. You also know you love your job and can make a lot more money to support the kids than your spouse can. Use your head and accept the recommendation. Now is not the time to propose you be the primary parent.

ALERT!

Some resolutions may be hard to swallow, especially if they involve your children. But now is not the time to throw a fit and fling threats at your ex-spouse. Such a tantrum might very well validate some of the findings and cause even more problems. If it's something you feel very strongly about, discuss it with your lawyer.

On the other hand, if you have serious concerns about your spouse's ability to care for the children, now is the time to address them. Just make sure your concern is valid and not a result of your anger toward your spouse. If you allowed your spouse to care for the children for the last five years and that was fine, he probably didn't magically become unfit in the last six months since your separation.

Going Ahead

Let's say you and your lawyer decide to attend the pretrial even though you're still waiting for a report from your financial expert. Your attorney figures the judge may be annoyed but won't assess sanctions or fines, so you prepare as much of the required paperwork as you can.

When you get to court you tell the judge that you and your spouse have an issue about the value of the business, but that you can't say much more because you're still waiting for the expert's report. At the same time you include a reasonable settlement proposal. Your lawyer should try to set up a meeting with the other side before pretrial so you can say you've discussed a settlement with them. Finally, the other side agrees to meet at the courthouse an hour before the scheduled hearing, so at least you'll be able to tell the judge you've met to discuss something.

The First Scenario

Here is one possible scenario. You, your attorney, and the other side find a conference room at the courthouse. In the hour before the scheduled pretrial, you make some agreements. When the judge's clerk checks with you at the appointed hour you say, "We're making progress," so the clerk suggests you continue to negotiate, which you do for another hour. Now the clerk tells you the judge no longer has time to see you and gives you a new pretrial date. You're pretty disappointed you didn't even see the judge but glad that you've made some settlement progress.

The Second Scenario

Pretrial could go also like this: You meet at the courthouse a few minutes ahead of time. The judge's clerk calls the attorneys into the judge's office, called chambers. You and your spouse sit uncomfortably on benches outside the courtroom for what feels like forever. Finally the lawyers come out to tell you what the judge has said, and the four of you now talk a bit, using the judge's input to resolve some issues. The lawyers go back to see the judge, and this time they come back with a new date for a second pretrial.

FACT

Trial can mean preparing written arguments with supporting documents on unresolved issues and submitting them to the judge by a certain date. The judge also may give each side one chance to respond in writing to the other's arguments, with a due date for these responses. Then the judge will review the written submissions and decide.

Lawyers often go into the judge's chambers without their clients. Sometimes lawyers prefer this and sometimes judges prefer this. Lawyers can snipe at each other there: "She hasn't sent me her pretrial statement or answered my interrogatories." "He doesn't return my phone calls." They can also tell the judge they could settle the case if their clients—that's you—weren't so unreasonable. The judge can speak more openly about her thoughts on your case. After talking to the judge, the attorneys come back with the judge's wise words. Trouble is, each lawyer may hear those words differently. Lawyers may also have their own agenda about proceeding to trial because of their desire to win cases, preserve their reputation as a hard nose, or simply to charge you more fees. Because you weren't there, you're in no position to question what your attorney tells you.

Staying in Control

An experience like this will help you understand that by going to court you lose control of your divorce. Think how it felt to sit in the corridor while your lawyer met with the judge. They were talking about your life, your future, and you weren't able to provide input or even meet the judge. Did your lawyer say the right things? Did he tell the judge how bad and unreasonable your spouse was? Did he defend you or did he let your spouse's lawyer do all the talking? You won't know the answers to any of these questions, which is why you need to find a lawyer you can trust. If you go to trial, you'll turn all decision making over to the judge. Compromise looks better and better. At least you'll know everything that is going on.

Judges are free to decide how conferences with lawyers and parties will occur. You should assert your preference with your lawyer to be included in all conferences with the judge. Your lawyer knows the judge, so listen to her advice regarding making such a request. The reality of pretrial conferencing is that you may not be included.

Judges like to have clients and their lawyers work on a settlement, so they'll usually let you take some time, sometimes all day, to try to resolve issues. Because you'll experience a letdown if you never see the judge, you'll want your lawyer to ask the judge's clerk if all of you can go into chambers at the appointed hour. If you all hear what the judge has to say, you'll all get the same direction, which may help resolve or at least narrow issues. And you'll at least meet the judge who is probably going to try your case and get some sense of what he is like. If you don't get to meet the judge, you will have to rely on your lawyer for information. Listen carefully and make sure that what she is saying sounds reasonable. If there are options you can see that she hasn't mentioned, don't be afraid to say so.

A Typical Pretrial Hearing

Here's how many pretrial hearings play out, so try to imagine yourself going through these motions. You and your lawyer arrive a few minutes before your pretrial is scheduled. You're dressed conservatively to show you respect the process and the judge. You've thought about this day for months and are willing to negotiate with your spouse and give up some things you had previously wanted. You haven't brought friends along, although you may bring your accountant in case you need his expertise.

Your spouse shows up with a lawyer and an entourage: mother, sister, best friend, and new significant other. Your spouse is wearing new clothes that accentuate her appearance and is sporting a new hairdo and overall look, including gaudy jewelry. You all go into the courtroom and sit in the spectator seats. Your spouse's new significant other and your ex-mother-in-law whisper and giggle while pointing and staring at you. All of your conviction to settle your case leaves you and is replaced by the desire to drag your spouse through the mud and make her suffer for what she's done to you and the children.

Inside the Chambers

The clerk comes through a door at one side of the judge's bench and makes sure everyone is present. The clerk asks for copies of documents that are supposed to be in the court file but aren't, while your spouse's lawyer sputters a bit about the slowness of the mail and the fact he failed to bring copies with him. (Remember, you haven't seen these papers, either, because they aren't ready.)

ALERT!

Men should never wear caps or hats in the courtroom or judge's chambers. Women should not show cleavage or wear short skirts or wear a lot of noisy jewelry. Dress conservatively in professional clothing. Wear only clothes that show you respect the judge. Judges like to be respected.

You've told your lawyer you want to be present for whatever happens, so your lawyer asks if all four of you can see the judge. You all go into the judge's chambers and sit around the judge's desk as the lawyers explain the issues to the judge. Because you're present, you get to hear exactly what goes on and assess for yourself whether your lawyer is doing a good job. The judge may give you useful information such as, "Unless there is some information I haven't seen, I am disinclined to award spousal maintenance in this case" or "I can't find any documentation for this nonmarital claim. If there is no proof, there is no claim." These kinds of observations can be very helpful in prompting you to modify your expectations of settlement.

Proper Behavior

Remember, you're a guest in a judge's office, so show respect. Judges like old-fashioned good manners, so be polite to your spouse. And don't bring your enormous briefcase full of divorce papers into chambers. It makes you look obsessed with the divorce. In addition, don't speak unless the judge asks you a direct question, and then answer only the question the judge asks. Your lawyer is there as your representative, and the judge will speak to her directly. If your lawyer needs more information, she might turn to you and ask that you answer the judge's question. Listen carefully and provide only the information requested. This is not the time for you to tell the judge that your spouse is a louse.

After meeting with the judge, you're sent to a nearby conference room to discuss settlement. Activist judges are likely to keep you talking until your lawyers report nothing more can be settled because of missing information. If both sides are missing information, the judge probably won't impose sanctions. If only one side has failed to bring required documents, the judge may impose fines, but he will make them conditional. (For example, if the case settles within the next thirty days, the fine will be forgiven.) Even if you lack actual numbers you may be able to settle certain issues. For example, if your spouse has a pension that was earned during the marriage, you may be willing to agree that it will be divided equally even though you don't know the exact value.

Too often one party is stuck on the behavior and actions of the other and unable to think of resolving issues for the family's benefit. You can be sure the judge will pick up on this, and you won't look good. Even if you have hostility toward your spouse, don't let it show in court. If you let it out, your case will suffer.

Still Moving Toward Trial

At the close of negotiations, the four of you troop back into the judge's chambers and report on progress or lack thereof. The judge, the judge's law clerk, or a stenographer records the information, or the judge may direct one of the lawyers to prepare the pretrial order. The order will spell out any agreements, set out a schedule for completing any unfinished discovery, set a date for exchanging exhibit and witness lists, and set any sanctions for failing to complete tasks on time.

The judge may schedule another pretrial hearing depending on her preferences. Some judges really like to try cases. They like sitting up on their benches, hearing testimony, making rulings on evidence, and appearing wise. These judges probably will set a trial date after one pretrial hearing.

On the other hand, some judges really don't like to try cases at all. They have trouble making decisions, especially in divorce cases. They'll give you every opportunity to settle your case, and they may schedule several pretrials. If that doesn't work, they'll give you time to discuss settlement on the day of trial, then they'll probably reschedule the trial. Another reason a judge will schedule a couple of pretrials is to make sure the parties are complying with discovery and financial disclosure. In order for a fair settlement to be reached, disclosure must occur, and most judges follow this closely to make sure that it does.

In most states, parties can change their names as part of a divorce. You should decide before the trial whether you want to change your name at this time because this will be the easiest way to get an order. Some parents choose to keep the same name as their children while they're in school.

Last Chance to Settle

Some wise judges realize divorce trials mean all other alternatives have failed—that the parties won't take responsibility and the buck has stopped in the judge's courtroom because someone else has to make the decisions. These judges probably will schedule a second pretrial with some serious sanctions for failure to exchange necessary documents. These judges will enforce sanctions because they know you can't settle the case if you don't have the information you need. Judges who understand divorce dynamics try to get the parties to make as many of their own decisions as possible. They then work with the divorcing spouses and their lawyers to devise a plan for resolving any remaining issues.

It's All about Preparation

The pretrial hearing is a tool to prepare for trial. It makes lawyers complete their preparation, gets everyone organized, and sets the trial rules. It's common for the parties to reach agreement on at least some issues at the pretrial. In fact, if you and your spouse have completed discovery, it's possible you will be able to resolve all the issues of your divorce at this time. Most divorce cases actually settle without the need for trial. Make your divorce one of these and you will save yourself and your family a ton of money, stress, and aggravation.

CHAPTER 14

The Trial

Most people have some preconceived notion of what a trial will be like. Whether you've seen one on television or heard stories from your friends, nothing can fully prepare you for the uncertainty and emotional roller coaster of a trial. In a perfect world, a trial offers you the chance to present what you believe to be a slam dunk case. The problem is that after hearing all the evidence, the judge may find that it was really your spouse who had the slam-dunk case.

14

Final Preparations

Being prepared for trial will take time and effort from both you and your lawyer. You'll need to meet with your lawyer to decide on a final witness and evidence list, review your testimony and make sure you have all the information you need to present your case. Most states provide timelines for the exchange of witness and exhibit lists so it's likely you will have already given this information to your spouse and received her lists as well. When you provided your list to your spouse, you probably included every possible person who you could think of to call to help you. Now is the time to pare down your list and fine tune your case presentation.

ALERT!

Make sure your lawyer meets with the witnesses who will testify at the trial. He needs to get a feel for these witnesses and how they will present themselves to the judge. It's critical that your lawyer know if potential witnesses have any negative information about you because this will probably come out at trial.

If you're contesting custody, your witness list will probably include family and friends, but your lawyer will streamline this group of witnesses. The judge assumes family members and friends are going to say nice things about you, so their testimony is noteworthy only when they don't (or if your spouse's family has good things to say about you). Select a family member who has seen both you and your spouse with the children and can provide recent information. Then select one really good witness from among your friends, which is probably enough, because the judge doesn't need to hear six people say the same thing. Choose the friend or two who'll be the most effective and who really knows you and your children well. Also choose the witnesses that have firsthand knowledge of facts that could help your case.

Double-Check Financial Information

For financial issues, you'll be using experts. If you haven't been able to agree on independent neutrals, both sides will bring their experts to the trial. You and your lawyer need to review the experts' testimony with them ahead of time and make sure they have all the accurate and current information. If your experts are interesting and easy to understand, they should be given ample time on the witness stand. If they're dull but very bright, you may want to limit their testimony to explaining charts and exhibits clearly and concisely. Most importantly, you want to make sure that your experts have considered alternatives that may be offered by your spouse's expert so they can be prepared with good explanations as to why your spouse's expert is wrong. You don't want to bore the judge, but you do want the judge to understand your position and the weaknesses of your spouse's position.

As you and your experts prepare for trial, you'll be able to see whether you can prove your position on certain issues. If your experts can't convince you, they can't convince the judge. On the other hand, if you see the weaknesses in your argument, you may choose to give in on those issues and focus on the areas where you're strong. Considering on an issue you are unlikely to succeed with at the trial is a small sacrifice to you and may produce some movement toward settlement from the other side as well.

Use Current Numbers

Both sides need to give each other and the court up-to-date financial information. Recent pay stubs, the most recent tax returns available, current stocks, real estate values, and any other financial document related to your particular financial assets should be in your lawyer's file, ready for court. If your lawyer plans on using these as evidence at trial, she may have to subpoena a witness from your place of employment, investment company, or other source in order to get the documents into evidence at trial. Make sure your lawyer has made all the necessary arrangements well in advance of trial.

In order to value assets, you and your spouse will need to agree on a date in time or rely on the court to set a date. If you and the other side haven't agreed on a date for valuing assets, it's possible the court will use the date the divorce was filed or a pretrial or trial date. You need to have values as of all possible dates the judge could use. If you want the judge to use a different date, you'll need a persuasive reason. If stock market values have been fluctuating widely, real estate prices have been booming, or some other factor has affected your holdings' values, the judge will want to pick a valuation date that doesn't create a crazy result. The judge will want to use a value that is valid at the time he makes his decision.

Review Your Exhibits

Exhibits are the documents given to the judge during the trial. They include budgets, financial statements, expert reports, charts, graphs, e-mails, text messages, police reports, psychological records, medical records, and any other documents that will help you prove your case. Exhibits are intended to validate testimony and, sometimes, to flesh it out. Your trial will go much more smoothly and you will please the judge if both sides meet beforehand to review exhibits.

While you may have copies of all your exhibits, these documents are not automatically admissible at trial. Rules of evidence typically require a witness from the company that keeps the records to bring the documents with them to court. This ensures the accuracy of the documents accepted into evidence.

During this review, it'll be clear to the lawyers that some exhibits are going to be received by the judge, no matter how much they object, like tax returns and pay stubs. It's in everyone's best interests to stipulate, or agree, to admit these documents. As one side presents its case and these exhibits are offered into evidence, the other side can simply say, "stipulated." This saves a lot of time during the trial, and judges like trials that move along. It's also a good way to save money because you won't have to subpoena a witness to validate the document.

Laying Foundation

Even if you have agreed with your spouse that certain documents will be admitted, your attorney will still have to establish their authenticity. In lawyer language, this is called laying the foundation for the records. Let's say you're trying to admit documents from the bank. Ordinarily, this would mean you have to bring a bank employee, the record keeper, to the courtroom to testify these are indeed your records from the bank. The other side knows you can get the bank employee to come to court with the records by issuing a subpoena *duces tecum*, which is Latin for "show up with the stuff." Your spouse's lawyer might well agree to waive her foundation objection to the bank records. That way you don't have to pay for the subpoena, for getting it served, and for having the guy from the bank come to court.

Laying foundation for an exhibit can be unnecessarily expensive and time consuming. For this reason, it is to both your and your spouse's benefit to agree on the authenticity of exhibits if at all possible. If you object to all of your spouse's exhibits—even the ones that are clearly accurate—the judge will be irritated, and it's rarely to your advantage to irritate a judge. However, both sides will probably have exhibits that will require bringing a person to court to lay foundation. Lawyers will be happy to negotiate a deal here: "I will waive my foundation objection to your bank records if you will waive your foundation objection to my medical records." This way neither side has to bring a witness to authenticate the records. The judge will be happy, and a happy judge will do a better job of listening to evidence.

ALERT!

Sometimes litigants bring a storage box of canceled checks to court as an exhibit. No judge has time to go through this box of checks. Pull out the checks that prove something like an extravagant purchase or outrageous spending for a period of time. This will allow the judge to focus on the problem you are trying to prove.

If you're using charts and graphs as exhibits, take a hard look at them. Make sure you have the necessary backup documents to support the information contained in the graphs and exhibits. Do you understand them? If you don't, what makes you think the judge will? Only present exhibits to the judge that will help her understand issues and your position on them. In these situations, sometimes less is more.

Making Agreements or Stipulations

We just talked about the lawyers meeting to review exhibits and make agreements about getting them into evidence. Lawyers can stipulate a number of things prior to trial. They can put together a statement of the facts—including all of the facts to which both sides agree—and reserve the right to argue about any contested facts. They can even agree about which facts are contested.

Lawyers can agree to have witnesses testify out of order, which can be a bit confusing, but it's far better than spending a lot of time arguing about it. For example, say one of your witnesses is a doctor who is only available on Thursday afternoon, but your spouse's case will probably be presented Thursday afternoon. The lawyers can agree the doctor can testify when he shows up at the courtroom. Lawyers and judges will usually make accommodations for expert witnesses because of the cost of bringing these folks to court. Many experts bill by the hour or half day, so it will cost a fortune if they end up sitting around for hours. Don't forget that money spent on experts is less money left in the marital pot to divide.

ALERT!

If your spouse's lawyer sets your teeth on edge, try to remember that this lawyer, like yours, has a job to do here. Although your spouse's lawyer may seem completely unreasonable, don't forget that she is representing your spouse's wishes. Part of a lawyer's job may be to get you upset, so don't play into the plan. Bite your tongue and stay calm.

Lawyers can agree to have a witness testify by deposition or video deposition. Suppose an expert who can help explain the value of your business has just gotten a contract to work in Bali for six months. Obviously, it would be too expensive to bring him back to trial, so his testimony can be preserved in a deposition where the lawyers conduct direct and cross examination as if they were in trial. Similar testimony can be presented by conference call, too.

Stipulations to exhibits, facts, valuation dates, and the order of witnesses are important aids to making the trial go smoothly. However, they can happen only if the lawyers meet prior to trial and reach these kinds of agreements. If real issues need to be litigated, it's probably wise to stipulate the less important stuff and focus on these disagreements. In other words, pick your battles.

The Big Day Arrives

The day of your divorce trial marks the culmination of all your painstaking preparation. You will get a chance to present your side to an impartial judge. But what should you expect, and how should you conduct yourself?

A Last-Minute Proposal

Let's say you, your lawyer, and several bankers' boxes of documents arrive at the courthouse a few minutes before the trial is to begin, and you'll need some time to unpack and get organized. Then the other side arrives, at which point your spouse's lawyer beckons to your lawyer. The other side has a last-minute settlement proposal, so the lawyers huddle. When the judge's clerk appears to ask if everyone is ready, the lawyers ask for a few minutes to talk. Now what?

It may surprise you to know that many cases scheduled for trial settle the day of trial. This is usually because after doing all the pretrial preparations, you or your spouse decide that a less-than-desirable settlement may still be better than the uncertainty of what the judge could order. Your lawyer comes to you with the other side's proposal. The offer is good only if you agree not to go to trial. If the trial starts, all bets are off. What should you do?

Remember that it's always best to negotiate whatever you possibly can. You may not get exactly what you want, but at least you'll maintain some control over the issue instead of allowing a third party complete control. You should also consider the value of settlement to your long-term relationship with your spouse, particularly if you have children.

In the best-case scenario, you spent much of the week before trial clarifying your bottom-line position. You can now evaluate the proposal with that bottom line in mind. If you don't have a bottom line in mind, you'll need to huddle with your lawyer to review the proposal. If it's reasonable, you should probably accept it or make a reasonable counterproposal. A settlement, even on the courthouse steps, is usually better than letting a judge decide.

Trial Attire

If possible, wear a suit. If you don't have a suit, wear formal clothing, not jeans and a T-shirt. If you are worried about not having proper attire, consult with your lawyer or her paralegal about what is appropriate. Wear comfortable clothes because you'll be in an uncomfortable setting all day long. And remember, a judge can see your legs and feet under the counsel table, so be sure your socks match, and sit appropriately if you wear a skirt.

Who Should Come to Court?

Do not bring children to the trial. Judges do not let children testify and won't let them listen to the trial unless they're adults. If the judge wants input from the children, he will talk with them on a day other than the day of your divorce trial. Find a babysitter and leave your children at home.

Limit your entourage. Don't bring your new love interest unless that person is going to testify. If she is, have her there only for testimony. Usually judges won't allow witnesses to sit in a courtroom until after they've testified. Keep that in mind when you ask people to come to your trial. If you want your best friend to be there for moral support, remember that he can be in the courtroom only if he isn't going to testify or has already done so. Think about how much of your personal life you want to share, even with your best friend.

Judges Rely on Their Eyes and Ears

Judges notice what people wear and how they behave, and they draw conclusions from these observations. A rich woman who comes to court casually dressed in a cashmere sweater and Gucci loafers sends a message that she does not take court seriously. A spouse who stares angrily at the other spouse throughout the proceedings will give the judge information about the relationship.

FACT

Most courts prohibit food and beverages in the courtroom, but they will provide water at your table. Do not bring soda or munchies, and absolutely do not chew gum. Judges are truly offended by gum and feel it is a sign of disrespect. The last thing you want is for the judge to think you are disrespecting his court.

Judges notice who makes the trial take longer, who is angry, and who is unreasonable. While they don't consciously punish these people, decisions on close issues may be influenced by their frustration with them. Although judges are supposed to be unbiased, they are human, and all humans get frustrated with unreasonable behavior.

The Trial Begins

Let's assume the last-ditch settlement effort failed, and the trial is about to begin. Most civil cases begin with opening statements from the lawyers.

Opening Statements

Sometimes lawyers will waive their right to present an opening statement as a means to save time. However, opening statements are a good idea because they make each side state its perception of issues. They also help frame important issues for the judge and focus her attention on what is important to you.

Trial Paperwork

You, your lawyer, and your lawyer's staff have prepared a mountain of documents for the trial.

These documents will include most of the following:

1. Exhibits. There should be three copies of each: one for the court to mark into evidence and one for each lawyer.
2. A trial notebook prepared by your lawyer. At a minimum, it should contain an outline for the presentation of your case, including a topical outline of what needs to be covered, the order of witnesses to be called, and the order of exhibits to be admitted and by which witnesses. It should also include testimony outlines for your witnesses and how each contested exhibit will be admitted. The notebook will also include strategy reminders and topics or questions to ask the other side's witnesses.
3. Proposed findings to submit to the judge at the close of testimony. In some jurisdictions, courts allow lawyers to submit proposed findings at the end of trial. It's really your final argument to the judge put into the form of the judgment and decree.
4. Memorandum of law. A memorandum of law is a written document that sets forth the law on a particular topic and applies the law to the facts in your case.
5. Closing statement. Some jurisdictions will allow lawyers to submit a written closing rather than give an oral statement at the end of trial. This can be beneficial because it allows lawyers the time to review the testimony and evidence submitted at trial and concisely present a closing argument that will help persuade the judge to find in your favor.

Procedure and Evidence Rules

You hired a lawyer in part to navigate your divorce through the legal process. Your lawyer knows the procedure and evidence rules—he'd better, because it's a given you don't know them. Focus on the content of the testimony, and let your lawyer flex legal muscles on your behalf. That being said, if you are concerned that your lawyer is sitting at the table not paying attention to what's happening, speak up!

Procedure Rules

Procedure rules apply to how things are done in the legal process. For example, in a divorce, the plaintiff or petitioner presents her case first and the defendant or respondent goes second. There are the rules that govern how many days before trial you have to provide your witness list to the other party or exchange exhibits that are to be used at trial. They're kind of a cookbook on how to make a lawsuit.

Evidence Rules

Rules of evidence govern what evidence and testimony is allowed to be considered by the judge at trial. This issue provides a lot of confusion for most litigants because the rules of evidence are confusing, even for lawyers. For example, it may be hard to understand why a letter from your employer stating what you pay for the cost of your spouse's health insurance isn't enough to prove what you pay. After all, you got the letter from your employer. But the judge and your spouse don't know that for sure, having only your word to rely on. For this reason, you will have to subpoena someone from your job to come in and verify what you pay.

FACT

A counselor may not be able to testify about what your spouse said unless your spouse has given a release to provide the information. Otherwise, it may be considered privileged, like communications between a lawyer and client. Under some situations, a court can order a spouse to provide a release for a counselor to testify or face a negative outcome if he refuses.

The rules of evidence are designed to make sure the court is considering the most reliable evidence and testimony in making decisions. Because the rules of evidence differ from jurisdiction to jurisdiction, you will have to rely on your lawyer's expertise to understand why a particular piece of evidence or testimony is admissible or not.

Here are some examples of important rules of evidence:

1. **Hearsay rule.** This rule says you can't tell the judge what someone else has said unless that person is going to testify and unless you heard it yourself. So, you can tell the judge what your spouse said because she is a party to the divorce, will hear your testimony, and will be able to respond. But you can't tell the judge your marriage counselor said your spouse was behaving irrationally. If you want this information to come in, the marriage counselor will need to be a witness. There are numerous exceptions to the hearsay rule, which your lawyer will know and use at trial to get testimony and documents admitted.

2. **Relevancy rule.** All testimony and documents must be relevant to the proceedings at hand. For example, if you have already resolved custody, the court is not going to hear you testify about what a bad parent your spouse is just to make him look bad.

3. **Privileged communication.** You will not have to testify about information that you gave to someone if a privilege exists. Examples include conversations and some written exchanges between lawyer and client, doctor and patient, psychologist and patient, and drug counselor and patient. Be aware that just because a privilege exists, that doesn't mean that it can't be waived, either by your actions or your words. For example, if you tell your lawyer that you broke into your spouse's business and stole $1,000 from the register, your lawyer cannot tell anyone about this. However, if you told your best friend what you did, the fact that you also told your lawyer doesn't protect you.

4. **Self-incrimination.** A court cannot force you to testify about facts and circumstances that would result in your admission to a crime. Be aware that if you admit to your lawyer that you committed a crime, you cannot then get on the stand and say you didn't commit the crime; you can only say that you refuse to answer on the grounds that it could incriminate you. Your lawyer cannot knowingly allow you to lie to the court.

5. **Perjury.** The lawyer's code of professional conduct does not allow your lawyer to put you on the stand and allow you to lie. This means that you cannot tell your lawyer one version of the story and then get up on the stand and tell a completely opposite version in order to make yourself look better.

Testifying at Your Divorce Trial

Ordinarily the petitioner, or plaintiff, goes first. If your spouse is the petitioner, her lawyer may call you as the first witness. This is a tactic some lawyers use to unnerve the other side and perhaps get the person to say things he will regret. Be prepared for this possibility. Don't panic. Take deep breaths. And remember, your lawyer will give you a chance to expand on the answers you give during cross-examination.

Direct Examination

When it's your turn, your lawyer calls you to the witness stand. You swear to tell the truth and then sit down in the witness chair. Your lawyer starts the questioning, which is called direct examination. The first few questions will be preliminary: your name, address, age, and employer. These questions help you get adjusted to testifying. After that your lawyer takes you through the outline you prepared together. You are on your own here, and your lawyer cannot tell you what to say. Don't look to her or anyone else in the courtroom for assistance in answering questions.

Be confident and self-assured and focus on the questions being asked. Do not make the mistake of feeling like you have to explain yourself or your choices. Answer only the question asked. If your lawyer feels like more information is needed, she will ask additional questions. If some facts don't make you look so good, you should be the one to introduce them, if possible. You know your spouse will if you don't. If you can bring up the bad news first, you can give your perspective and potentially soften its impact. Don't try to alter the facts to make yourself look better because your spouse's lawyer will pick up on this and make you look like a liar when he gets the chance to cross-examine you.

Cross-Examination

When your lawyer finishes her questions, your spouse's lawyer will conduct cross-examination. Your spouse's lawyer will try to ask questions that can be answered only "yes" or "no." Try to answer the questions in this way and do not give additional information. In trying to explain, you might give your spouse's lawyer additional ammunition to make you look bad. Also, if you try and explain your answers, the lawyer probably will say, "This question calls for a yes or no answer." Sometimes a judge will let you explain, but if she doesn't, don't get upset. Your lawyer will give you a chance during redirect examination. If your children are represented by a lawyer, he will also get a chance to ask you questions about the testimony you provided on direct examination.

Redirect Examination and Re-cross-examination

After cross-examination, your lawyer will get another chance to ask you questions about what you testified to on cross-examination. This is called redirect examination. Your lawyer will use this time to clarify information and try to reframe negative information in a more positive way. After redirect, your spouse's lawyer will get a chance to re-cross or ask you questions about the testimony you provide on redirect.

Rules for the Courtroom

There are some helpful guidelines for how to conduct yourself when you give or listen to testimony.

Rules for Testifying

If you can follow these rules when you testify, you'll do a better job.

1. Listen to the question, then answer it. Don't volunteer additional information. Answer the question asked. Don't begin an answer about your behavior with, "My spouse . . . "
2. Pause before answering questions to give your lawyer time to object. If two people talk at the same time, it's a nightmare for a court reporter or a tape recorder to sort out who's talking.
3. Look at the judge when you speak. This is the person you want to hear you.
4. Don't try to match wits with your spouse's lawyer. She has been doing this for a long time, or at least longer than you have. This is her turf. You may win a skirmish but lose the war with smart retorts. You will also

appear confrontational to the judge, which will not help him form a positive opinion about you.

5. Don't argue with the attorneys or the judge—especially not the judge.
6. If you need a break, ask for it.
7. If you have children, always refer to them as "our" children, never "my" children.
8. Maintain your composure. It's acceptable to show emotion as you discuss upsetting or frightening events, but keep it in check.

Testifying in court is scary and stressful. It's important to remember you're trying to give information to help the judge decide contested issues. The judge doesn't have to like you, but he does need to understand the facts of what happened. Keep in mind that he really isn't interested in your spouse's small failings unless they resulted in the health department or social services getting involved. Tell the judge what he needs to know, then stop.

When the Other Side Testifies

Have a pad of paper and pen ready. If the witness says something you disagree with, make a note. Don't elbow your lawyer or whisper in her ear, because this will distract her from following the testimony. Don't roll your eyes, flail your arms, breathe heavily, make comments under your breath, or proclaim that your spouse is lying. Let your lawyer do her job.

ALERT!

The judge will watch you while your spouse testifies. Remember that the judge pays attention to nonverbal as well as verbal communication. Try to let your reactions be genuine. Don't make faces. Don't make comments, and don't shoot your spouse evil looks from across the room.

When your spouse's lawyer finishes examining the witness, you and your lawyer can confer briefly before your lawyer begins cross-examination. This is the time to have your lawyer review your notes on issues on which you and your spouse may have very different perceptions of certain events of your marriage.

Where Does Time Go?

A typical court day runs from 9:00 A.M. to noon, with a fifteen-minute morning break. Courts typically resume at 2 P.M. and run until 4:30 P.M., with a fifteen-minute afternoon break. Judges may have other cases scheduled for conferences or motions that may take longer than scheduled and run into your trial time. What's more, those fifteen-minute breaks can stretch into thirty minutes or more. If the judge has an obligation after work, he may want to stop promptly at 4:30 P.M. If you're lucky, you'll have four hours of actual trial time during a court day. Of course, you'll pay for at least eight hours of attorney time!

Suppose your case is set for a two-day trial. You start late on the first day and are about sixty percent of the way through the case by the end of the second day. The judge doesn't have time to hear the rest of the testimony the following day, plus your attorney has another trial starting then. So the judge and the lawyers confer and agree to finish the trial about sixty days from now. At this rate, it may take several months to complete your trial.

After all the testimony is in, the judge has ninety days in most jurisdictions to issue a decision. Attorneys often ask for the opportunity to submit written final arguments and a proposed judgment and decree. They usually get another couple of weeks to do that. The judge's ninety days doesn't kick in until all papers have been submitted. As you can see, it's going to take some time before you actually have a ruling from the court.

CHAPTER 15

The Judge Rules

The trial is over. The attorneys have submitted all arguments and the judge is considering the case. When will the judge decide, and what will you do with the decision once you get it? Is your life about to be turned upside down or will justice prevail? Chances are the judge's decision will fall somewhere in between. Whatever the outcome, you'll need to review the decision with your lawyer to determine your next move. Hopefully, you're almost finished and ready to embark on your new life.

Can You Hurry a Judge?

A judge has a specific time period in which to issue a decision. This usually is ninety days from the date of the last submission, although it may vary from jurisdiction to jurisdiction. Some judges get decisions out quickly, while some take months to issue decisions. Some don't do their work on time. The wait can be nerve-wracking, but unfortunately there is nothing you can do to make the judge move faster.

Some actions may slow the judge's decision. The temporary orders in effect when you went to trial remain until they're changed by another order. However, sometimes it's necessary to get an order changed while you're waiting for a judge's decision if, for example, you lose your job or your spouse gets one. The new circumstances require a motion, complete with paperwork such as affidavits and exhibits.

FACT

You now have time to reflect on your trial. You and your lawyer may sit down and review what went well and what went poorly. You can make a settlement proposal to the other side, even at this late stage of the process. The certainty of a final resolution outside of court may appeal to your spouse as well.

If you bring a motion after trial but before a final decision, you can expect a further delay in the final decree. The judge first will have to rule on the motion. If the motion's substance changes facts presented at trial, the judge will probably treat it as a new submission, which may extend the time it takes for her to issue a new decision.

Finally, the Judge's Decision

Your lawyer may call to tell you about the decision, or he may just mail it to you. Read the decision carefully, then read it again. Write down your questions and concerns, and then schedule a meeting with your lawyer. You should meet within a week of getting the decision because there are time limits on challenging it, often thirty days from receipt of the order. The judge's decision will usually be in three parts: the findings of fact, the conclusions of law, and the order.

Findings of Fact

In findings of fact, a judge makes decisions about facts contested at a trial. These findings reflect which party the judge found credible, which witnesses the judge believed and what evidence the judge relied on in making her decision. Sometimes when two competing experts present evidence, a judge will rely on the evidence she understands better. When witnesses present very different values for something, such as a business, a judge is likely to select a value somewhere in between. If you and your spouse do a lot of mudslinging and foster care isn't an option for your children, a judge will have to decide which of you is the lesser evil, and she will make findings to support that choice.

Conclusions of Law

From the findings, a judge will draw legal conclusions. A legal conclusion would be something like this: "From the findings about the parties as parents, I conclude that it would be in the best interests of the children to live with their father." Or, like this: "From the facts presented at trial, I conclude the spouse has met her burden in proving the parties' home has a 30 percent nonmarital component." When a judge talks about meeting the burden, she is saying a person has provided enough evidence to support a claim.

The All-Important Order

Judge's orders are derived from the findings of fact and the conclusions of law. For example, say the judge finds that Dad is the one who provides stability and nurturing for the children. From this finding, the judge concludes it would be in the best interests of the children to live with their father. Considering the best interests of the children, the judge issues an order saying something like this: "Dad is granted (or awarded) sole physical custody of the children."

When the findings, conclusions, and order are stated separately, you can follow a judge's thinking pretty easily, even if you disagree with it. In some courts, a judge prepares a document called Findings of Fact, Conclusions of Law, Order for Judgment, and Judgment and Decree. In such a document, findings and conclusions are combined in one portion, and the order simply says "Let Judgment Be Entered Accordingly." This means you and your lawyer have to go through the findings to make sure the judge got the facts right, then review those same findings to ascertain the legal conclusions. This is pretty confusing, and it's why you hired that good divorce lawyer.

In some courts, after a judge makes a decision, she directs one of the lawyers to prepare the judgment and decree based on the judge's findings and conclusions. Both lawyers sign off on the document saying it's consistent with the judge's order, but this doesn't mean they agree with the decision. If the lawyers have to prepare the judgment and decree, this lengthens the process.

An Unwelcome Decision

Chances are you'll be unhappy with a judge's decision. In fact, some judges say they know they've done a good job when both sides are unhappy with a decision. What they're really saying is that mutual dissatisfaction reflects the impartiality of the decision.

On the Lookout for Mistakes

When you and your lawyer review the judge's decision, be on the lookout for certain things. Did the judge get the facts right? Did he make computation errors? Did he confuse the parties? Did the judge make enough findings to support his conclusions? Does he have a basis for facts he found after hearing contested evidence? Parts of the judge's decision may reflect the use of judicial discretion, where the judge interprets the evidence after considering words, documents, and behavior. Remember, what the judge sees in the courtroom influences his interpretation of the evidence.

Did the judge make a legal error? Here you'll have to rely on your lawyer. If the judge did make an error based on the law, does this mistake support a motion asking the judge to reconsider? Can the mistakes be corrected easily by conferring with the judge? That is, would the other side agree to these changes, too, because they're clearly the result of confusing the parties or making a computation error? Do the mistakes require going back to the trial judge before considering an appeal? Can you go back to the trial judge? Should you appeal?

Don't get an attitude if you find the judge has made a mistake. This doesn't mean you'll end up getting what you wanted. Mistakes can be corrected without changing the judge's decision. If the mistake is serious enough, your lawyer may have to appeal the decision to a higher court. Even then, it doesn't mean you will get what you wanted.

Conferring with the Judge

If a judge has made obvious factual errors, such as a mathematical error in computing child support or getting the parties mixed up, your lawyer and your spouse's lawyer can correct these by conferring with the judge. If the judge is willing, this can be done by conference call. If correcting these errors leads to an outcome the judge didn't intend, she may want to have a hearing about these errors, with arguments on what the outcome now should be.

If the judge believed your spouse instead of you, you'll have a hard time getting the judge to change her mind, even if you can correct certain factual errors in your favor. On top of that, appeals courts are very reluctant to reverse trial court judges' decisions when these decisions are, in effect, a judgment call (rather than a factual error) on the trial judge's part. This is that judicial discretion concept. Unless a trial judge was clearly wrong, an appeals court will affirm a trial judge who has had the advantage of seeing witnesses and determining their credibility.

You might consider making your spouse a new settlement offer, a better one than before trial but still preferable to the judge's decision. If the judge was skating on thin ice in the decision, your spouse may choose to settle rather than let the courts take another shot at both of you.

Here's an example. You might offer to pay your spouse a lump-sum payment instead of paying monthly alimony. Your spouse could invest the money and live on the income. The two of you wouldn't have to deal with each other every month and could move on with your lives. Plus, spousal maintenance wouldn't depend on your staying alive and employed.

Back to the Trial Judge

If you and your lawyer think the judge made mistakes that support an appeal, you probably should first ask the trial judge to take another look. This is called making a Motion for Reconsideration or a Motion for Amended Findings or a New Trial. Some states make such a motion a precondition for appeal. The appeal is based on denial of a new trial, assuming the judge denies the motion, and that's a pretty safe bet.

FACT

Judges hate to be reversed by appeals courts. Appeals court decisions are public, and all the lawyers and other judges can read them. Your judge will take your motion for amended findings seriously and may make corrections in response to your motion.

In a motion for reconsideration or amended findings, you'll raise the issues you would raise on appeal. You might argue the judge simply didn't make enough findings about your parenting skills to deny custody. Or you might argue the judge ignored some important evidence, but this is a little chancy because the judge might flat out say he didn't believe that testimony. Or you may cite other cases to show the judge applied the law incorrectly.

Should You Appeal?

After the judge rules on your motion, look at the whole picture to decide whether to appeal. If you got most of what you wanted from your motion, maybe you should pick up your marbles and go home, because appeals courts are unpredictable. Appeal only if the trial court missed a very big issue and your lawyer says you have a good chance to prevail. Otherwise, it's too expensive in time, money, and emotions to prolong your divorce by another year or so.

Rules of Appellate Procedure

The rules of appellate procedure give you a specific time limit to appeal a judgment. You'll need to decide fairly quickly whether to appeal because you'll need to accomplish a lot in the thirty to ninety days allotted. You need to order a trial transcript from the court reporter, which, if the trial was long, will take awhile for the court reporter to type up—and you're probably not the only case wanting one. Your lawyer needs to put exhibits into order and write an appellate brief. And you need to submit certain papers in a specific format dictated by your state's rules of appellate procedure. Different states have different time periods for "perfecting" an appeal. Perfecting is the term used to describe that point in time which the appellant has submitted all the necessary paperwork to the court.

While you should always consider negotiation, don't give in to issues you feel strongly about just to be done with it. Spending so much time in the courts may be a tactic your ex-spouse is using to wear you down. Maintain focus on your objectives and think through negotiations before signing on the dotted line.

If you're the appellant, you will prepare all your papers, submit them to the appellate court, and serve them on the other side. The other side, called the respondent, has a chance to respond. When all the paperwork (yours and the other side's) has been submitted to the appellate court, the clerk of that court will schedule oral argument. The lawyers then go to the court to make spoken arguments and answer the appellate judge's questions about their positions. You're permitted to attend oral argument, but you won't be permitted to say anything.

The appeals court will issue a decision within six months or so. While you're waiting to get on with your life, you again may consider making a settlement proposal. Negotiating a settlement is always an alternative.

Appeals Court Outcomes

There are three possible outcomes from an appeal. The appeals court may affirm the trial court's decision, which means that, unless you appeal to your highest state court, the trial court decision stands. It may affirm part of the decision and reverse another part, issuing its own decision where it reverses the trial court. If this happens, you can appeal to the highest appellate court of your state. Finally, the appeals court can reverse and remand (send back to court) all or part of the trial court's decision. When it remands a portion of the trial court's decision, it sends it back to the trial court for another hearing. It would be possible to have that hearing, get the trial court's decision, and appeal again. And again. And again.

ALERT!

The various levels of appellate courts have different rules regarding which cases they will hear on appeal. There are usually special rules that govern whether your case is eligible to be heard in the highest court in your state. Many divorces are not eligible. Your attorney will know the rules of your state and whether an appeal is possible.

When a case is appealed to the highest court, the issue presented is: Did the appeals court make a mistake? The high court can affirm the appeals court or reverse it. It also can send the case back to the trial court. In some states, the highest court can refuse to hear the case in certain situations. It probably would be possible to spend the rest of your adult life in the courts if you had enough money and nothing else to do.

Implementing the Final Order

At some point, the case will be over. However, even when the judgment and decree is final, work still needs to be done. Some decree provisions require you to do something to implement them. For example, if the court has awarded you the house, you'll need to get the title transferred into your name. To do this, you get a certified copy of the judgment and decree along with a Quit Claim Deed signed by your ex-spouse, and take both these documents to your county's clerk or registrar of titles of deeds where the title transfer is processed.

If you agreed to remove your ex-spouse's name from the mortgage and take over payments for mortgage, insurance, and taxes yourself, you'll have to refinance your home. To ensure this happens, you may be directed to hold your ex harmless should you not meet this responsibility. This means you'll reimburse your ex-spouse for any and all loss or harm you may have caused her because you didn't make the necessary payments.

ALERT!

Though you may breathe a huge sigh of relief once the divorce is final, it's probably at this time that you'll feel the effects of prolonged stress. Your muscles may ache, you may feel sick, or you may just want to crawl in bed and stay there for the next three years. Take care of yourself both physically and mentally, and these effects will soon subside.

Suppose you got the house and your spouse got a lien against it for a specific amount. That lien will be due and payable at some point, maybe when your youngest child turns eighteen or after a set number of years. When you pay off the lien, you'll want to get a Quit Claim Deed giving you the property free and clear. If you sell the property before paying off the lien, you will have to pay the lien from the proceeds of the sale. There may also be additional paperwork that you will need your ex to sign in order to transfer the property to your name, so be sure to check with your lawyer to make sure you get all the necessary documents. When you record your new deed, there will probably be fees that you have to pay to the clerk. You may want to call ahead to make sure you have all the paperwork and the necessary funds.

New Names and Titles

You'll need to transfer titles to cars, boats, trailers, or snowmobiles according to decree terms. Usually you and your spouse can simply sign off on the title documents and apply for new titles. If you changed your name, you'll need to change your Social Security registration as well as the name on all your accounts—bank, credit, and utility—and apply for a new driver's license.

Money Matters

If the decree divides retirement funds, your lawyer may need to draft a Qualified Domestic Relations Order for each account that is to be so divided. Each employer has different requirements for this order, so your lawyer will have to contact the company's legal department to get the appropriate form. Other retirement money may be divided by providing a certified copy of the judgment and decree.

Drafting DROs and QDROs requires specific expertise, so make sure your lawyer has experience drafting this kind of document. It is important for you to get everything from the retirement benefits the judge awarded. Once a DRO or QDRO is signed by the judge, it is difficult to change. In some cases, your attorney may recommend that a different attorney draft the DRO or QDRO in order to make sure it is correct.

The decree will order child support and spousal maintenance, if warranted. You may have had a support order in place while the divorce was pending. Perhaps you and your spouse had an informal arrangement to pay support that didn't involve the formal system.

If income withholding is in place when the decree is issued, you'll only need to give the new numbers to the employer or the child support enforcement agency that implements the withholding. If payments are being made directly and you want withholding, you'll have to make arrangements to get it set up. This usually requires an order from the court, so make sure you asked for this during the trial. Usually it takes several months between the request and the implementation. You'll need to pay the agency or your ex-spouse directly during that time.

Is It Really the End?

With any luck, you're now finished with the legal divorce. If you had to go to trial, you've invested several years, a lot of money, and your sweat and tears in the process. For some people, the divorce is only the beginning of years of litigation. Repeated requests to modify provisions of your decree, endless court appearances, and fighting with your ex can prolong the process. Unless you and your ex-spouse learn to resolve issues through negotiation, you may meet again in the halls of justice as your lives and circumstances change.

CHAPTER 16

Being Parents after a Divorce

Now that you're divorced, you need to develop your plan for being parents to your children until they're legally adults. This may be extremely difficult if you had a very contentious divorce, but try and put the past behind you and move forward in a positive way. Learn from your divorce and try to leave the battle-ground mentality behind—for the benefit of your children if nothing else.

Creating a Plan When You're Friends

The courts can serve as your backup only as long as the children are considered dependent under the law. Most state laws label children emancipated when they reach eighteen, marry, join the military, finish high school, or obtain full-time employment and become self-supporting. When one of these things happens, the courts lose jurisdiction over the children because the law considers them adults. However, a few states retain jurisdiction until the children reach age twenty-one, so you need to check your state's laws with your lawyer.

On Friendly Terms

Assume for a moment that you and your spouse are on reasonably friendly terms. You can talk to each other on the phone about the children, and you've been flexible, trading weekends to accommodate activities and special events. If you both show up for your son's baseball game, you can even sit together and cheer. This is terrific. Your ability to work together bodes well for the ongoing mental health of all members of the restructured family. This is the ideal relationship and one that all parents should strive to achieve and maintain.

ALERT!

All parents need to have a written parenting plan. Even when you and your spouse get along well and can operate under a flexible, reasonable, and liberal plan for visitation, you may disagree at times. When you do, a written parenting plan can serve as the tiebreaker, the fallback position to resolve the disagreement.

Be Realistic

As you design a parenting plan, you and your ex-spouse need to consider the practicalities of implementing it, not just for yourselves but for the children. For example, you may both philosophically agree that the children should spend as much time as possible with each of you, so you're considering taking the kids half of each week. But does this fit the needs and wishes of your children? And can you make this happen? How does it fit in with the reality of your work schedules? For example, if you plan to exchange the children on Wednesdays after school, this means you have to keep Wednesday afternoons clear for the foreseeable future. Can you? Nothing is more devastating for a child than to be left waiting at the school door while all his little friends hop on buses or bikes to go home.

What about weekends? To keep your division equal, you'll need to exchange the children on Saturday evening or Sunday morning. Religious, sports, or other commitments may make this awkward. In addition, this would mean neither of you would have a full weekend with the children. This may or may not be a problem, but you need to think about it.

Creating a Plan When You're Not Friends

Now assume you and your ex-spouse don't get along well—you're both still angry and find it hard to be civil to each other. But despite your animosity, you both want to create your own parenting plan, rather than let the judge decide. What can you do?

FACT

You can include the use of a parenting consultant in your divorce decree. You can give the person you choose authority to resolve parenting disputes between you and your ex. You will pay less than it would cost to go to court to settle your disputes about the children, and you can get your dispute resolved immediately.

You can enlist the help of a third person—a mediator or a parenting consultant—to help formulate your plan. You've already learned a bit about mediators, so if you use one be sure to pick a person who knows about children's needs as well as divorce laws. A parenting consultant is usually a mental health professional with experience working with divorcing parents. This person understands the developmental needs of children and the dynamics of relationships between parents who are still hurting and angry. A parenting consultant can propose a plan that you can review with your lawyer to make sure you're not creating legal pitfalls down the road.

Nonverbal Communication

In addition to having a parenting consultant available to resolve disputes, you can use a children's notebook, a book in which you communicate with each other about the children. You can tell the other parent what happened during the week, any illnesses that require medication, or any special concerns. You can, in effect, keep each other up to date about the children without meeting face-to-face or talking on the phone. A children's notebook works as long as both parents use it properly and not as another opportunity to take shots at each other. Remember, it's about the children.

Another way to discuss the children is through e-mail exchanges. E-mails can be exchanged regarding scheduling, issues that impact the children, concerns that come up, or any other information that needs to be exchanged. Many parents with high conflict relationships find that e-mail can be an effective way of managing their parenting relationship without having to actually see one another. It also allows each parent to maintain their own documentation regarding agreements on scheduling changes and other issues. Unlike a children's notebook, you have control of the documentation all the time and it cannot be lost in transit.

For a fee you can subscribe to a service that lets you do your scheduling and discuss the children online. One such service is *www.ourfamily wizard.com*. This service allows you access to a confidential website where you can set up schedules, communicate about changes in parenting time, and maintain a journal regarding your children.

Regardless of the nonverbal method you choose, your focus needs to be on the children. This is so easy to say but not so easy to accomplish. Sometimes it means you will have to give in to your ex and let her make the decision about whether your son will go to swimming lessons on Tuesday night or Thursday night. Other times it means you will have to ignore a sarcastic comment about how often you ask to change the schedule and re-focus the conversation on who will be picking up the children tonight. Nonverbal communication can help reduce negative interactions between you and your spouse, but ultimately it is going to be up to the two of you to limit the negativity.

Considerations for Angry Parents

Even though you're angry with your ex-spouse, you don't want your anger to harm your children. You must consider their needs first and take into account each child's age and developmental level. For example, if you want to minimize your ex-spouse's involvement with the children and maximize your own, ask yourself if this fits your children's needs. A father who has attended every football practice since your son started playing shouldn't now be denied because you're angry. If he was a good enough parent to come to every game for three years before you were divorced, he's probably a good enough parent to come now. If he stops coming because you verbally attack him every time you see him, your son is going to be the one who is really hurt.

FACT

Parental conflict—often with children in the middle—has the most harmful long-term effects on the children of divorce. Whenever possible, parents need to keep children out of their conflict. If this means you are never in the same room together, acknowledge it and just do it. Don't keep fighting about it.

If you and your ex-spouse are hostile, you also need to consider how you'll exchange your children. Exchanges and transportation are the most difficult issues to resolve between hostile parents. You should try to plan on making as many exchanges as possible in public places and avoid exchanges at each other's house. If you can, try making exchanges where you don't even see each other, such as pickups at school or day care, providing you pick up the children on time and don't get into arguments with teachers and care providers. If you are running late, be sure to call.

Nothing is more frightening to a child than to feel abandoned . . . again. You can also pick a public place such as a restaurant or convenience store. Both of you can stay in your cars and let the children get out and change vehicles. In your situation, it is best to minimize the number of exchanges each week, because the fewer opportunities you have to find fault with each other, the better.

Details, Details

Once you and your ex-spouse agree on a parenting plan, you'll need to look at the details. Details can consist of anything from exchange locations to who's going to provide transportation to who's going to be responsible for getting the children to their religious education classes. It's often in the details that parents run into conflicts. As a result, you should consider your parenting plan, reconsider your parenting plan, run it by your relatives and friends, and then consider it again. Accept the fact that regardless of how carefully you review it and address every possible problem, at some point you will find an overlooked detail that causes a conflict.

Exchanging the Kids

If you think exchanges are going to be a problem, you should be as detailed as possible in your parenting plan. That means you should state specifically how exchanges will be accomplished. If parents live near each other, many simply pick up their children from their ex-spouse, take them to their home for their scheduled time, and then bring them back. So long as this can be accomplished without angry words between the parents, this is by far the simplest arrangement. This has the additional advantage of making sure your children get to your home on time. You aren't stuck waiting and worrying when the children are late.

If you and your ex-spouse need to exchange the children without coming into contact with each other, your parenting plan should specify exactly where the transfer is going to take place and at what time. Include a provision that states how long you have to wait if the other parent fails to show up. For example, "the parents shall meet at Fast Food Palace at 6:00 P.M. every Friday to exchange the children." If the parent picking up the children for her parenting time is more than fifteen minutes late, that parent forfeits her parenting time until the next scheduled transfer of the children.

Exchanges can be a very emotional time for all involved, especially at first. But you must remember that you're the adult. The sooner you learn to accept the new situation, the easier it will be on your children. You should also remember that you are a model for your children and they will absolutely replicate your behavior!

Parents who have great difficult seeing each other sometimes use an exchange service. One parent delivers the children to this service thirty minutes before the other is to pick them up. Staff at the service care for the children until the other parent arrives. Using such a service means setting the exchange times during the agency's hours, and, of course, paying for the service, usually on a sliding fee scale based on your ability to pay.

In the most extreme cases of parental conflict, exchanges may have to occur at a local police station in order to make sure the children are not exposed to any angry or violent outbursts. Clearly, this is the worst-case scenario for the children and sends a strong message to them that one or both parents are out of control. If parental conflict is this high, you should really take a look at whether any additional steps should be taken to protect yourself and the children. Some steps might include obtaining an Order of Protection or restricting visitation to a supervised setting.

Importance of Being on Time

Being on time is a simple principle, but one that seems to pose significant challenges for some parents. What parents fail to remember sometimes is that the children are also impacted if a parent is late to a transfer. Children are left wondering if the parent will show up and may even blame themselves for the parent's tardiness.

Whether it's a result of a busy schedule or the desire to inconvenience the other parent by making him have to wait, timeliness is often the issue that brings people back to court. Think twice before you make a habit of disrupting transfer times. Judges hate to see parents back in court over this issue. If a judge finds that one parent is intentionally disrupting the schedule to get back at the other parent or is simply irresponsible in making transfer times a priority, the result could be a reduction in parenting time for the guilty parent. Parents should treat the parenting time transfer schedule like a job schedule. It's not something that can be altered on a whim. If you are late too often, there will be penalties.

FACT

Many children of divorce are left with the belief that one parent or the other doesn't want to spend time with them or that they have done something to make that parent angry. Although you may reassure your children that this is not the case, actions speak louder than words. A chronically late parent sends the message that the children are not important enough to make them a priority.

Distance Complicates Logistics

When you and your ex-spouse live far apart, logistics are tougher. Schedules have to be carefully planned. Weather can make travel difficult or impossible, and transportation costs are higher. To lessen these problems, some parents choose to meet halfway between their respective homes and exchange the children at a local restaurant so they have a comfortable place to wait. Other parents alternate making the round trip from one home to the other. This works well when the driver has family or friends near the other parents and can combine the exchange trip with a visit. If one parent does all the driving, the other may help pay for gas and maintenance on the vehicle that carries the kids. Sometimes, the visiting parent comes to the city where the custodial parent lives and stays with friends or relatives so the visit can take place on the children's home turf.

It's also important to remember that if you are the parent who voluntarily chose to move away from the children, a judge may decide that you are the one responsible for all transportation. The rationale here is that since you chose to make the move, you assumed the responsibility of arranging for contact with your children. Judges typically won't order custodial parents to assist with transportation or the cost of transportation if the noncustodial parent has chosen to move far away. You may want to think about the impact of distance before you choose to move, and make that move only when no other choice is available.

ALERT!

Experts agree that younger children should not spend long periods of time without seeing the other parent. If you have young children and want to do what's best for them, you may want to postpone a long-distance move (if at all possible) until they're a little older.

Dealing with Very Long Distances

What if you or your ex-spouse has moved to a different state? Here again, parents who can work together have more options than those who are dependent on a judge's decision because they can't get along. You may choose to split the year into school and nonschool segments, making one of you the primary parent during the school year and the other parent primary during school holidays. Then all you need to work out is how to get the children from one place to the other, how and when to have telephone contact, and who gets the children on which holidays. If you can negotiate a plan, you can figure out a way to make it work.

Parents need to keep in mind that it is very difficult for children to transition distances as they get older. Teenagers are not going to want to leave their friends for an entire summer to go visit a parent far away. A parent who is considering moving a great distance from the children should take this into consideration in making the choice.

Phoning Your Kids

Regular phone contact is very important to most parents, particularly if you are the noncustodial parent and only see your children every other weekend and one day during the week. It's also very important to most children, It provides them with the feeling that their absent parent is interested enough in their day-to-day lives to call and speak with them routinely. Phone calls offer children time to bond with the absent parent and increase their feelings of security.

Whatever method of contact you use with your children, try to keep conversations focused on their activities and interests. You sabotage communication when you use it to complain about the other parent or to lay guilt on the child for not spending more time with you.

Again, if the parents are civil to one another, they can usually agree to reasonable telephone contact without any limitations. Some can agree on some general parameters for calls, like between 8 A.M. and bedtime. Other parents need a specific schedule for calls, like Tuesday evening between 7 and 8 P.M. Still others require very specific parameters, such as limiting phone talk to one call of no more than fifteen minutes in length every Saturday to avoid abuse of phone calling privileges.

Abusing Telephone Calls

Sometimes a parent calls to badmouth the other parent or to tell the children how lonely she is. Sometimes one parent refuses to answer the phone at all or says the children can't come to the phone or are in bed. In more extreme cases, a parent will completely interfere with telephone contact in other creative and destructive ways. For example, an angry parent may record telephone conversations between the children and the other parent and then talk to the children about things that were said. Or, an angry parent will listen in on an extension phone and make nasty remarks to the other parent during the phone call or to the children after the phone call is concluded. These tactics are extremely detrimental to children and often result in them distrusting the guilty parent.

Other Alternatives for Contact

Today, alternatives to the telephone exist. E-mail makes frequent contact with your child possible and allows you to have private conversations with your child that aren't time dependent or intrusive. While it's not the same as hearing your child's voice, it's a good substitute. Also, with cell phones, you and your child can talk to each other when the other parent is somewhere else, giving you the opportunity for a private, pleasant exchange.

Surviving Holidays and Vacations

Holidays are supposed to be a pleasant time for families and friends to come together and celebrate religious or other traditions. For children, holidays are supposed to be magical and relaxed. Reasonable parents figure out ways to share holidays so children can develop traditions with both sides of their family. Unreasonable parents fight over birthdays and major holidays and make everyone dread what should be happily anticipated events.

Be Reasonable

Some parents alternate holidays, while others celebrate the same holidays with their children every year, either to develop traditions or to accommodate traditional family gatherings. If Christmas is a big event in your ex-spouse's family, you might agree to divide the winter school break so Christmas falls in his half every year. Then you and the kids can develop your own special event for your half of the school break. Kids don't object to celebrating a major holiday or birthday twice. It's the parents who have a hard time with this.

Sometimes a holiday may fall during the other parent's scheduled weekend. For example, your spouse might be scheduled for the first weekend in every month, which in September ends up being Labor Day. You're supposed to have the kids on that holiday, so what do you do? Reasonable parents switch weekends.

When drafting parenting plans, it's important to include language that states that holiday and vacation periods will supersede the regular scheduled parenting plan. By doing this you make sure you will get your scheduled holiday or vacation period even if it falls during the other parent's scheduled parenting time. You need to think about these schedules carefully in order to make sure everybody is getting what they need.

ALERT!

You can never be too careful or too detailed in drafting a parenting plan. While flexibility works well if you have a good relationship with your spouse, it will not work well if you do not. Sometimes it is worth sacrificing flexibility for predictability in your parenting plan in order to guarantee that you will have specific holiday and vacation periods with your children.

In planning holiday and vacation periods, you will want to consider how they fall with respect to the regular parenting time schedule. For example, let's say you have parenting time every weekend from Friday to Monday and you tack your ten-day vacation period on to the end of your regularly scheduled parenting time. Now the other parent doesn't get to see the children for a fourteen-day period. This may work out well for you, but does it work well for the children? Consider the opposite result. Let's say the other parent has parenting time every Monday through Friday and he tacks his ten-day vacation period on to the end of his regularly scheduled parenting time. Now you are the one who doesn't get to see the children for a fifteen-day period. If this is the result that works best for you and your family, that's fine. Just make sure when you make the deal, you understand what it means and how your parenting time will be impacted.

Cozy, But Not Too Cozy

Some restructured families get along well enough to celebrate holidays together. This is great because the children get to have a pleasant holiday with both parents present. If no disputes erupt and everyone focuses on the event, the strategy can be a pleasant experience for everyone. But beware of giving your children false hopes about your family reuniting.

New Family Members

As you move on with your life, it's possible you'll develop a new relationship, even remarry. You'll want to use good judgment in introducing your new love to your children. For one thing, you want to be sure this relationship is likely to be permanent before encouraging your children to get to know and love the new person. There is no need or benefit to the children to introduce them to every boyfriend you may have. It will be very hard for children to become attached to this new person, only to have him disappear.

FACT

Children never give up hope that their parents will get back together. When you share an activity with your ex-spouse and the children, be careful to avoid fueling that fantasy. Particularly if you have a new relationship, children may be confused and angry. They may feel the new person is an intruder who is ruining the chances of their parents reuniting.

It's probably not a surprise that a new relationship can change an amicable relationship with your ex-spouse. Maybe the ex still had thoughts about getting back together and now has to accept that this won't happen. Maybe the ex-spouse sees your new love as trying to take his place with the children. Whatever the reasons, your ability to cooperate may evaporate.

This is one reason it's so important to have a written parenting plan to enforce when you need it. With any luck, your ex-spouse will adapt, and you can go back to a reasonable and liberal parenting time. If not, at least you have a written schedule and can stay out of court.

Some Final Thoughts

When parents amicably negotiate a parenting arrangement, they can put together a plan that works. They can take into account distances, work schedules, family traditions, special activities, children's preferences, and everyone's needs. They can build flexibility into their plan and agree to make changes as their lives change and as their children's needs and interests change.

As children get older, they tend to get very busy with school, activities, and friends. In fact, teenagers often aren't very interested in spending time with their parents, particularly if they are always arguing over transfers and parenting time.

As things change, reasonable parents work with the realities of their lives and their children's lives. On the other hand, an angry parent has a much harder time focusing on reality and on her children. All she wants to do is hurt the other parent, regardless of what that may do to the children. She takes custody issues to court over and over again because she and the other parent can't cooperate in developing a parenting plan. She is constantly messing around with child support and spousal maintenance to try to cause an economic crisis. Often, she isn't really interested in rearing her children anyway. She just wants to make life miserable for her ex-spouse.

Try to put this whole parenting thing into perspective. Your children will be grown and on their own before you know it. The years that fall within the court's jurisdiction are a small percentage of your years as a parent. After they are grown there will be engagements, weddings, baby showers, grandparenting, and a whole host of other events that can be joyful times for families. You can lay a positive foundation for many years of enjoying your children and grandchildren after they become adults. The choice is yours. One fact is certain, though. As your children become adults, it is now their choice when and how much to include you in their lives.

CHAPTER 17

Special Considerations in Divorce Actions

While many divorce actions result because couples just can't get along, have grown in different directions, or found new partners, others are a product of much more grave issues. If domestic violence, child abuse, physical disability, mental health disability, or substance abuse is a factor in your divorce, be sure to read this chapter. Whether any of them is a direct cause of your divorce or just one problem among many, you and your lawyer need to closely evaluate these special considerations as you navigate a divorce.

What Is Domestic Violence?

Domestic violence is a pattern of abusive behavior used by the batterer for the purposes of maintaining power and control over the victim. According to the National Coalition Against Domestic Violence, an estimated 1.3 million women are victims of physical assault by an intimate partner each year, and the majority (85 percent) of family violence victims are female. Domestic violence can take many forms, including verbal, emotional, physical, sexual, and economic abuse and stalking.

Power imbalances in a relationship can sometimes lead to psychological abuse. One spouse belittles the other, and the abusive spouse may even try to limit the victim's contact with others. As a result, the victim begins to believe the criticism. Her sense of self diminishes, and the abuser's ability to control her grows.

Some examples of abusive behavior include the following:

- Constant criticism of appearance or skills
- Name calling or other demeaning statements
- Displays of extreme jealousy
- Threats to harm you or people and things that you care about
- Controlling where you go and who you see all the time
- Preventing you from working or going to school
- Denying you access to medication or health care
- Denying you access to funds, credit cards, and financial resources
- Destroying your personal property
- Physically hurting you
- Using physical force to intimidate you
- Using your children to try to control your behavior
- Forcing you to have sex
- Following you to and from your home or job
- Showering you with unwanted and unsolicited gifts
- Calling, e-mailing, or texting you repeatedly

This list is not meant to be comprehensive and only provides some examples of abusive behavior and stalking. If you are being treated in a way you feel is abusive, it probably is.

Although many victims may have similar experiences of domestic violence, each victim's abuse can be dramatically different. Typically, abuse escalates over time and increases in duration and intensity. Abusive behavior may be random and unpredictable or it may be present all the time. Sometimes an abuser may not have been physically violent but may try to maintain total control over a victim, deciding who you see, where you go, if you can work, what you buy, and if you are allowed access to family funds. Control is maintained by threats or intimidation.

Some victims may experience a cyclic pattern of abuse. It can take weeks or months to go through the cycle. An abuser may be kind and loving for a time, but anger begins to escalate. This usually ends with some critical event—perhaps a physical or sexual assault on the victim. It is followed by apologies and promises to change, and the cycle begins again.

In many cases, there is no cycle at all. While victims' experiences and batterers' behavior may differ from case to case, if your spouse is engaging in behaviors that are designed to maintain power and control over you, then you are a victim of domestic violence.

QUESTION?

If I look for information on the Internet, will my abuser know?
It is quite possible that your abuser can track your movements on your computer. Even if you think you have erased your tracks, there may still be hidden files on your computer that will show where you have been. Use a computer at a friend's or the local library if you are afraid of being caught by your abuser.

To find out where to get help in your state, contact the National Domestic Violence Hotline at 1-800-799-SAFE (7233) twenty-four hours a day, seven days a week. Most states also have a domestic violence hotline that can refer you to local services. That number can usually be found in the phone book, on the Internet, or by calling information. If you are afraid for your safety or the safety of your children, find out how to get help. If you are speaking to a lawyer, ask him what steps you can take to protect yourself.

New Attitudes Toward Victims

For many years, domestic violence victims stayed in abusive relationships because they believed they had no other choice. The typical victim was an unemployed woman with minimal job skills and no ability to support herself and her children. She had no safe place to go. She knew cries for help were likely to be dismissed by others: "You must have done something to make him mad" or "It's your duty to abide by your marriage vows."

She knew if she tried to leave, her husband (her abuser) would track her down and would probably beat her badly as punishment. She lived a terrible life of fear and pain, never knowing what might trigger an outburst. Sometimes the only reason a victim would seek help was to protect her children from the violence.

Today, laws provide protection to domestic violence victims. The laws of all states permit victims to get restraining orders either through a criminal or family court proceeding. The rules about how to obtain a restraining order differ from jurisdiction to jurisdiction. You will need to check with your local court regarding the options available in your state.

FACT

Many protection orders issued in domestic violence cases are good for only one year. If the abuser continues to threaten harm or violates the terms of the order, it can be extended. Depending on the facts of your case, you may be able to get the court to issue a longer order. Check with your attorney or the district attorney to see if your case qualifies.

In many states, a restraining order can also include an award of custody, child support, or spousal maintenance for the victim, helping the victim and the children to survive financially. The abuser can be ordered to stay out of the family home, giving the victim and the children a safe place to live. Sometimes the abuser is ordered to stay away from the children's schools and to have no contact at all with the victim. The prohibited contact can include all forms of communication such as telephone calls, letters, and e-mails.

The Criminal Justice Response

In the last twenty years the criminal justice system has become more sophisticated in its understanding and treatment of domestic violence. Significant money and energy have gone into educating law enforcement and court personnel. The police no longer assume a woman struck by her husband must have done something to deserve it. Instead of walking him around the block to cool off, they arrest him.

In every jurisdiction around the country, laws are in place to protect victims of domestic violence who are harassed, threatened, or assaulted by their abusers. Batterers who are found guilty are placed on probation or receive jail time depending on the severity of the crime. Restraining orders are routinely issued to victims in order to offer them additional protection from further abuse.

If your spouse is arrested, you are probably going to want to know when he is released so you can take steps to protect yourself from retaliation. Many jurisdictions have a victim notification system that will call you when he is released. Ask the district attorney if this service exists in your area. Be aware that these systems sometimes fail, so don't rely on them completely.

Safety Planning

Think about safety and what you will do to protect yourself and your children, particularly as you move forward with a divorce. Safety planning means thinking about every possible scenario and what additional steps you need to take to stay safe. From how you get from your car to the front door of your house at night to what you would do if your spouse broke into your house, safety planning could save your life. While the thought of safety planning can be overwhelming and terrifying, there are people who can help. Your local domestic violence service agency will have advocates who have received special training in safety planning that can help you work out your own personalized safety plan.

While a restraining order is a good way to protect victims, it is only a piece of paper. Even after you obtain a restraining order, you should do safety planning just in case your spouse decides to violate the order. That way you will be prepared and know what to do just in case the worst happens.

Victim Service Providers

Support networks for domestic violence victims exist in all states. Shelter and safe homes are widely available and offer victims and their children a safe place to stay for weeks or even months while they look for housing and employment or wait for a court date to get a restraining order that will let them return to their home. Advocates trained in domestic abuse law; safety planning; and the practicalities of finding housing, child care, employment training, and the money to pay for them are accessible through most shelter programs. Advocates often accompany victims to the courthouse to help them fill out the necessary papers and attend hearings. In addition to safe shelter, many of these programs have nonresidential services that offer the same kinds of supportive services to victims who don't need shelter.

Divorce or Separation Can Be the Most Dangerous Time

Statistics show the most dangerous time for a domestic violence victim is when she's trying to get out of the abusive situation. This includes the time period following the issuance of a restraining order. The abuser's behavior can get very scary, violent, and even deadly. In the worst case scenario, the abuser decides, "If I can't have her, nobody can have her" and takes steps to isolate or kill her. Sometimes children end up in the middle of this violence.

In other cases, abusers may go to great lengths to try to gain an advantage in the divorce case. Some may think that if they can win custody and many of the assets, the victim will return home and they will be able to maintain their control. For example, if a divorce is filed, the abuser is likely to hide as much of the marital estate as he can and try to convince the kids their mother is to blame for the destruction of the family. This type of abusive father is especially likely to persuade teenage sons to side with him. Children, particularly boys, are easy targets because they have been raised in a setting where their mother is constantly demeaned and belittled. Having witnessed this kind of behavior from their father for a long time, they may now believe that it is acceptable for them to treat their mother the same way.

ALERT!

If your spouse is trying to manipulate or intimidate your children, try to get them into counseling immediately. A good mental health professional will probably be able to uncover what is happening, which will help you make your case for sole custody. It will also provide your children with some help in dealing with the situation.

Domestic Violence and Custody

You may think that a judge will automatically give you custody if you are a victim of domestic violence, but this is not always true. Abusive spouses often try to characterize domestic violence as an angry outburst or a one-time thing. Some deny it altogether and are often successful. Because it is often hard to prove, you may have trouble even getting the judge to believe your story. If your spouse has been arrested or there are witnesses or other evidence that supports your claim, it will be easier. But because domestic violence often happens behind closed doors, you may not have any evidence. Talk to your lawyer about a strategy for dealing with this situation. If you can prove that your spouse is an abuser, the judge will probably award you sole legal custody. Most judges understand that joint parenting is impossible when one parent abuses the other.

This is a very difficult part of the law, and you should try and find a lawyer who is familiar with domestic violence cases. Don't be afraid to ask that question when you are interviewing lawyers. Also, don't be afraid to ask your lawyer to tell you how he defines domestic violence. This may tell you a lot about the kind of lawyer you are hiring and whether he has the skills to represent you.

Dealing with Child Abuse and Neglect

Child abuse, like domestic violence, can come in many different shapes and sizes. Child abuse can be physical, sexual, and/or emotional. Most people think of a bruised or bloodied child when they think of child abuse. The reality is that abuse can occur in far more subtle ways, and the signs can be much more obscure. Child abusers can be very clever in hiding what they do to children, using manipulation, threats of violence, or other tactics to keep children from telling the truth.

Child Neglect

Child neglect usually occurs in three different ways: physical, education, and emotional. Examples of physical neglect include a parent's failure to provide food, clothing, or needed health care. Examples of educational neglect include failing to send children to school or causing them to be late all the time. Examples of emotional neglect include repeatedly belittling a child's self-worth or isolating the child.

If you think one of your children is the victim of child abuse or neglect, get help. To find out where to get help in your state, you can contact the National Child Abuse Hotline at 1-800-4-A-Child (1-800-422-4453). You can also contact your local child protection agency. This agency will usually do an investigation of any allegation of abuse or neglect it receives. If the agency finds evidence of abuse or neglect, it will take whatever steps it deems necessary to protect the child.

If you have reason to believe that your spouse is abusing one of your children, talk to a lawyer immediately or call a child abuse hotline. Your failure to take steps to protect your children from abuse or neglect could make you just as guilty as the actual abuser. You may not be charged criminally, but your children could be removed from your care and you may not get them back if they were severely abused.

False Allegations of Child Abuse During Contested Divorce Proceedings

In some divorce and custody cases, one parent will make false allegations of physical or sexual abuse against the other parent. This usually plays out in a couple of different ways. One scenario is that the mother accuses the father of sexually abusing the children. Another scenario is that the father accuses the mother's boyfriend, an older male child from another relationship, or another male family member of physically or sexually abusing the child. Whatever the situation, false allegations of this kind can tear families and children apart. If you truly believe your spouse or someone associated with your spouse is harming your children, you have a duty to act. Just be sure you are acting out of concern for your children and not as a way to get a leg up in your divorce.

If you are a parent who is wrongfully accused of abuse, do not discuss this issue with anyone but your lawyer. Follow his advice closely because you risk losing your children if the allegations are found to be true. The problem with allegations of this kind, especially with small children, is that there is not usually much evidence to support a finding one way or another. It may be hard to prove your innocence.

Physical Disability and Divorce

Individuals who have physical disabilities can face unique challenges in a divorce proceeding. If you become disabled during your marriage, this may have placed strain on the marriage that has now resulted in your spouse wanting a divorce. If this is the case, try to focus on obtaining the best possible financial settlement. Your spouse has an obligation to pay for your support—maybe not indefinitely, but at least for a time. Physical disability is one factor that can be used to support a claim for receiving more alimony or a larger distribution of the marital estate. While you may feel uncomfortable relying on your disability to support such a claim, don't. If you are physically disabled, you need to take care of yourself. If your spouse is still able to work, he can start over on his own; you may not be able to.

If you are a parent who has become disabled during the marriage, your spouse may try to suggest that you are incapable of providing care for the children. Don't think for a second that a physical disability makes you unfit to take care of children. Before bending to his will, think about what steps you can take to make the situation workable for you. For example, let's say your spouse worked while you stayed home with the children. You were able to provide for their care with the help of a part-time housekeeper who prepared meals because you were not able to. Now that you're divorcing, your spouse claims you can't feed the children on your own. While that may be true, you can still ask for enough child or spousal support to be able to hire a part-time housekeeper to help you. You may also be able to resolve the problem by hiring a business that prepares the meals for you and only requires you to throw the food in the oven. Be creative in figuring out how to deal with your physical disability and parent your children.

Mental Health Disability and Divorce

Managing mental health issues can be challenging enough under everyday stresses, but adding a divorce into the mix can be disastrous. If you are living with mental health issues, speak to your mental health provider about how the emotional strain of a divorce may impact your condition. There may be steps you can take or supportive services you can use that will provide you additional help in managing your condition. If you think you're headed for a divorce, make sure you're in compliance with your doctor's treatment recommendations. Once you get to court, missed appointments or unfilled prescriptions may become an issue.

There are many laws that protect people with mental health conditions from discrimination. Your lawyer should know if these laws are applicable in your case. Sometimes the judge will appoint a special lawyer, typically called a guardian *ad litem*, to make sure your mental health issues aren't used against you to gain an unfair advantage in court. This person has specialized knowledge regarding disabilities. Her role is to make sure that decisions regarding your financial and personal interests are made in good faith and in your best interests. You will still have your own lawyer, but you will also have a guardian *ad litem* to make sure you are treated fairly.

Custody and Mental Health

Just because you have a mental health condition doesn't mean you can't be successful in fighting for your children. While it may be terrifying to think that your entire mental health history is going to be displayed in open court for all to see, the end result may be worth it. If you have a mental health condition, it is quite likely that your spouse is going to bring it up during the divorce. While your spouse may have once been sensitive to your condition and understanding of the struggles you face, his lawyers may depict you as a crazy person who can't be left alone with your children. Careful planning with your lawyer will be necessary to effectively address these concerns.

The judge may want you to sign over your mental health records or even undergo a new mental health evaluation. While this is very invasive, it is probably the only way to overcome allegations that your mental health status impacts your ability to parent. Sometimes the judge will order a forensic evaluation, which will include both spouses and the children. This will typically be conducted by a psychologist. As part of this evaluation, the evaluator will review your mental health records, treatment history, and progress. The evaluator is also likely to call your treatment providers to speak with them about your progress, abilities, and limitations. She will meet with you personally and may conduct some written testing of her own to further assess both you and your spouse. After thoroughly analyzing your situation, the evaluator will submit a report to the court that may include recommendations about custody. This type of evaluation is common in many custody proceedings, not just in cases where someone's mental health status is questioned.

If your mental health condition is going to impact your ability to parent once divorced, be realistic and reasonable. Ask for parenting time that will allow you to spend quality time with your children while giving you the time you need to manage your mental health. A judge will appreciate the fact that you know your limitations and are able to balance your mental health condition and your parenting responsibilities. Be careful here because how you present yourself will definitely impact your success. Your lawyer should be able to help you develop a winning strategy.

ALERT!

While you may have to sign releases for your spouse or the court to get certain records, always consult with your lawyer before agreeing to release any records. A privilege may exist that allows you to object. Before exercising this privilege, you want to make sure that you are not going to negatively impact your case.

If you don't think you can do it on your own, put supports into place that will allow you to be able to spend as much time with your children as possible. For example, ask a family member or friend to help out during your parenting time. Try to build a better relationship with your ex if possible so the two of you can work together to accommodate your limitations. Children need to be with both parents. You don't have to let your mental health condition dictate your relationship with your children.

Substance Abuse and Divorce

Anyone experiencing a substance abuse problem should consider treatment. Be it alcohol, prescription drugs, or illegal drugs, the long terms effects of substance abuse are devastating. If you are actively using while you are going through a divorce proceeding, it will be especially important for you to seek help. This can be a time of severe emotional distress and depression that can trigger increased abuse.

Talk to Your Lawyer

You may think that hiding your substance abuse problem from your lawyer and the court is a good strategy. It is not. Your spouse probably knows about your problem and may have anticipated your denial. Your spouse may have spent time gathering evidence against you prior to filing for divorce and now will be using it to prove that you are not only an addict but that you are also a liar. Consult with your lawyer about the best strategy to deal with this issue. If you don't want to admit your problem even to your lawyer, ask him a hypothetical question using your situation as the basis. Listen carefully to his answer and follow his advice.

Custody and Substance Abuse

If you are actively using or very recently clean and sober, you may not be successful in obtaining custody of your children. Judges have grave concerns about awarding custody or parenting time to a person who is or was recently abusing drugs or alcohol. Instead, they will order supervised visitation to make sure you are clean and sober when you are in contact with the children. Most judges like to see a period of clean time of six months to a year before they will consider awarding custody and lengthy periods of parenting time. This lets you take care of your addiction first before you make parenting your priority, which benefits both you and your children.

CHAPTER 18

Moving On

It's really over. Your divorce is final, and one way or another you have your judgment and decree. If you <u>negotiated </u>that decree, you can hit the ground running toward a new life. If you went to court and suffered through an appeal or two, you may be less ready to move on. But move on you must. Start over without the hostility of the past and you will find the future will be a much brighter place.

Tying Up Loose Financial Ends

Before you leave the system behind, you need to pay your lawyer. If you and your lawyer are still friends—yes, that's really possible—you don't want to jeopardize that friendship. After all, you'll have other legal matters to address, such as changing your will, setting up trust funds for your children, or drafting a prenuptial agreement the next time you get married. And, unfortunately, it's always possible divorce issues will erupt again. If you maintain a positive relationship with your lawyer, you can call upon him for new needs. You'll save time and money because this lawyer already knows a lot about you and your history.

The divorce decree may order your ex-spouse to pay part or all of your attorney fees, but if your spouse doesn't obey this order, you may have to go back to court to get a judgment against her for unpaid fees. However, the bottom line is you are responsible for the bill (recheck your retainer agreement to make sure). If your ex fails to pay, you'll have to pay first and then try to collect from your ex.

Resolve Issues Promptly

If you have issues with your lawyer, resolve them as soon as possible. The first step is to talk with him directly, so make an appointment to review whatever is troubling you—your file, your bill, his handling of certain issues. Don't hesitate to ask your lawyer hard questions, such as "Why didn't you raise the issue of my spouse's mental health history?" or "Why are these phone bills so high?"

FACT

If you still think your lawyer's fees are too high, you can go to fee arbitration. Your local bar association can tell you how to set it up. Usually a fee arbitration committee is made up of lawyers and nonlawyers who listen to each side and make a decision. Their decision is final, and you'll have to pay whatever fee the committee determines.

Making a Complaint

After you've discussed your concerns with your lawyer, you still may feel your lawyer didn't satisfactorily answer your questions. You may believe your lawyer's behavior was unethical, or you have discovered billing statement discrepancies. Maybe your lawyer can't account for funds that were to be held in his trust account during the divorce. Maybe your lawyer hasn't forwarded the property settlement to you—the check your ex says was sent to the lawyer weeks ago.

These are issues for the Lawyers Professional Responsibility Board. However, you should evaluate your concerns carefully before making a complaint to be certain it is valid. Dissatisfaction with trial results, a lawyer's inconsistent return of telephone calls, or insensitivity to your emotional response to the divorce are reasons to hire a different lawyer in the future, not reasons to make an ethical complaint. Many of the complaints made to the board come from divorce cases, but the board finds cause to go forward in very few of these complaints. Even so, unfounded complaints take up a lot of lawyer and board time, so be sure your complaint is legitimate. If it isn't, let go and move on. Realistically, the best time to evaluate your attorney's performance is before your case is finished. If you think there is a problem, address it with your lawyer promptly to avoid a bad outcome. If necessary, hire another lawyer before going to trial.

Other Litigation Expenses

If you hired any experts for your divorce, you probably have to pay bills for their time, too. There's the accountant, the home or business appraiser, the private custody expert, and any other expert who testified on your behalf. Making necessary arrangements to get these people paid is an important step in getting on with your life. The fewer reminders you have of the past, the easier it will be to look toward the future.

Talking to Your Children

Now that the divorce is over, you're ready to have a heart-to-heart talk with your children. With any luck, your own psyche is in pretty good shape, and you can tell the kids again that the divorce wasn't their fault. Tell them you love them—you can never do this too often. You can emphasize that your ex-spouse is a good person who loves them, too, and explain the parenting arrangement that has been worked out.

ALERT!

Never give papers from the divorce to your children to read or leave them out where the children can find them. Children have enough to deal with and they will not understand how their parents could say such terrible things about one another. Don't enmesh them in the adult details of a divorce.

If your kids are of appropriate maturity, ask them for input and help in making the schedule work. This doesn't mean you have to follow every request or suggestion they make. Children often feel they have to say what one parent or the other wants to hear after a divorce. They may tell you one thing and your ex another. That doesn't necessarily mean your ex is behind their change of heart. It could just mean your children are doing the best they can not to upset anyone.

Mending Fences with Your Ex

Let's assume you and your ex-spouse have no children and that, after dividing your assets, neither of you has an obligation to make monthly payments to the other, either as spousal maintenance or as part of your property settlement. If that describes your situation, you're in a good position to move on. You may be leaving the relationship on a friendly footing, or you still may be harboring bad feelings from the breakup and divorce experience. If you do want to clear the air, you can always go to a counselor who does exit counseling. Perhaps you can have a last supper together, reminisce about the good times, commiserate about the bad, and part on a friendly basis. Only you can decide whether it's important to mend fences.

On the other hand, if you have children, you'll have to deal with your ex until death—yours, his, or the kids'. Under these circumstances, at least you'll want to have a civil relationship with your children's other parent. Of course, counseling is always an option, but in your day-to-day interactions with your ex, you can do a number of things, and avoid doing others, to improve dealings between you. For example, if your ex has primary physical custody of the children, here are some do's and don'ts:

Recent literature suggests an apology often goes a long way toward healing past hurts. So, even if you believe it was all your ex's fault, you might consider saying you're sorry. You might also consider being the one to extend the olive branch even if you feel your ex is to blame for everything. Forgiveness and acceptance has to start somewhere.

1. Do pay any support on time and in full.
2. Don't send support checks with the children.
3. Do spend time with your children on a regular, consistent basis.
4. Do pick up and return the children on time. If you're going to be late, notify the other parent.
5. Do tell the other parent where you and the children will be if you're taking them on a trip. Write down an address and telephone number and the dates of the trip.
6. Don't say negative things to your ex-spouse when exchanging the children. Be respectful and pleasant.
7. Don't show up at your ex's home unannounced. Respect boundaries.
8. Don't say things to the children such as, "I can't take you to the movies because your mother has all my money."
9. Do work with your ex-spouse to pay for extras for your children like camp and music lessons. After all, these things benefit your children.
10. Do try to find housing near the children's primary residence to make commuting easier and to make it easier to be on time for picking up and returning the children.

If you have primary physical custody of the children, here are some do's and don'ts:

1. Don't have the children ask your ex-spouse for the child support.
2. Don't schedule activities for the children that interfere with their time with the other parent.
3. Do encourage the children to contact the other parent on a regular basis.
4. Do make sure the children are ready to leave when it's time for them to go with the other parent.
5. Don't threaten to prevent the children from seeing the other parent in an attempt to get your ex-spouse to do something such as paying for hockey or ballet lessons.
6. Don't refuse to let the other parent have visitation because he hasn't paid his child support. Children do not understand this tit for tat way of thinking. In any case, they shouldn't know that child support is past due.
7. Do give the other parent complete information about the children's school, doctor, dentist, orthodontist, and church.
8. Do share activity schedules so the other parent can attend games, practices, and recitals.
9. Do list the other parent on all school and medical records and church registrations.
10. Don't try to change your children's names.
11. Don't raise adult issues when exchanging the children. Be respectful and pleasant.
12. Don't try to move the children's home a long way away from the other parent. Long-distance parenting is hard on everyone.

These do's and don'ts address many of the issues that most often upset and make parents angry with each other.

ALERT!

A major factor in getting on with your life is getting along with your children's other parent. The parent who continues to relive old hurts and angers harms herself and the children. Ongoing anger drains your energy for no useful purpose. Getting back at your spouse may feel good in the short term, but it has long-term negative effects on the children.

Be aware of the sensitive spots and do your best not to pour salt into old wounds. Try to remember your ex-spouse is your children's other parent, a person you once loved. Try to remember conflict is the number one cause of problems for children of divorce. You're using negative energy when you stay angry and upset, and the children will feel it.

Building a New Nest

You're now ready to begin a new life, and the question becomes whether you want a new place to live. The answer is probably yes if you moved out of the house when you and your spouse separated. At that point you may not have thought very hard about housing. You may have hoped for reconciliation or award of the family home, so your current housing wasn't a big issue. But even if you're now living in the house you lived in during your marriage, you may be ready for a change for a variety of reasons. Now is the time to decide.

The Marital Home

If you were awarded the family home in the divorce, you were given a mixed blessing. The family home is often an affordable choice. The mortgage payment may be more manageable than comparable rental housing, and the children don't have to adjust to a new place and, possibly, a new school. On the down side, this home is where the marriage fell apart, and it may hold some unhappy memories. The home may need repairs and maintenance beyond your budget. You may be wise to sell the house and use the proceeds to start over in a place that is truly yours. However, bear in mind that you might not be able to replace the marital home with one of equal quality if you can't qualify for a big enough mortgage.

Distance Matters

If you decide to look for new housing, think about where the other parent is living and about the impact of distance on your shared parenting. Parenting is a full-time job, so if you can share this responsibility, both of your lives will be less stressful. Every parent needs time alone. Often the only time you get for yourself is when the children are with the other parent. If you live far from each other, the other parent may not be able to spend time with the children on a regular and frequent basis. When the commute time is less than half an hour, each parent can more easily meet his share of the parenting responsibility.

While you should look upon your new life as a great adventure and an opportunity to meet your goals and make your dreams come true, don't go overboard. Especially if you have children, there will always be something tying you to your former life. If you try to cut those ties, you'll likely regret it in the future.

You may also have to consult with your ex before moving the children out of their present school district. If you have joint or shared legal custody, you cannot unilaterally decide to move to another school district. You must obtain the other parent's consent. Also, if you move any distance away, even if it is in the same school district, you will be the one most likely providing transportation to accommodate the parenting time schedule.

Sharing Housing

When divorced parents have little money, they sometimes have to live with their parents or share housing with a friend. It's not uncommon for a parent with the children to move home with the folks some distance from where the family lived before the breakup. Now the visiting parent has both a long commute and a frosty reception from former in-laws when coming to see the kids—not a very inviting prospect. No good solution may present itself here, except to encourage telephone and e-mail contact in those long periods between visits. Even if you don't have primary responsibility for the children, you may be financially strapped after paying support and monthly debt obligations. You may not have enough money to rent a place of your own, so you, too, may have to move back home or share an apartment.

Whether you're the custodial parent or the visiting parent, it's important to find housing that enables the children to stay with you overnight. They need to have their own beds and some privacy. It's not a good idea to share sleeping quarters with them. Sleep on the couch or put a sleeping bag on the floor if you have to. Make sure your roommates know about and accept having children stay with you on a regular basis.

Living with a New Love

If your roommate is your new romantic relationship, you need to tread very carefully. Your children are adjusting to the divorce, and they may not be ready to accept a new person in your life. The last thing children usually want is to share the limited amount of time they get with their parent with a new love interest. You may need to ask your honey to be absent when the children are with you, at least for a while. It takes a special person to put children's needs first.

Get Back to the Future

You've found a place to live and have furnished it so it feels like yours. You've established a routine that includes work and the children. Now, what are you doing for yourself? On those evenings when the children aren't with you, do you go home, flip open a beer, turn on the TV, and vegetate until bedtime? Do you call your ex-spouse and leave nasty messages on her answering machine?

Following the pain of divorce, many people are eager for acceptance. Therefore, it is easy to "fall in love" with the first person who shows interest in you. Remember that you're on the rebound and emotionally fragile. It will be better for everyone concerned if you take your time and make sure to pick the right person with whom to start a new life.

It's normal to feel sad after a divorce. It's normal to be angry. It's even normal to feel sorry for yourself. For a while. Divorce is a lot like experiencing the death of a loved one. The loved one didn't die, but your feelings for them did. It's easy to keep the wound open by dwelling on the past.

Take Inventory

With time, you may even revise history to make yourself the undeserving victim. For instance, as you nurse your second or third beer, you feel more and more angry or sad, so you call your ex-spouse hoping to aggravate her, or maybe cry on her shoulder. Your ex, however, is out for the evening and Grandpa is watching the kids. How sad that you spent so much energy focusing on your ex-spouse when you were so far from her thoughts.

If you find yourself stuck in the past, it's time to take inventory. Who are you, and where are you going? What choices are open to you, and what are the consequences of these choices? If you can't do this yourself, consider working with a counselor or therapist to develop a plan for breaking free of the past and really starting that new life.

Testing the Waters

You're finally ready to think about life beyond the couch. The first step is to realize living alone is okay. This may be a totally new experience because you went from living at home with your parents to living in a dorm or an apartment with a roommate to living with your spouse. At first, life on your own may feel really strange; however, you can learn to luxuriate in time that is yours alone. Once you're adjusted to your single status, you're ready to look for new adventures.

Getting off the couch and getting involved in activities is good for your mind and your body. Active people generally have better health and a more positive outlook on life. When you feel good, you communicate positive things to others. Your children will notice, and so will people who could provide potential new relationships.

What if you've never taken time to develop hobbies or interests outside work and family? A whole new world is out there, waiting to be discovered. Most communities offer adult education classes in subjects ranging from drawing to French to woodworking. Many local school districts publish their offerings quarterly. Health clubs offer classes, too. Their offerings range from exercise programs like Jazzercise to competitive athletics such as tennis. Many religious organizations sponsor programs just for singles.

Taking such classes is a way to develop new interests and to meet new people. The choices are many, and the cost is usually modest. You just need to take advantage of the opportunities out there.

Involve Your Kids in New Interests

In addition to developing interests for yourself, you can look into new activities involving your children. Kids are a great excuse to do things you might be embarrassed to do on your own, like going to the zoo or watching a Disney movie. You and your children might learn a new skill together, like golfing or playing the piano. Competing with a parent is often an incentive for children, and, to your surprise, you may find yourself having fun, too. Participating in activities with the children helps avoid the sugar mommy syndrome, where visiting parents just take their kids out and spend money on them or give them stuff. Giving of yourself is much more meaningful than loading up your kids with material things.

A New Relationship?

If you began a new relationship before ending the marriage, your spouse probably didn't react well to being replaced. His anger and hurt may have increased the hostility level of your divorce. The relationship that triggered your leaving the marriage may or may not survive the divorce.

Take It Slowly

In any case, it might be wise to give yourself some time alone before re-entering that relationship or beginning another. A new relationship has its best chance for success if you're feeling okay with yourself. If you get involved with someone new to show your ex-spouse you're still desirable or to fill those empty evenings, you may discover you haven't traded up. Amazingly, people tend to select new spouses who are much like the original model. You may want to take some time to figure out just what you want in a new companion and what characteristics of Spouse Number One led to the marriage's end.

Again, Consider the Children

If you have children, you need to be candid with your new love about the importance of your children. If that person doesn't have children, chances are she will want some of her own. Do you have the energy and financial ability to support a second family? Under the law, obligations to your first family take precedence over any new obligations you take on.

While you should look upon your new life as a great adventure and an opportunity to meet your goals and make your dreams come true, don't go overboard. Especially if you have children, there will always be something tying you to your former life. If you try to cut those ties, you'll likely regret it in the future.

If your new love interest does have children, how they will fit into the equation? You'll need to introduce your children to a new person in your life and a whole new set of siblings. If your children see your love as having caused the divorce, they may be pretty hostile. Even if you stay single for a while, they may resent the new love taking your time and attention away from them, so be sure to focus your energy on making the children feel safe and loved.

Second Marriages

If you remarry, continue to be sensitive to your children's reaction. Sometimes they're really happy to have this new person as part of the family. Sometimes they're not. It may be wise to establish guidelines with your new spouse regarding the children. Discipline can be an especially sticky issue. If the kids know you're the only one who will enforce rules, they can make your new spouse's life a living hell.

A second marriage is harder than a first, and national statistics show an even higher percentage of second marriages fail. Second marriages have new stresses brought about by circumstances resulting from the dissolution of the first marriage. Your new spouse may push you into fighting for a different parenting arrangement. A lot of new spouses pressure their partners to go after joint custody. Or your new spouse may resent supporting your children and may pressure you to take your ex-spouse back to court for more child support. Whatever the pressures, you need to stay in charge in your second marriage, just as you needed to stay in charge during your divorce.

ALERT!

Do not require your children to call a new spouse Mom or Dad. They already have a mom and a dad. Little kids will be confused. Big kids will be resentful. Your ex-spouse will be mighty angry. After all, how would you like it if your spouse had your children calling a new love interest Mommy or Daddy?

If you wait until you're ready, if you establish open lines of communication with those important to you—your new spouse, your kids, your ex—and if you stay in charge, you stand the best chance of success.

Glossary

action
The legal name for a lawsuit.

administrative process
A court hearing using a commissioner or hearing officer; often used in setting and collecting child support.

affidavit
A written factual statement sworn to under oath; a required companion to a motion.

agreement
A written document setting out areas of agreement, which is signed by the parties and their lawyers.

alimony
Money paid to a former spouse for his or her support; same as maintenance or spousal maintenance.

allegation
A statement by one of the parties as to what he or she believes—and intends to prove—is true.

appearance
Accepting the court's jurisdiction, either by actually appearing at a hearing or by submitting pleadings with the court.

appeal
A challenge to a court decision by taking the case to another, higher court.

appeals court
See appellate court.

appellant
The person who initiates an appeal.

appellate court

Also called appeals court. Most states have two levels of appellate courts. The first hears appeals from trial courts; the second hears appeals from the first appellate courts.

arbitration

A form of dispute resolution in which parties submit issues to a third party who decides how they should be resolved; can be binding or nonbinding.

brief

A written argument of facts and law, with references to other relevant decisions, submitted by a lawyer at trial or on appeal.

chambers

A judge's office.

child support

Money paid for the support of children.

collaborative law

A form of alternate dispute resolution in which the lawyers agree that they will put their energies into settling the case. If they are unsuccessful, they will withdraw and other lawyers will take the case to trial.

complaint

See petition.

community property

The name given to the property acquired during a marriage in so-called community property states, which refers to the property belonging to the married couple.

contempt

Disobeying a court order.

court reporter

A person trained to use a stenograph, who takes down what is said at a trial, a motion, or a deposition. The court reporter will provide a transcript of the matter upon request. The person who requests the transcript pays for it.

cross-examination
Questions put to a witness by the other side's attorney.

custody
The care and upbringing of the children of divorce.

custody evaluation
A study done by trained professionals—social workers, psychologists, or child development experts—to make recommendations to the court about a custody arrangement that is in the children's best interests.

decision
The judge's conclusions in a case; includes the judge's reasoning and how the judge saw the facts.

default
A hearing at which only one side appears, either because an agreement has been reached before the hearing or because one side does not show up despite having notice of the hearing.

defendant
One who defends against a lawsuit brought against him or her by the plaintiff. (See respondent.)

deposition
The testimony of a potential witness to a trial taken out of court and under oath. The deposition is ordinarily transcribed into a written document for later use.

direct examination
Testimony produced when a lawyer questions the witnesses on his or her side.

discovery
Gathering information needed for settling or trying the divorce case.

discretion of the court
The latitude given a trial court judge by appellate courts in interpreting evidence.

dissolution
The current word for divorce.

domestic violence

When one member of a household causes harm, makes threats of harm, or acts in a way to create fear of harm against another household member.

emancipation

When parents are no longer legally responsible for the children. Parents are legally responsible for their children until the kids reach a certain age (eighteen or twenty-one in most states), marry, join the military, or choose to live independently.

equitable

Reasonable under the circumstances. Usually refers to property division.

evidence

The information provided to the court at trial, or the information used by the parties and their lawyers to reach agreement.

ex parte

When one side goes to a judge for relief, usually in an emergency. Most states require the party seeking relief to notify the other, who may choose whether to appear in response.

expert

A person with specialized knowledge about issues within the divorce.

forensic

Done for purposes of providing testimony in court. For instance, a forensic psychologist is one who does studies, then testifies to explain them to the court.

foundation

The factual background that tells the court the witness has the necessary knowledge and information to testify about something.

grounds

The legal basis for claiming that the marriage is over. This may be marital misconduct, incompatibility, or irretrievable breakdown. Some states require the parties to have lived apart for a time, ranging from ninety days to two years.

guardian *ad litem*

Also called law guardian. A lawyer appointed by the court—and usually paid for by the parties—to provide information about what custodial arrangement would be in the children's best interests.

hearing
An appearance before the court at which evidence is produced and arguments are made.

hold harmless
One of the parties agrees to be responsible for a debt and protects the other from any expenses or losses related to the debt collection.

homestead
The real estate that was the parties' residence during the marriage.

impeachment
Using a statement made at another time—like a deposition—that is different from current testimony to show a witness is lying.

indemnification
To promise to reimburse another person if he or she suffers harm or loss; same as to hold harmless.

independent neutral expert
An expert selected by both sides to provide information the parties can then use to resolve issues.

interim order
Same as temporary order.

interrogatories
Written questions submitted by one side to the other to be answered under oath within thirty days.

joint custody
When divorcing parents share responsibility for child rearing.

joint legal custody
When the parties make major decisions about their children's education, medical care, and religious upbringing together.

joint petition
When people getting divorced are in agreement from the outset, they may prepare a joint petition for dissolution that sets out the facts and a stipulation that

sets out their agreements. Both parties sign this document. They do not need a summons, and papers do not need to be served.

joint physical custody
When parents share physical care of their children. While the time division need not be fifty-fifty, it is usually close to that.

judgment
A court order, based on the parties' agreement or following a trial on the issues.

judgment and decree
The document that says the parties are divorced and containing the court's decisions on issues before it.

jurisdiction
The authority of the court over persons and things, usually based on where the people live and where the property is located.

law guardian
See guardian *ad litem*.

legal custody
Parental decision making about the child's education, medical care, and religious upbringing.

legal separation
Some people don't want a divorce (often for religious reasons) but need a court order setting rules for their behavior. They may seek a decree of legal separation that addresses custody and support but usually cannot divide real estate. The decree does not dissolve a marriage.

litigation
Bringing issues to court and presenting them in the form required by the rules.

litigator
An attorney who specializes in trial work.

maintenance
See alimony.

marital property
The property acquired by the parties during the marriage not by gift or inheritance. This property is subject to division in a divorce.

mediation
A form of dispute resolution in which the parties meet with a third person, a mediator, to resolve their differences. Most mediators want the parties to be represented by lawyers who can advise them of the implications of their agreements because the mediator cannot give legal advice.

modification
A change to an existing court order, usually because of a change in circumstances.

motion
The legal document used to bring issues to the court.

negotiations
The communications among the parties and their lawyers as they work to resolve the issues.

no-fault divorce
The rule in most states today. It is only necessary to prove an irretrievable breakdown of the marriage has occurred, not that one of the parties is "at fault."

noncustodial parent
The parent with whom the children do not live.

nonmarital property
Property acquired before the marriage or by inheritance or gift. The court can only award nonmarital property to the other party if it is necessary to avoid "substantial hardship."

notice to remove
The one free shot at getting rid of a judge assigned to hear your case.

order
A written court decision directing behavior. An order can be based on an agreement of the parties or a court decision after a contested hearing.

order for protection

An order issued in a domestic violence matter that directs one party to stay away from the other and not to harm that person. Violating an order for protection is a basis for arrest and criminal charges.

order to show cause

An order directing a person to come to court and show cause why the judge should not order specified relief. A judge signs this order. Failure to come to court as ordered can result in issuance of a warrant for the person's arrest. If the judge finds a person in contempt, the judge may send the person to jail.

parenting consultant

A person designated by the court to make parenting decisions when the parties are unable to do so. These decisions have the effect of a court order.

parenting plan

The actual practical arrangement worked out by the parties that says when each will provide care and take responsibility for the children.

paternity

Fatherhood. In court, this means verifying a man is the father of a child. Today sophisticated testing makes this determination nearly 100 percent accurate.

perjury

Lying under oath.

petition

Also called complaint. This document, together with a summons, begins a divorce. It sets out the facts required by state statutes and asks the court to grant certain things.

petitioner

The party who initiates the divorce; also called the plaintiff.

physical custody

The actual hands-on care of the children.

plaintiff

See petitioner.

pretrial

A hearing shortly before the trial to narrow issues, set a final timetable, and try to persuade the parties to settle.

privilege

Information shared between lawyer and client or doctor and patient that cannot be released without consent of the client or patient.

pro se

Acting as your own lawyer, also sometimes referred to as *pro per.*

record

The written version of a deposition, a hearing, or a trial, together with all the exhibits that were made a part of them.

referee

A judicial officer hired by a judge to help handle the caseload; also called a magistrate, commissioner, or hearing officer.

removal

When a custodial parent wants to move a significant distance away from the noncustodial parent and asks for court permission to do so; also called relocation.

removal for cause

Shows actual prejudice on the part of the judge. If you've used your free shot to remove a judge (notice to remove), and you get another judge you don't want, you must show cause for removing this new one.

request for admissions

A document sent by one side to the other with a list of statements and a provision that if there is no response within thirty days, these statements will be deemed admitted to the court record. (Example: The other side submits to you the statement, "I have a secret bank account in Switzerland.")

request for production of documents

A document sent by one side to the other asking for documents believed to be in its possession or that it has the ability to obtain. The documents asked for must be produced in thirty days.

respondent
The person who responds to divorce papers served by the petitioner. If the initiator is called the plaintiff, then the responder is called the defendant.

retainer
Money paid to a lawyer to obtain the lawyer's services.

retainer agreement
The written contract between lawyer and client governing fees and, perhaps, behavior. (For instance, the lawyer writes, "I will return telephone calls within twenty-four hours.")

rules of civil procedure
The legal rules governing how lawsuits are run. (The lawsuit cookbook.)

rules of evidence
The legal rules governing what information can come before a court.

settlement
An agreement reached by negotiation.

settlement conference
A meeting of parties and lawyers to discuss settlement. This conference can be convened voluntarily, or a court can order one.

sole custody
One parent is responsible for the children.

sole legal custody
One parent makes all the decisions about education, medical care, and religious upbringing

sole physical custody
One parent provides most of the actual child care.

special magistrate or special master
A person hired by the parties and their lawyers to act as judge in their case. In counties that have long waits to get before a judge, parties may prefer to hire their own judge. They then give this person the same authority as a judge to decide their contested issues. Appeal of a special magistrate's decision goes to the first-level appellate court.

spousal maintenance
See alimony.

stock options
The right to purchase shares of stock in the company at a specific price after a specific holding period. Often part of an executive's bonus package. If one chooses to buy the stock, it is called exercising the stock option.

subpoena
A legal document requiring a person to appear before a court to testify

subpoena *duces tecum*
A legal document requiring a person to appear before a court to testify and to bring certain documents listed.

summons
The initiating document of a divorce that requires a response in twenty or thirty days and usually contains restraining orders governing behavior and assets.

temporary order
Also called an interim order. An order issued during a divorce to set rules until a divorce is final. A temporary order is usually not subject to appeal.

testimony
Oral evidence given under oath at a deposition or a trial.

transcript
The written record of a deposition, motion, or trial provided by a court reporter who recorded all the testimony.

trial
A contested hearing before a judge.

visitation
The time spent by a noncustodial parent with children.

vocational assessment
An evaluation to determine a person's employability and job interests.

APPENDIX B

Worksheets

Monthly Expenses Sheet

Expense	Petitioner or Plaintiff	Respondent or Defendant
Residence		
Rent or mortgage payment	$	$
Contract for deed payment	$	$
Real estate taxes	$	$
Insurance	$	$
Utilities		
Heating fuel	$	$
Water, sewer	$	$
Electricity	$	$
Gas	$	$
Telephone	$	$
Waste disposal	$	$
Home maintenance		
Housecleaning	$	$
Household repairs	$	$
Yard and landscaping	$	$
Snow removal	$	$
Laundry and dry cleaning	$	$
Food and other grocery store household items		
	$	$
	$	$
	$	$

Expense	Petitioner or Plaintiff	Respondent or Defendant
Automobile		
Gas and oil	$	$
Repairs and maintenance	$	$
Licenses	$	$
Insurance	$	$
Installment payments	$	$
Clothing		
	$	$
	$	$
	$	$
Grooming, cosmetics		
	$	$
	$	$
Medical		
Insurance	$	$
Unreimbursed doctor and hospital	$	$
Unreimbursed drugs	$	$
Unreimbursed dental and orthodontics	$	$
Counseling or therapy	$	$
Life insurance		
	$	$
Personal property insurance		
	$	$
	$	$
	$	$

Expense	Petitioner or Plaintiff	Respondent or Defendant
Miscellaneous personal		
Newspapers, magazines, books	$	$
Club or association dues	$	$
Vacations	$	$
Gifts	$	$
Education		
Tuition	$	$
Room and board	$	$
Transportation	$	$
Books and supplies	$	$
Activities	$	$
Charitable contributions		
	$	$
	$	$
Debt payments (list each separately with monthly payment)		
	$	$
	$	$
	$	$
	$	$
Child care		
	$	$
	$	$
	$	$
Animal care		
	$	$
	$	$

Expense	Petitioner or Plaintiff	Respondent or Defendant
IRA contributions		
	$	$
	$	$
Savings		
	$	$
	$	$
Other (list each item)		
	$	$
	$	$
	$	$
Children's Expenses		
Clothing	$	$
Grooming	$	$
Formula/diapers	$	$
Tuition	$	$
School lunches	$	$
Athletics/other activities	$	$
Allowances	$	$
Medical	$	$
Dental or orthodontic	$	$
Total expenses	**$**	**$**

Asset Summary Sheet

Asset	Wife's values	Husband's values for settlement only	Values stipulated
Personal property			
Furniture	$	$	$
Furnishings (pots, towels, etc.)	$	$	$
China, silver, crystal	$	$	$
Jewelry and furs	$	$	$
Homestead (purchase date)			
Market value	$	$	$
Mortgage	$	$	$
Second mortgage	$	$	$
Net equity	$	$	$
Other real estate (purchase date)			
Market value	$	$	$
Mortgage	$	$	$
Net equity	$	$	$
Back taxes	$	$	$
Boats and vehicles			
	$	$	$
Automobile			
Market value	$	$	$
Encumbrance	$	$	$
Net value	$	$	$
Second automobile			
Market value	$	$	$
Encumbrance	$	$	$
Net value	$	$	$
Other vehicles			
Market value	$	$	$

Asset	Wife's values	Husband's values	Values stipulated for settlement only
Encumbrance	$	$	$
Net value	$	$	$
Securities			
Stock (purchase date)	$	$	$
Bank accounts	$	$	$
Savings (account number)	$	$	$
Checking (account number)	$	$	$
Life insurance			
Company/policy number	$	$	$
Face amount	$	$	$
Cash surrender value	$	$	$
Loan	$	$	$
Retirement accounts			
Deferred comp./account number	$	$	$
Company/Plan name	$	$	$
Owned by	$	$	$
Profit sharing	$	$	$
Pensions	$	$	$
Keoghs	$	$	$
IRAs	$	$	$
Business interests			
Name			
Type			
Ownership interest	$	$	$
Debts			
Credit card name			
Loans	$	$	$
Total	**$**	**$**	**$**

Proposed Division of Property

Asset	Wife	Husband
Homestead	$	$
Other real estate (list separately)	$	$
	$	$
	$	$
	$	$
	$	$
Furniture	$	$
China, silver, etc.	$	$
Jewelry and furs	$	$
Automobiles	$	$
Boats	$	$
Other vehicles	$	$
	$	$
	$	$
Bank accounts	$	$
	$	$
	$	$
Stock	$	$
Deferred comp.	$	$
Life insurance cash value	$	$
Other retirement assets	$	$
Debt	$	$
	$	$
	$	$
Business	$	$
Cash equalizer	$	$
Grand total	**$**	**$**

APPENDIX C

Resources

Books with General Information on Divorce

Ahrons, Constance. *The Good Divorce*. New York: HarperCollins, 1994.

Feizenbaum, Alan, and Heather Linton. *The Complete Guide to Protecting Your Financial Security When Getting a Divorce*. New York: McGraw-Hill, 2004.

Friedman, James T. *The Divorce Handbook*. New York: Random House, rev. 1998.

Margulies, Sam. *Getting Divorced Without Ruining Your Life*. New York: Simon & Schuster, rev. 2001.

Talia, M. Sue. *How to Avoid the Divorce from Hell*. Danville, California: Nexus Publishing, 2nd ed. 2004.

Books for Children

Brown, Marc, and Laurene Krasny. *Dinosaurs Divorce*. Boston: Little, Brown, 1986.

Lansky, Vicki. *It's Not Your Fault, Koko Bear*. Minnetonka, Minnesota: Book Peddlers, 1998.

Thomas, Pat. *My Family's Changing*. Hauppauge, New York: Barrons' Educational Series, 1998.

Books about Children and Parenting

Aldort, Naomi. *Raising Our Children, Raising Ourselves: Transforming Parent-Child Relationships from Reaction and Struggle to Freedom, Power, and Joy.* Book Publishers Network, Washington, 2005.

Condrell, Kenneth N., and Linda Lee Small. *Be a Great Divorce Dad.* New York: St. Martin's Griffin, 1998.

Faber, Adele, and Elaine M. Mazlish. *How to Talk So Kids Will Listen and Listen So Kids Will Talk.* London: Piccadilly Press, 2001.

Kohn, Alfie. *Unconditional Parenting.* New York: Atria Books, 2005.

Lansky, Vicki. *Divorce Book for Parents.* Minnetonka, Minnesota: Book Peddlers, 2000.

Ricci, Isolina. *Mom's House, Dad's House.* New York: Simon & Schuster, 1997.

Thomas, Shirley. *Parents Are Forever.* Longmont, Colorado: Springboard Publications, 1995.

Books about Domestic Violence

Bancroft, Lundy, and J. Silverman. *The Batterer as Parent: Addressing the Impact of Domestic Violence on Family Dynamics.* Thousand Oaks, CA: Sage Publications, 2002.

Bancroft, Lundy. *When Dad Hurts Mom: Helping Your Children Heal the Wounds of Witnessing Abuse.* New York: G. P. Putnam's Sons, 2004.

Evans, Patricia. *The Verbally Abusive Relationship: How to Recognize It and How to Respond.* Avon, Massachusetts: Adams Media, 2nd ed. 2003.

Jones, Ann. *Next Time She'll Be Dead: Battering and How to Stop It.* Boston: Beacon Press, 2000.

Wilson, K. J. *When Violence Begins at Home: A Comprehensive Guide to Understanding and Ending Domestic Abuse.* Alameda, CA: Hunter House, 1997.

Books about Alternative Dispute Resolution

Allen, Elizabeth L. and Donald D. Mohr. *Affordable Justice.* Encinitas: West Coast Press, 1998.

Meek, Susan B. *Alternative Dispute Resolution.* Tucson: Lawyers and Judges Publishing, 2007.

Moffitt, Michael L. and Robert C. Bordone, eds. *The Handbook of Dispute Resolution.* San Francisco: Jossey Bass, 2005.

Tesler, Pauline H. *Collaborative Law, Achieving Effective Resolution in Divorce Without Litigation.* Chicago: American Bar Association, 2001.

Other Resources

American Academy of Matrimonial Lawyers
150 N. Michigan Ave., Suite 2040
Chicago, IL 60601
312-263-6477
Fax: 312-263-7682
www.aaml.org

The academy is a resource for finding the top divorce lawyers around the country. It also has several outstanding publications available for purchase, and articles of interest on its website.

American Bar Association, Family Law Section
www.abanet.org/family/advocate

Publishes the *Family Advocate,* a quarterly magazine that often has useful information for the divorce client. Copies can be ordered from ABA Publications Orders, P.O. Box 10892, Chicago, IL 60610, or call 1-800-285-2221.

Association for Conflict Resolution

1527 New Hampshire Ave. N.W., Third Floor
Washington, DC 20036
202-667-9700
Fax: 202-265-1968
www.acrnet.org

This organization was formed by the merger of the Academy of Family Mediators, the Conflict Resolution Education Network, and the Society of Professionals in Dispute Resolution. The association publishes the *Conflict Resolution Quarterly*, directed primarily to professionals in mediation. It is also a source of referrals if you're looking for a mediator.

Association of Family and Conciliation Courts

6515 Grand Teton Plaza, Suite 210
Madison, WI 53719-1048
608-664-3750
Fax: 608-664-3751
www.afccnet.org

Association members are lawyers, judges, and mental health professionals from all over the world. The organization has excellent pamphlets, books, and audio and videocassettes available for purchase.

National Domestic Violence Hotline

1-800-799-SAFE (7233)
www.ndvh.org

This site offers professional services and confidential help for anyone who has been affected by domestic violence.

International Academy of Collaborative Professionals

www.collaborativepractice.com

This site offers information about the process of collaborative divorce as well as an attorney referral service to collaborative professionals across the country.

Index

A

Abuse, 4, 29-30. *See also*
    Domestic violence
Acceptance, 17
Addiction. *See* Substance abuse
Alternative dispute resolution,
    91-103
    arbitration, 93, 102, 103
    collaborative law, 95-98
    mediation, 92, 98-101
    negotiation, 92-95
    special master, 103
    trends in, 102-3
Appeals, 230-32
Arbitration, 93, 102, 103

B

Budget, 172-73, 200-1

C

Child abuse and neglect, 258-59
Child support, 157-67, 171-73
    and budget, 172-73
    college expenses, 166-67
    enforcement of, 165-66
    deviation from guidelines,
        163-64
    guidelines, 158-59
    health care and childcare
        costs, 166
    and income, 160-63
    joint custody and, 164-65

modification of, 171-72
Children, 33-46, 76-77. *See also*
    Custody; Parenting plan
    marital problems regarding, 3
    and new family members, 249
    parental alienation of, 46
    and parental conflict, 38
    phone contact with, 245-47
    psychological needs of, 40-45
    reactions by, 39
    and respectful behavior by
        parents, 78
    talking to after divorce, 268-69
    telling about divorce, 34-36
    therapy for, 40
Collaborative law, 95-98
Counseling, 4-6, 16-17. *See also*
    Therapy
Courts, 75-90. *See also* Decision;
    Judges
    change of circumstances,
        89-90
    defined, 79
    expectations about, 79-83
    and fairness, 80-81
    and papers, 81
    and selective information,
        83-84
    and settlement, 84-85
Custody, 37-38, 137-55. *See also*
    Children; Parenting plan
    and children's preferences,
        143-44
    decision by court, 152-53
    and domestic violence, 257-58
    and experts, 133-36

    and information about child, 140
    joint, 142-43
    legal, 37-38, 139-40
    litigation example, 145-51
    negotiating, 144-45
    and parentage, 155
    physical, 38, 141-44
    and relocation, 153-54
    understanding, 138-39

D

Decision, 225-35
    appealing, 230-32
    conclusions of law, 227
    findings of fact, 227
    implementation of, 232-35
    mistakes in, 228-30
    order, 227-28
Definition of divorce, 76-78
Depositions, 124-25, 126-28
Discovery process, 121-36
    cost of, 128
    depositions, 126-28
    experts, 128-36
    interrogatories, 124, 125-26
Domestic violence, 252-58

E

Emotions, 21-25, 30, 273-75. *See
    also* Stress
Expectations, 79-80
Experts, 128-36, 184

THE EVERYTHING® SERIES!

BUSINESS & PERSONAL FINANCE

Everything® Accounting Book
Everything® Budgeting Book, 2nd Ed.
Everything® Business Planning Book
Everything® Coaching and Mentoring Book, 2nd Ed.
Everything® Fundraising Book
Everything® Get Out of Debt Book
Everything® Grant Writing Book, 2nd Ed.
Everything® Guide to Buying Foreclosures
Everything® Guide to Fundraising, $15.95
Everything® Guide to Mortgages
Everything® Guide to Personal Finance for Single Mothers
Everything® Home-Based Business Book, 2nd Ed.
Everything® Homebuying Book, 3rd Ed., $15.95
Everything® Homeselling Book, 2nd Ed.
Everything® Human Resource Management Book
Everything® Improve Your Credit Book
Everything® Investing Book, 2nd Ed.
Everything® Landlording Book
Everything® Leadership Book, 2nd Ed.
Everything® Managing People Book, 2nd Ed.
Everything® Negotiating Book
Everything® Online Auctions Book
Everything® Online Business Book
Everything® Personal Finance Book
Everything® Personal Finance in Your 20s & 30s Book, 2nd Ed.
Everything® Personal Finance in Your 40s & 50s Book, $15.95
Everything® Project Management Book, 2nd Ed.
Everything® Real Estate Investing Book
Everything® Retirement Planning Book
Everything® Robert's Rules Book, $7.95
Everything® Selling Book
Everything® Start Your Own Business Book, 2nd Ed.
Everything® Wills & Estate Planning Book

COOKING

Everything® Barbecue Cookbook
Everything® Bartender's Book, 2nd Ed., $9.95
Everything® Calorie Counting Cookbook
Everything® Cheese Book
Everything® Chinese Cookbook
Everything® Classic Recipes Book
Everything® Cocktail Parties & Drinks Book
Everything® College Cookbook
Everything® Cooking for Baby and Toddler Book
Everything® Diabetes Cookbook
Everything® Easy Gourmet Cookbook
Everything® Fondue Cookbook
Everything® Food Allergy Cookbook, $15.95
Everything® Fondue Party Book
Everything® Gluten-Free Cookbook
Everything® Glycemic Index Cookbook
Everything® Grilling Cookbook
Everything® Healthy Cooking for Parties Book, $15.95
Everything® Holiday Cookbook
Everything® Indian Cookbook
Everything® Lactose-Free Cookbook
Everything® Low-Cholesterol Cookbook

Everything® Low-Fat High-Flavor Cookbook, 2nd Ed., $15.95
Everything® Low-Salt Cookbook
Everything® Meals for a Month Cookbook
Everything® Meals on a Budget Cookbook
Everything® Mediterranean Cookbook
Everything® Mexican Cookbook
Everything® No Trans Fat Cookbook
Everything® One-Pot Cookbook, 2nd Ed., $15.95
Everything® Organic Cooking for Baby & Toddler Book, $15.95
Everything® Pizza Cookbook
Everything® Quick Meals Cookbook, 2nd Ed., $15.95
Everything® Slow Cooker Cookbook
Everything® Slow Cooking for a Crowd Cookbook
Everything® Soup Cookbook
Everything® Stir-Fry Cookbook
Everything® Sugar-Free Cookbook
Everything® Tapas and Small Plates Cookbook
Everything® Tex-Mex Cookbook
Everything® Thai Cookbook
Everything® Vegetarian Cookbook
Everything® Whole-Grain, High-Fiber Cookbook
Everything® Wild Game Cookbook
Everything® Wine Book, 2nd Ed.

GAMES

Everything® 15-Minute Sudoku Book, $9.95
Everything® 30-Minute Sudoku Book, $9.95
Everything® Bible Crosswords Book, $9.95
Everything® Blackjack Strategy Book
Everything® Brain Strain Book, $9.95
Everything® Bridge Book
Everything® Card Games Book
Everything® Card Tricks Book, $9.95
Everything® Casino Gambling Book, 2nd Ed.
Everything® Chess Basics Book
Everything® Christmas Crosswords Book, $9.95
Everything® Craps Strategy Book
Everything® Crossword and Puzzle Book
Everything® Crosswords and Puzzles for Quote Lovers Book, $9.95
Everything® Crossword Challenge Book
Everything® Crosswords for the Beach Book, $9.95
Everything® Cryptic Crosswords Book, $9.95
Everything® Cryptograms Book, $9.95
Everything® Easy Crosswords Book
Everything® Easy Kakuro Book, $9.95
Everything® Easy Large-Print Crosswords Book
Everything® Games Book, 2nd Ed.
Everything® Giant Book of Crosswords
Everything® Giant Sudoku Book, $9.95
Everything® Giant Word Search Book
Everything® Kakuro Challenge Book, $9.95
Everything® Large-Print Crossword Challenge Book
Everything® Large-Print Crosswords Book
Everything® Large-Print Travel Crosswords Book
Everything® Lateral Thinking Puzzles Book, $9.95
Everything® Literary Crosswords Book, $9.95
Everything® Mazes Book
Everything® Memory Booster Puzzles Book, $9.95

Everything® Movie Crosswords Book, $9.95
Everything® Music Crosswords Book, $9.95
Everything® Online Poker Book
Everything® Pencil Puzzles Book, $9.95
Everything® Poker Strategy Book
Everything® Pool & Billiards Book
Everything® Puzzles for Commuters Book, $9.95
Everything® Puzzles for Dog Lovers Book, $9.95
Everything® Sports Crosswords Book, $9.95
Everything® Test Your IQ Book, $9.95
Everything® Texas Hold 'Em Book, $9.95
Everything® Travel Crosswords Book, $9.95
Everything® Travel Mazes Book, $9.95
Everything® Travel Word Search Book, $9.95
Everything® TV Crosswords Book, $9.95
Everything® Word Games Challenge Book
Everything® Word Scramble Book
Everything® Word Search Book

HEALTH

Everything® Alzheimer's Book
Everything® Diabetes Book
Everything® First Aid Book, $9.95
Everything® Green Living Book
Everything® Health Guide to Addiction and Recovery
Everything® Health Guide to Adult Bipolar Disorder
Everything® Health Guide to Arthritis
Everything® Health Guide to Controlling Anxiety
Everything® Health Guide to Depression
Everything® Health Guide to Diabetes, 2nd Ed.
Everything® Health Guide to Fibromyalgia
Everything® Health Guide to Menopause, 2nd Ed.
Everything® Health Guide to Migraines
Everything® Health Guide to Multiple Sclerosis
Everything® Health Guide to OCD
Everything® Health Guide to PMS
Everything® Health Guide to Postpartum Care
Everything® Health Guide to Thyroid Disease
Everything® Hypnosis Book
Everything® Low Cholesterol Book
Everything® Menopause Book
Everything® Nutrition Book
Everything® Reflexology Book
Everything® Stress Management Book
Everything® Superfoods Book, $15.95

HISTORY

Everything® American Government Book
Everything® American History Book, 2nd Ed.
Everything® American Revolution Book, $15.95
Everything® Civil War Book
Everything® Freemasons Book
Everything® Irish History & Heritage Book
Everything® World War II Book, 2nd Ed.

HOBBIES

Everything® Candlemaking Book
Everything® Cartooning Book
Everything® Coin Collecting Book
Everything® Digital Photography Book, 2nd Ed.